Bridges
between Times and Continents

The Story of Three Generations
of a German Missionary Family on Sumatra

By Herbert Windolf

With an new Afterword by the Author

Content   **Page:**

Acknowledgments	ii
Preface	iv
Maps	viii

1. Hermann and Martha Weissenbruch

Hemann Weissenbruch's Journey to Sumatra	1
Martha Weissenbruch's, née Schmidt, Journey to Sumatra	7
Weissenbruchs' Journey from the Coast to Si Piak	11
The first Year in Si Piak	17
Settled in	42
The Year 1910 with the larger Family	56
Gertrud, their second child, is born	65
The Transfer to Balige	79
The Weissenbruchs' second Departure to Sumatra	100
The Weissenbruchs' Retirement in Germany	115

2. Heinz & Else Otto, née Weissenbruch   119
and their Offspring

3. Alfred & Gertrud Rutkowsky, née Weissenbruch

The Rutkowskys' Journey to Sumatra	133
The War Years on Sumatra	149
Alfred's Internment in India	172
Returned to Germany	224
Off again to Indonesia	230
Final Return to Germany	247

4. The Rutkowsky Children   249

Christa Rutkowsky, married Wuliger, Minas, and Schubert
Michael Rutkowsky
Dorothea Rutkowsky, married to Günter Klingebeil
Ute Rutkowsky, married Windolf

5. Epilog   257
A Third Generation's Visit to Sumatra

Glossary & Final Note   272

Acknowledgments

The title *Bridges between Times and Continents* was suggested by my now long departed friend, Lucy Jane Jackson.

This story of three generations, told in 'Bridges,' begins with Hermann and Martha Weissenbruch, née Schmidt. It is largely based on family records.

Chapter 1 was mostly assembled from Martha's and Hermann's Sumatran correspondence with Martha's parents and relatives in Germany. The latter years of their activities on Sumatra were extracted from Martha's diary and Hermann's correspondence with Mission Headquarters in Barmen, Germany. I am indebted to Mrs. Töpperwien in Germany, who had performed the laborious task of transcribing some of Martha's and Hermann's handwritten letters from the old German Sütterlin script into our contemporary script, putting the approximately 200 pages in a computer. Reams of written records and pictures were supplied by Dorothea Rutkowsky in Berlin.

Chapter 2 recounts the experiences of Else Weissenbruch, married Otto, and her children, Irmgard Seiffert and Renate Rhode on Borneo, Japan, Germany, and Denmark.

Chapter 3, the story of the second generation, the Rutkowskys, also came together through letters and diary notes from similar sources.

Chapter 4, about the third generation, becomes partly autobiographical, when the author became acquainted with the Rutkowsky siblings. The events described in this chapter took place in Germany, Canada, and the United States.

In chapter 1, I have taken the liberty to severely edit the mentioning of family matters from my translation, such as well-being, illnesses, marriages, and deaths, etc., since those occurring in Germany were of little if any importance to the account of 'Bridges.' I have, of course, condensed the available material substantially, especially Hermann's extensive 'sermons,' to make the story more readable. However, since this is essentially the story of two generations of missionaries, I believe I have retained enough religious references to give them their due. Rest assured, though, that, while I left aside plenty of information of interest only to the people of that bygone time, the essence, everything that I think makes this story and the spiritual and physical "Bridges" of the participants interesting, has been retained.

In the Epilog I tell about my/our impressions traveling the area around Lake Toba in 1991 together with my wife Ute, Dorothea, and Günter Klingebeil.

And, last not least, I am greatly indebted to Manfred Wenner and Zene Krogh for editing this extensive manuscript to give it the final touch.

Herbert Windolf   Prescott, Arizona, 2011   Edited 2021

Preface

Indonesia, called by this name only after W.W.II, is with its many islands equal in size to the United States in its extent from east to west. In colonial times, it was called the Dutch or Netherland East Indies. The Dutch concluded their acquisition of the archipelago only in the early nineteen hundreds with the conquest of Bali, a remnant of the once unifying Buddhist empire, Sriwijaya, which was succeeded by the Hindu empire Majapahit. Upon the latter's decline, various Islamic sultanates were established across the archipelago.

The largest island, Sumatra, is the home of orangutans, tigers, rhinos and elephants, and was, in places, until the latter part of the nineteenth century a land of cannibals. Beginning in the eleventh century, Muslim traders introduced their religion to parts of the islands. Except for the northernmost part of Sumatra, Aceh, the interior of Sumatra remained largely a heathen place. South of Aceh, in the highlands around the shores of Lake Toba, lived the tribes of the Batak people.

It is thought that the Batak arrived on Sumatra more than four thousand years ago, settling in the highlands around Lake Toba. They evolved in almost complete isolation from other tribes on the island. Their language and culture experienced little outside influence. Each of the six ethnolinguistic groups had its own rituals, architectural styles, kind of dress, and, most importantly, their own writing.

Marco Polo, Portuguese explorers, and William Marsden, a British historian of Sumatra who visited there in 1820, all claimed that cannibalism was practiced by the Bataks. Some of the earliest missionaries were Henry Lymann and Samuel Munson, from the American Board of Commissioners for Foreign Mission, who arrived in the Similung valley in 1934. The Bataks, expecting another forced conversion – as had happened in an earlier Islamic incursion – killed the two and ate them, as was reported. An earlier visit by the British Baptist missionaries, Richard Burton and Nathaniel Ward in 1824, had however been peaceful.

The 'Rheinische Missions Gesellschaft,' in English the 'Rhenish Missionary Society,' nowadays in German called 'Vereinigte Evangelische Mission, V.E.M.,' was established in 1828 in Wuppertal-Barmen, Germany. The evangelical mission awareness found its expression under the influence of the religious revival movement. It was marked by a skeptical view of the Enlightenment and secularization. This belief arose from the perceived security of a village milieu and its emotionally-oriented perception of God. Individual experiences of salvation became the motive for missionary work and thus the saving of souls through Jesus Christ.

In 1830, the Rhenish Mission Society's first mission station was established near Cape Town, South Africa. Beginning in the mid-nineteen hundreds, the Society began to dispatch missionaries to the Dutch East Indies, ranging from Sumatra to western New Guinea. New Guinea, in particular, became a kind of death trap for missionaries. During the first twenty years, many lost their wives and children to illness. In 1859 the missionary Ferdinand Rott was killed on Borneo by natives, followed by the missionary Ostermann in New Guinea in 1904. We do not know the reasons for the killings; however, since, in the manner of their time, some missionaries, ignorant of native customs, may have dealt somewhat forcefully with natives, the natives' reaction could be understandable.

Missionaries of the Rhenish Missionary Society were expected to leave by themselves, then, after a waiting period of two years, 'apply' to find a wife in the homeland, if they had not previously found a match. Once done, the fiancée had to pass an 'exam' before she was permitted to depart for her destination.

With many missionaries coming from modest social backgrounds, it appears that their mission work raised them to a higher social position, especially when their wives came from pastoral families. While males were called 'Brothers', females were called 'Sisters,' whether they were the wives of missionaries or nurses.

In 1862, Ludwig Ingwer Nommensen was sent to Sumatra by the Rhenish Missionary Society. He was born in 1834. At age twelve, a horse cart had rolled over his legs, crushing them. He was not expected to walk again, but, after daily prayers for recovery, he was able to do so three years later. His miraculous recovery led him to take up mission work among the Batak. He reported encountering difficulties at first, but three years after his arrival had converted 2,000 Batak to Christianity. By 1878, he had finished his translation of the New Testament into the Batak language.

In 1878, Nommensen acted as interpreter and consultant to the Dutch Army in its war with the Batak king-priest Singamangaraja. Eventually, events calmed down and, by the time of his death, on May 23, 1918 – he was 84 years old – the church he had helped to build numbered 180,000 members with 34 Batak pastors and hundreds of native teachers. Nommensen was buried in Sigumpar on the south shore of Lake Toba. Today, his simple grave is still visited by many people, remembering him as the 'Apostle of the Batak,' also as *Ompu*, grandfather. Shortly after his death, Hermann Weissenbruch wrote, "The old, patriarchal conditions are gone now." In 1954, the Batak Christian University at Medan and Pematang Siantar was renamed Nommensen University. Today, the Lutheran Batak Church has close to four million members and is known as H.K.B.P.

In 1935 Hermann Weissenbruch translated a narrative of Pandita Joseph, a Batak Elder of the Mission from the Batak language, to German. The following is an excerpt of this story: The Bataks were in fear of the *begus*, evil spirits. The Bataks' thinking was *soehar*, wrong or bad, but they also had something good, *adat* , their customs and tradition, which included love for their relatives and tribal members, and honoring their chiefs and elders, although infractions took place. They knew their ancestors all the way back to Raja Batak, their progenitor. The Batak have a keen sense of right and wrong in their encounter with others and always remember it, especially the wrongs. They are very adept at copying that which they have once seen. Rhetoric is highly prized, which is also the reason why they often engage in quarrels and lawsuits. Those Bataks who converted to Christianity, and in the process had acquired other knowledge, were preferentially employed by the Dutch Government over pagans. The realization that knowledge, especially scientific and organizational knowledge, meant making money, drew many to attend schools in order to further themselves.

This story begins with the grandfather, Karl Hermann Weissenbruch, who, among many others, joined the 'Rheinische Missions Gesellschaft' to go to Sumatra to continue Nommensen's work. Once there, these Lutheran missionaries not only had to overcome pagan beliefs, but had to struggle also with the inroads of the Muslim religion and that of Catholic missionaries and, eventually, with heretical offshoots of their own Protestantism. The following account describes the journeys of three generations of this family through the turbulent times of two World Wars. The first generation, the Weissenbruchs, had it relatively easy, since Germany respected Dutch neutrality in W.W.I and did not invade Holland. Nevertheless, the Dutch expressed their resentments about the war Germany had initiated to the German civilians living in the Dutch East Indies.

The Huria Kristen Batak Protestan (H.K.B.P.) Church was established in Balige in September, 1917. By the late 1920s a nursing school was training nurse midwives there. In 1941, the Gereja Batak Karo Protestan (G.B.K.P.) was established. Although missionaries ceded much power to Batak converts in the first decades of the 20th century, Bataks never pressured the missionaries to leave and only took control of church activities as a result of the forced departure and internment of thousands of missionaries after the 1942 invasion of Sumatra by the Japanese.

While W.W. I and W.W.II raged, first the Weissenbruchs, then the Rutkowskys made no secret of their patriotic feelings for the Fatherland, largely based on the scant or distorted information available to them on Sumatra. During W.W.II, things were very different for the second generation, the Rutkowskys, when Germany invaded Holland. German civilians living in the colony were immediately arrested and interned, with the men separated from women and children. Prior to the Japanese invasion of Indonesia, all male internees were evacuated to Dehradun, the Allies collective internment camp in the foothills of the Himalayas. The Japanese, allied with Germany (also Austria & Italy) 'liberated' the women and children, who were now 'free' to largely fend for themselves.

When British and Dutch military forces retook Indonesia, they immediately had to cope with a native independence movement, which had been abetted by the departing Japanese. This, in turn, pitted many native people against each other, some taking the side of the independence movement, others that of their former colonial masters. During these chaotic years, the German women and children lived in a semi-freedom, waiting and waiting, longing for nothing more than their eventual repatriation to their beloved homeland, which had little to offer them during these postwar years. Eventually, after seven years of separation, the Rutkowsky family was reunited in Germany in 1947.

The third generation did not follow in the footsteps of their forebears. Some remained in Germany, others dispersed to the United States of America, Canada, and Denmark.

Sumatra

century, Bataks never pressured the missionaries to leave and only took control of church activities as a result of the forced departure and internment of thousands of missionaries after the 1942 invasion of Sumatra by the Japanese.

While W.W. I and W.W.II raged, first the Weissenbruchs, then the Rutkowskys made no secret of their patriotic feelings for the Fatherland, largely based on the scant or distorted information available to them on Sumatra. During W.W.II, things were very different for the second generation, the Rutkowskys, when Germany invaded Holland. German civilians living in the colony were immediately arrested and interned, with the men separated from women and children. Prior to the Japanese invasion of Indonesia, all male internees were evacuated to Dehradun, the Allies collective internment camp in the foothills of the Himalayas. The Japanese, allied with Germany (also Austria & Italy) 'liberated' the women and children, who were now 'free' to largely fend for themselves.

When British and Dutch military forces retook Indonesia, they immediately had to cope with a native independence movement, which had been abetted by the departing Japanese. This, in turn, pitted many native people against each other, some taking the side of the independence movement, others that of their former colonial masters. During these chaotic years, the German women and children lived in a semi-freedom, waiting and waiting, longing for nothing more than their eventual repatriation to their beloved homeland, which had little to offer them during these postwar years. Eventually, after seven years of separation, the Rutkowsky family was reunited in Germany in 1947.

The third generation did not follow in the footsteps of their forebears. Some remained in Germany, others dispersed to the United States of America, Canada, and Denmark.

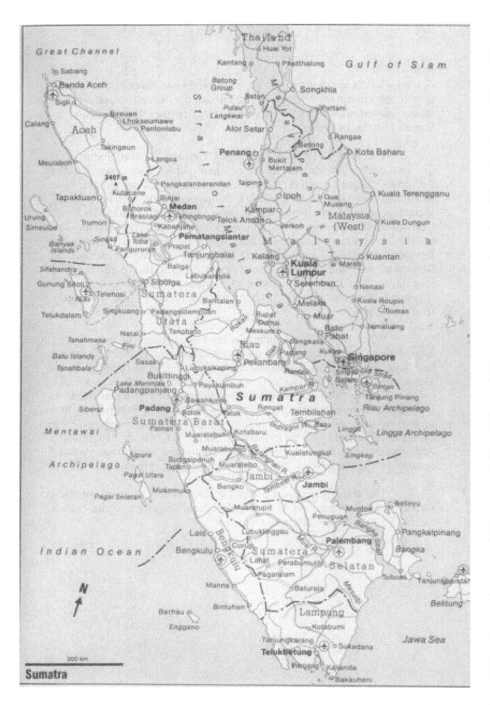

Sumatra

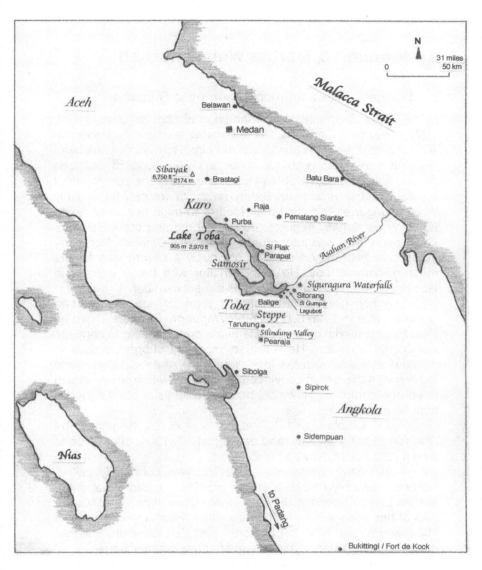

North Sumatra

1. Hermann & Martha Weissenbruch

Hermann Weissenbruch's Journey to Sumatra

Karl Hermann Weissenbruch was born on January 20, 1877 in Barmen, Germany. His father was a simple tradesperson – a carpenter, as Hermann described him. Hermann's curriculum vitae is very brief, with close to half consisting of religious declarations, indicative of his pious nature and the conditions of his time and environment. Barely seven years old, he and his three younger siblings lost their mother through her early death. (One of his sisters, Auguste, eventually married the missionary Ostermann, who was later murdered on New Guinea). Not many years later his father also died, obviously a severe loss for the thirteen year-old boy. He found shelter with foster parents in Isselhorst, where he apprenticed as a machine fitter.

When he reached eighteen years of age, he returned home to what in 1928 had become Wuppertal-Barmen. There he found accommodation with some aunts and was able to continue working in his trade. He received important support, mostly in religious matters, from the local Young Men's Association. Bible studies with this group convinced him that he was a sinner and in need of redemption. However, he also remarks about the joyous time he experienced there.

On October 1, 1897, at the age of 20, he joined the Rhenish Mission Society, and on August 10, 1904, after close to seven years of study, was ordained.

Hermann Weissenbruch, as he was commonly called, became upwardly mobile when he married a pastor's daughter, Martha Luise Friederike Schmidt. In her curriculum vitae, Martha tells of her engagement to the missionary Hermann in August of 1904, which must have been shortly after his ordination. She had made his acquaintance a year earlier at her parents' house.

Dutifully, she wrote that she was looking forward to doing the Lord's work.

Martha was born on July 4, 1882 in Miehlen, Germany, the second daughter of pastor Gustav Schmidt and his wife Christine, née Schlocker. Martha described having had a pleasant childhood with four siblings. At age thirteen she and a

Hermann Weissenbruch

sister were sent to Bielefeld to live with an aunt, Mrs. Rott, whose missionary husband had been killed on Borneo. For three years, Martha attended school there with a number of missionary children. At sixteen, together with a younger brother, she was confirmed by her father in the local village church. The following years were spent in the family fold with her sister and younger brother. The two older brothers visited only during vacations. At a later age, she worked at an orphanage, apparently run by relatives in Worms.

On October 6, 1904, Hermann boarded a ship in Genoa, Italy, which arrived in Sibolga, Sumatra, on November 1. As required by the Society's rules, a long wait now ensued until the betrothed couple was allowed to marry. In a letter dated July 27, 1905, from Lumban na Bolun, Hermann wrote that a year had already passed since he and his Martha solemnly promised themselves to each other, on the shady little bench in the peaceful rector's garden, until "death do us part." He thanked Martha's parents, whom he addressed as father and mother, for entrusting their daughter to him. At the same time, he apologized for writing them so infrequently. Alluding to the many letters he had written to his fiancée, he said, "Martha must have made you aware of some of their content, especially my description of life on Sumatra with its 'light and shadows.' " Precociously, he suggested to his father-in-law that he might like to take care of his grandchild in his older days, if that should still please him when the time comes. Unfortunately, none of his letters to Martha have survived the more than one hundred years since they were written.

On June 15,1906, Hermann wrote to Ria and Max, Martha's sister and her husband, from his station at Si Piak, a small promontory jutting into Lake Toba near the village of Parapat. He described some of the events which took place during his bachelorhood. In two areas, Girsang and Sipanganbolon, tribes which had risen against the Dutch colonials. He suggested that these people and their chiefs apparently wanted the old warring times to return. The rebels numbered about 400 to 500. "I tried my best to hold the people back," he said, "but they were obsessed, and my efforts were in vain, even endangering me. When things have calmed down, I think I can safely return to the villages in the Silindung and Toba regions.

"I'm looking forward to having Martha by my side as my faithful helper before too long. We have so many benefits here on Sumatra that it is difficult to talk of privation. This is why I understand more and more why some older missionary folks feel no desire to return home. Among our newcomers are several sisters; two of them brides of missionaries."

Hermann had shown his 'boy,' Gayus, his servant and cook, how to bake bread in an oven consisting of three stones and an empty petroleum container into which the bread mold was put and, voilà, in an hour, out came a loaf of bread. The boy even produced pudding and omelets in this contraption. Given a hunk of venison by some Christian Bataks from Laguboti, Hermann put it in vinegar in order to preserve it, but distributed most of it to the 'boys.' Happily, he reported that potatoes were also growing.

"The head of our synod, Ludwig Nommensen and his family, are expected to visit soon, and with other visitors showing up, my 'boy' usually loses his head. This is why I hope Martha will take over some of the tasks of hosting and representation, so that I can dedicate myself to the actual mission work.

"Simply by handing out medications to the locals gains me respect, since I do not ask for payment while their shamans do. They often bring me chickens or bananas, and are sad, even insulted, when I refuse to accept them. So, on occasion, I do. I frequently hear from them such remarks as, 'we Bataks are dear to the *tuan*, 'or 'the *tuan* thinks we aren't fat enough.' These remarks provide opportunities to explain to them some of the Christian teachings."

In a correspondence to his home town from Si Piak on July 15, 1906, Hermann described that about 6,000 heathen lived in his precinct. This is why he was glad to have received a bell from Germany where, in the town of Miehlen in Hesse, the residents had made a collection to pay for the bell. It arrived through the port of Sibolga, then took ten days to be carried to the shore of Lake Toba. From there it was taken on a ten hour journey by boat to his station. Upon its arrival he called the chiefs together and, referring to his nine month-long stay among them, said, "You should know by now why I have come. You have seen countrymen of yours who are teachers, policemen, and supervisors. All have gone to school. Don't you want your children to learn useful things, too?"

4

He urged them to build a school which was to serve also as a church until one could later be erected. He then produced the bell, telling them that its purpose was to call the people together, an idea to which the chiefs agreed. The carpenters, who were building the mission station, subsequently put together a framework up which the bell was hoisted. The station's native language teacher, Marinus, unable to wait to hear the bell's sound, rang it on Sunday before Hermann was able to tell him to do so. Now, past sunset, with only a few red clouds left hanging in the west, the bell's peaceful sound carried from the promontory across the lake to the nearby villages.

"So far no women have come to my services. I am often asked when the *njonja* will come to Si Piak. My teacher has indicated that eighteen women from different villages will come to listen to my teachings and services, once the *njonja* has arrived."

A cooking stove arrived from Germany, but with its stovepipe missing. Either it was forgotten, packed separately, or somehow misplaced. Hermann wrote that if it doesn't arrive soon, it meant continuing the use of the petroleum can-cum-three-rock oven. The construction of the house proceeded very well, but he had to keep close track of the workmen so that they did not mess up the expensive wood. The most difficult part of establishing his station now lay behind. Again, he looked forward to Martha's arrival, so that he could go to the villages and spend more time learning the Batak language by using it. He described Batak as not very difficult, but having an enormous number of words, many not even known to Ludwig Nommensen, who had translated the New Testament into Batak.

On September 25, the mission's new motor boat, christened 'Tole,' meaning 'Forward,' arrived for the first time at Sipiak with an entire complement of *tuans*, including Ludwig Nommensen. "My Gayus became rather agitated again, but we managed to feed our guests well with potato soup, duck eggs, and cake. The group paid another visit on their return trip on the 29th, and reported that the boat performed well even in high waves. Hermann remarked that, tomorrow, he would send his row boat for the last time across the lake to Toba, after which the Tole will do the circuit.

The people began to deliver the initial lumber for the construction of the school. Everyone had to contribute his share, whether he wanted to or not! "I have made it a requirement that all the lumber must be supplied this month, and that everyone not conforming, must pay four guilders in Dutch currency, two to the *Raja*, and two for the school. Dear father in Germany, you must think: 'So, then is this the way God's kingdom is spread.' Well, we cannot educate our 'children' to become good without some stringency, which means, even the lazy ones will be drawn from their hiding places. They will eventually be grateful to me for having been forceful."

On October 7, 1906, in a letter to Martha's parents, Hermann expressed how delighted he was to receive Martha's letter, in which she advised of her arrival on Penang, on November 2.

Incomprehensible for our time, with its almost instant communication, Hermann had sent her a postcard to Aden, where the ship was expected to stop. One must understand that such mail had to be addressed something like: "Aden Postmaster General. Attn: Martha Weissenbruch, on board of Steamship 'Bülow,' arriving from Genua." Once the 'Bülow' arrived in Aden her purser had to go on land to pick up any such mail from the Aden postmaster to deliver it to the ship's passengers. Hermann mailed another letter to Colombo, on Ceylon , the second-to-last of 'Bülow's' ports of call.

He expected to release the carpenters in eight to ten days, and hurried to get everything ship-shape so that their house would not look like a bachelor's digs. Some of the furnishings had arrived, and the rest was to arrive shortly from the mission's industrial training facility in Si Antar. "And how many guilders will I have to shell out for them?" he wondered.

On the evening of the 24th, he told of walking outside and, while returning to the house stepped on a soft, resilient mass. Exclaiming in fright, he jumped, then observed in the faint moonlight, how the snake, which is what it was, took flight. About six feet long, it was killed by a buckshot blast and turned out to be one of the most poisonous snakes found on Sumatra!

Martha Weissenbruch's, née Schmidt, Journey to Sumatra

In a letter sent from the Hotel 'Du Milano' in Genoa, Italy, dated October 9, 1906, Martha reported about her long journey from Germany. Most likely, the trip by train was her first long excursion beyond her hometown. She described the sights of Lake Luzern, Lake Lugano, and Lake Como in glowing terms. During a stop in Milano she had time to see the cathedral, then a train took her at night to Genoa and the Hotel 'Du Milano.' She was impressed by its spacious marble-clad rooms and oriental carpets. Looking to her like a tale from the 'Arabian Nights.' The 'wildly gesticulating' Italians unnerved her, but the number of waiters, maids, the many colors, the electric lights, and the flowers and palm trees, appeared magical to her. It must also have been the first time she saw the sea.

The next day she wrote that she boarded the steamship 'Bülow.' It left in the morning, followed for awhile by many small boats from which various kinds of goods were noisily offered. With many Englishmen as passengers, she found life on board very interesting. She shared a cabin way down in the ship with a fellow woman-passenger from Germany, an American woman and her five-year-old son. Since none of the Englishmen nor the American woman spoke German, she found it a good opportunity to improve her English language skills.

They arrived in Naples and Martha wrote: "The view of Naples, Pompeii and Vesuvius, and sideways to the island of Capri, is indescribably beautiful." The ship anchored outside the port. Locals arrived speedily in small boats to offer their wares, while others begged for coins, which the ship's passengers simply tossed into the water for them to dive for. She, and her German travel companion, had themselves rowed ashore, there to take a guide to see Pompeii and Naples. While she was impressed by the beautiful architecture, she found the begging and the garbage everywhere abhorrent.

Passing through the Straits of Messina, and later the Suez Canal, they arrived in the Red Sea on October 19. The heat was so terrible that passengers slept on deck, the cabins being too stuffy. Martha described it as, "a most comical scene, seeing deck chairs, benches and lifeboats full of sleeping people.

Martha Weissenbruch with daughters Else and Gertrud

By early afternoon, the deck crew flooded the deck with water to cool it. Everyone remained on their deck chairs, rescued their shoes if necessary and simply raised their feet and let the water run off.

"I am very much impressed by the flying fish and the luminescent sea life. The Southern Cross and Orion are still visible. The Big Dipper is gradually disappearing below the horizon. The starry sky is so clear that it appears as if Heaven and Earth are closer together here."

She complained about the taste of their drinking water. Meat is looked at suspiciously, although there were four butchers on board who prepared fresh meat every day. Lemonade and various kinds of fruit were readily available. The ship teemed with Chinese laborers, who scrubbed and cleaned every day.

On October 22, the ship having entered the Indian Ocean, she wrote that the voyage had begun to tire her. The passengers did not go on shore in Aden, since it looked too desolate from shipboard. They passed Socotra Island and Cape Guardafui. Once more, she described her delight with the ocean's changing appearance and the night sky. But then the ship encountered a severe storm. Now, Martha bemoaned: "Sea sickness struck us mightily. We are eating herring (even I) and sour pickles. Many of our fellow-passengers who have made this trip repeatedly, say that they have never experienced the Indian Ocean as stormy as we do now. For two nights we have not gone to bed in our cabins. With waves rising too high, the portholes have been shut tightly which has made the cabin air intolerable. There's no real peace on deck, but at least the air is fresh." Before arriving in Colombo, on Ceylon, she described how, two days earlier, one of the Chinese deckhands, who had died of heat stroke, was simply dumped overboard.

On the 30th, Martha's ship arrived at George Town on the island of Penang on the Malay Peninsula, where she was eagerly awaited by Hermann, who had come from Sumatra to meet her. The following day the couple was married there. They had experienced some difficulties with their wedding plans, because the Dutch on Sumatra required a certain missing document to wed the couple. However, the British on Penang did not need this particular paper if enough witnesses were present. With a number of other missionaries on hand, this posed no problem. Their wedding was celebrated with friends in the hotel where they were staying. The couple then spent two more days on the island.

On November 2, they boarded a Chinese steamship – and what a ship it was! Martha wrote that, "the smells and dirt cannot be imagined." Except for the couple, everyone else was either Chinese or Malay. The cabin they were to occupy was so dirty that they backed away at its entrance and fled to the bridge where they had fresh air. It was the cleanest place on board, which they now shared with the captain, a Malay. He let them use his chair, and having purchased one themselves on Penang, they now had two seats to make the trip more comfortable. When later the sea became rough, it was fortunate that their chairs had been tied down or they would have gone overboard.

The cook prepared what Martha described in her diary as, 'stink-fish,' whose awful odor permeated even to the bridge, and they were glad when the crew's 'dinner' was finished. The two travelers had provisioned themselves only lightly, so, at some point they managed to ask the captain, who spoke no English, for some fruit. He took a pineapple in his left hand and holding it over the railing, pulled his dagger from his belt and chopped off the peel. Handing it to them, they ate it with relish, despite the less than appetizing preparation.

The stormy night passed, but only after they had become violently seasick. In the morning land lay ahead. However, with the tide being out, they had to wait for hours before the ship was able to tie up.

The Weissenbruchs' Journey from the Sumatran Coast to Si Piak

The ship landed in Batu Bara, a swampy, unhealthy little port town. Shortly after debarking, they walked past a dead crocodile that had just been caught and was lying next to the pier. They were welcomed by a Dutch official and a Danish hotel owner who presented Martha with a bouquet of roses. However, for whatever reason, they had been warned not to take accommodation at the hotel. With the help of a small dictionary, Hermann was able to secure a couple of rickshas. Martha was unceremoniously packed into the first while Hermann was still negotiating with the second driver. Her ricksha speedily took off until she was no longer able to see her husband. Unable to ask or request anything, she was relieved when a ricksha appeared in the distance behind and turned out to be carrying her husband. Martha delighted in her first impressions of a jungle, claiming that she never again experienced one as beautiful, with such giant trees, grown over by lianas and orchids. Her enthusiasm was probably due to this overwhelming 'first impression.'

Several times during the day's trip they had to change horses, and, finally, by nine o'clock that evening arrived at a coffee plantation. It was owned by a Swiss bachelor named Sulger, who was known to Hermann. The planter had dinner cooked for them and provided them with a room for the night. Martha was impressed by the beautiful surroundings of the plantation amidst palm groves. "The rich green everywhere, the foreign bird calls, the wonderful coloration of the sky, and the peculiar tropical smells are indescribable," she enthusiastically wrote.

The next morning, Mr. Sulger had them driven in one of his carriages to the next village. It took them close to three hours to get there. They were then ferried across a river, where several men from Adji Bata had been waiting for them for several days. Martha wrote, "We walked to the home of a Christian Batak with whom Hermann organized a carriage for our continuing trip. While he did so, the woman of the house squatted on a mat on the floor, and I sat on a chair, with both of us staring at each other in wonder." Already then, she found the Bataks' teeth most ugly, caused by chewing betel nuts, a mild euphoric.

Continuing their trip, their carriage became stuck in mud every so often, for which she thought the monkeys were deriding them in the trees. In the afternoon, they arrived at friends, Missionary Simon and his wife. During their first night, they heard nearby the scream of a tiger. Their hosts invited them to stay for a few days. Some beautiful rattan furniture the Weissenbruchs had purchased on Penang had also arrived, and porters would carry it to its destination. Their hostess thought that Hermann's servant, Gayus, who had previously worked for the wife of another missionary, was quite good. She suggested that Martha leave the cooking, Batak-style, to him, at least in the beginning. European cooking was not easy, since there were barely any vegetables growing at these high elevations, and it was too early for fruit. Their host's three-year-old daughter spoke a lingo, half Batak and half German. She was afraid whenever she first met a new white person!

The couple used their stay as an opportunity for early morning rides, so Martha could get used to riding the small Batak ponies. She told of a scary experience, one, she said, "I do not wish to have for a second time. Hermann and I had taken a morning ride into the forest. We stopped to rest, and when we were ready to return to the station, Hermann helped me into the saddle. Precociously, I rode off, while Hermann was still busy with his saddle. My horse was trotting along rather briskly up a slope. When I turned around to see whether Hermann was coming, I saw a tiger jump from the bushes. He followed me with crouching leaps. Oddly, my first, rather ridiculous thought, was, 'what a long tail this fellow has.' Then, fear for my husband drove me almost out of my wits: Hermann was going to ride right towards the tiger. Because of a headwind, my horse had not caught the scent of the carnivore. Due to my riding lessons in Germany, I had it under control and pulled on the reins to slow its gallop. The tiger followed me for what must have been about three minutes. It is impossible to describe what all went through my head at that time. The watchword of our wedding stood before my eyes: 'I shall carry you until you age and become gray.' I did not fully realize the danger I was in and remained surprisingly calm. Only one thought occupied me: 'Hermann must not appear now, or he will be lost. I must remain faster than the tiger!' Then I saw Hermann approach, and, in the blink of an eye, the tiger disappeared into the woods. These animals are rather cowardly; once they sense danger behind, they take flight. Hermann hadn't even seen the tiger and had been worried about me since I had ridden so far ahead. I learned in that moment that we are in God's hands!"

Martha and Hermann left the Simons on November 12, with six porters and two guides, passing through jungle until noon. Often, their overgrown trail had to be cleared by one of the guides who walked ahead to slash it open with his machete. Martha wrote that, "when in the jungle, I did not feel the heat. But sometimes the monkeys were so bold that they grabbed for us, making me bend low over my horse's neck. The Sumatran horses climbed like cats over obstacles, even tree trunks. At one time, however, my horse fell and I found myself looking at the sky with four legs sticking up above me. One of our Batak guides had the presence of mind to take a hold of me and to drag me out from under my steed.

"Sometimes the jungle opens up and one enters beautiful palm-studded clearings. The strange animal voices, the chirping, humming and screaming, drive home that one is in a foreign land. Five-and-a-half hours later we rested in a small village settled by Chinese. The Mission maintains guest houses everywhere, usually vacant houses, in which evil spirits are supposed to dwell, as claimed by Batak shamans. At one o'clock we continued our ride through the forest, until we arrived in Siantar at five in the afternoon. We found shelter in the nice, unoccupied house of a chief. It had three rooms and a beautiful, open verandah. The boys cooked themselves their rice, and Gayus made tea for us. We still had enough bread, butter and chicken meat. The remaining three days travel on horseback to Si Piak will be taxing. In the village of Bandar, we visited the dwelling of a Batak noble with ten wives.

"On such Sumatran jungle journeys, travelers always carry mattresses, blankets, pots and pans, plates, cups, spoons, forks, knives, tea, coffee, bread, butter, a live chicken, in short, plenty of stuff. We were glad not to have come across elephants so far, although we have seen their tracks. The next morning, we were off by seven o'clock, always climbing higher. Sometimes we crossed deep, pretty valleys. Often the trail dropped steeply, but we remained in the saddle on our sure-footed horses. When it became very steep, they put their forelegs straight together to slide down, which, of course, required that we lean far back to

13

stay in the saddle. Rivers are also crossed on horseback. We pulled our feet up as close as possible to the saddle and took a firm hold of the reins. But often the water got so deep that our feet and clothing became wet after all. On the opposite side of a river, the process was reversed by having to lean far forward in order to stay in the saddle. It would simply be impractical and time-consuming to dismount at every river crossing.

"On the following day we rode only until noon, then took shelter in a newly-built teacher's house in a small village. The residents had never before seen a white woman and gaped openmouthed at me. Some greeted me with '*tabe tuan*,' mister. They did not know whether I was a man or a woman, as some Batak men also wear long hair and sarongs, a kind of skirt. The chief's wife brought me a chicken and rice, calling me '*opung*,' the highest address of honor, actually meaning 'grandfather of man.' I got the feeling that many people we came across on our ride thought me to be a ghost.

"The house we stayed in lay secluded in the forest, and while it had two entryways, it had no doors to shut. It was a bit eerie, so we closed the openings with some mats and kept a lantern burning and a rifle next to us. Light keeps animals away. This is how we slept among the heathen, the so-called savages. At two, in the middle of night, Gayus brought us coffee, of course by mistake. Not having a watch, he thought it was time to leave.

"We had trouble finding a guide for the next leg of our journey. When we entered the village, its residents fled into the jungle. With some effort, we were able to find and convince a *Raja*, a chief, to guide us. It was seven in the morning when we headed out. The chief rode ahead on his little pony, not using a saddle. It was a very narrow path, and at one point, skinny as he and his horse were, they slipped through between two thick tree trunks. I was right behind him, and my horse followed immediately. But for me the passage turned out to be too narrow, and I got stuck. The horse pulled mightily forward trying to get through, so that Hermann had to use all his strength to pull it, and me, back out from the obstruction. Everything was torn, the saddle as well as the bridle. It required a lengthy stop to repair the gear in a makeshift way with some string. Once more we climbed higher and higher, and I found it absolutely gorgeous in the mountains. Hermann and I were so happy, it being a wonderful experience to ride through God's beautiful nature.

14

Batak house

I had no trouble with riding, even though we had ridden twenty-one hours in three days.

"Our porters were, of course, on foot and heavily loaded. They are strong and have plenty of endurance, They cross the rivers with the water often reaching up to their arms. There are few bridges, and most consist of a single tree trunk. At one point, Hermann and I climbed on all fours across one of them. Our horses had to have their saddles taken off, since the river was too deep to ride across. At another time, four Bataks carried me across a river, because I refused to ride through the torrential waters."

Martha was very enthusiastic about the journey, finding Sumatra beautiful, and expressed her regret that her parents could not experience it. In her first letter on November 15, she wrote: "We arrived on the heights above Lake Toba, overlooking our future home at Si Piak, which is located 3,000 feet (900 m) above sea level. From this height, I saw the lake for the first time, a most beautiful vista. The horses were now taken down by a different, less steep trail. The *Raja* of Repa, a pagan, who met us there, insisted on leading me. Thus, I had Hermann on one side and the chief on the other to steady me on the steeply descending trail. A bit farther down the chief's wife joined us, taking Hermann's place. When we arrived below, the entire village had gathered, never before having seen a white woman. With lots of hollering a *solu* was made ready and we took off. The chief stood in the bow of the boat, commanding and beating the rhythm. In half-an-hour, twenty oarsmen rowed us across the lake to Si Piak. Suddenly, something moved and squealed under our seats, and several piglets surfaced, our welcome present from the chief! Unfortunately, they did not thrive under my, as yet inexpert care. Upon our arrival, the little bell was ringing, and Marinus, the Station's teacher, greeted us with his family. A big crowd had gathered to gawk at me. While we sat on the verandah, the people squatted on the ground before us. Hermann answered their continuous questions about our trip, about Germany, our forests, whether there were also tigers, snakes and elephants, and whether Hermann had 'bought' me. Many brought a chicken and some rice. Marinus was of great help in maintaining proper behavior and had the house very nicely decorated for my arrival."

The first Year in Si Piak

"Our home is beautifully situated," Martha wrote on November 15, 1906, in her first letter from her new home. "Hermann never described to me how very nice it is here. Wherever one looks, one sees the beautiful, deep-blue lake with its steeply-banked shores. Samosir Island across Lake Toba reminds me of the sight when my ship passed Sicily. The lake has so many bays that I'm still unable to make myself a clear picture of it. Our house lies high up, from where we look down to the lake on three sides."

It is important to remember that the Weissenbruchs were residing in the midst of pagans. Not many years earlier, this area still had a bad reputation and was greatly feared. The people living there were thought to be poison brewers, and no one from the area of Toba or Simalungen dared to stay overnight in the villages around Si Piak and Parapat. It was said that caves at the tip of the Si Piak promontory housed all kinds of rabble lying in wait for fishermen to come close. If they were of another tribe, they were attacked and sold as slaves or even eaten if they were not ransomed by their relatives. Just before Hermann had arrived at Si Piak in 1905, the Dutch government had freed several such captives. This action established a resemblance of peace and security. Such were some of the conditions they encountered at the beginning of their missionary work.

Martha described some of her first experiences: "Today is market, and the lake swarms with small *solus*, all headed for the market. Many people use the opportunity to come to us for medicine, especially for sores. I am sitting with Hermann in the *bilut raturata*, the study. All our rooms are nice, large, bright and airy, with good views from each. At first, I let Gayus work in his own way, because I was unable to enter his 'old' kitchen, a kind of hole in the ground. The stove pipe still hasn't arrived, so, Hilde Simon gave us one. Marinus made a 'knee' from a tin can. The oven stands right by the window with the tin can's knee taking the smoke out the window. I'm still unable to communicate with Gayus in words and all too frequently fall into the habit of trying to explain things in English. For the time being, manual signs and a few Batak words must suffice, yet I must often call on

Hermann to translate for me. I no longer need to concern myself with our main course for lunch. Gayus knows better than I how to prepare *ristafel* with all its ingredients, and he is also good at baking bread. To my delight, he makes every effort to do things well. Dressed in his white jacket and sarong, he sets the table, then calls for dinner, always looking neat. Prior to cooking, he always bathes in the lake. Many, but not all, Bataks are used to bathing twice a day. I, too, bathe daily in the morning without wearing anything. The beach, with its nice, white sand, is surrounded by large boulders, where no one is bothering us."

In another letter, Martha expressed her sorrow at not having received any mail from home, but hoped that the Mission boat Tole would bring some today. Since here, in the north and at the high elevation, few vegetables and potatoes were available, the meals consisted always of rice, chicken, curry, *pisang goreng*, and a spicy condiment made from coconut and other ingredients. Their fruit trees were too young to bear fruit; the ground was poor, and there was yet insufficient rainfall. Mountains surrounding the lake intercepted the clouds at this time of the year, preventing precipitation from reaching the lake basin. In two weeks she hoped to harvest beans and put the seeds she brought into the earth.

Gayus was not healthy, having been bitten by a snake three years ago. If he would not get better, they would have to take him to a hospital in Pearaja. Gayus did not know his age, as is common among Bataks. Hermann thought that he might be eighteen years old. Their other helper, Mitta, a good-looking little boy, may be fourteen years old. In the morning, he brought the little eggs laid by our small chickens, fetched water, swept the verandah and performed a few other tasks around the house. The Bataks were not used to working all day, it being difficult to do so in the tropics.

Martha wrote: "Let me describe to you how my day passes. I rise at six o'clock in the morning and walk to our new bath house, down by the lake, to freshen up. After dressing and breakfast and our morning prayers, I get our living room, the glass-enclosed verandah, the study and the bedroom, in order, and make sure that Mitta sweeps everywhere. When Mitta brings the eggs, I write the date on them. Then I clean the petroleum lamps, after which there's still plenty to arrange. Some people will show up. Chiefs with their village delegates are still coming to greet me. And women with their children, who, until I arrived, did not let themselves be seen at the station, also stop by. For the first time this Sunday, they came to the church service, but maybe it was only from curiosity. The service takes place in a very primitive building, not much more than a wooden shed. We take a couple of chairs along for ourselves, and the people sit on the floor. By eleven o'clock Gayus starts to prepare our meal, which we have at one o'clock. A bit later, after our coffee break, we take Batak language lessons from Marinus. Afterwards, Hermann sometimes plays his French horn, and I accompany him by singing. Around six o'clock we go for a walk and admire the sights of the lake and, sometimes, a beautiful sunset. After our simple supper, we have a service with the boys in Batak, of course. Then we jointly sing German melodies with the words coming from a Batak-language hymn book."

The Weissenbruchs now had the first eleven students, some of them the sons of chiefs, one of them from the island of Samosir. Martha described the people living there as being wild, a band of robbers and thieves, a scary people. Samosir, with an area of 240 square miles (620 sq. km), was still independent, that is, not under Dutch authority. The island was located right across the lake from the Si Piak mission station.

When the Samosir chief brought his son, he requested that Martha educate him since he was misbehaving at home. This required that he cross the lake on a daily basis. As a gift, he brought her a small billy goat, and for the teacher's wife, a rooster and some rice.

By now the neighborhood folks appeared to have satisfied their curiosity, and not as many people showed up any more to gawk at Martha. Gayus had acquired the habit of strictly expelling them from the kitchen if they peered in too closely. These visitors were not permitted to enter the verandah. There was a secondary verandah for picking up of medicines right next to the examination room. Many ill people showed up, including some lepers. Most of the illnesses dealt with fever, the eyes, and ulcers. Marinus, who had been baptized, was married and had three children. He frequently helped with the task of treating people.

19

Beautiful Lake Toba could be seen from every window of the Weissenbruchs' house, which was only a few steps from the shore. They heard the waves lapping on the beach, which consisted of pure white sand, some small shells and, in places, pumice. It is the world's largest wet caldera, produced by a volcano that erupted approximately 75,000 years ago. It is huge, about 60 miles (100 km) long, and 20 miles (32 km) wide, with its deepest point being 1,680 feet (505 m). Its elevation is close to 3,000 feet (900 m), making for a cooler climate, which Martha said was rarely above 70 degrees Fahrenheit (21 deg. Celsius). While the lake was usually peaceful and pleasant, storms could whip up serious waves.

A *prau*, a sailboat, was expected to arrive shortly, bringing, as was hoped, some crates, mail, and a guest. It was already the second Sunday before Christmas with the Holy Day approaching quickly. Every evening the boys practiced singing 'Silent Night, Holy Night.' It was now raining daily without it being gloomy. The rain made for good growing weather, if only they had good seed material. Martha asked her mother to send some well-wrapped in a letter. She was able to get some lettuce and radish seeds into the ground but expected little, since a subsequent rain may have washed the seeds away. The rainy season was brief, followed by a long dry period.

Martha reported on her collection of animals, consisting of an unknown number of chickens, unknown, because new ones were constantly added, and every week a couple of older ones were butchered. In addition, there were seven ducks, a billy goat and a ram, the latter two gifts from Bataks. Of the four little black pigs she had been given, one soon died and a second the boys butchered, since it would not eat any more.

She explained that, "such gifts are not pleasant to accept, and whenever possible, we refuse them, but those made upon my arrival had to be accepted. A Batak never makes a present without an ulterior motive. He may be thinking of some quarrel he is dealing with, to which the *tuan* may be of help to him, or he expects to receive, who knows what kind of major present in return. They never seem to work, rather fight their quarrels and figure out some new deceit. But they must find the necessary daily rice, and they do fish. They do not grow fruit, and they do not plant much, both requiring care and maintenance."

The Weissenbruchs, though, had many banana, orange, papaya and lemon trees, with a number of other local fruit trees. All were still very small, including the coconut trees.

Martha described the air as refreshing, the heat quite tolerable, and her health as being very good. Life passed at a slower pace to avoid tiring quickly. When they had visited the market a short while earlier, the people pressed closer and greeted them joyfully with loud shouts. Bataks have a much closer personal space than Westerners, which can become uncomfortable until one gets used to it. It was precious to observe how a shaman, a former foe of Hermann's, acted the policeman by pushing the people back to make room for the Weissenbruchs to move forward. There was not much to be had at the market, except some fruit, fish, chickens, and mats. Goods the Weissenbruchs were used to, like butter, milk and cheese, came in cans, the first from Germany, the second from Switzerland, and the third from Holland. And these items, even salt, were very expensive because of the cost of shipping. And everything they need had to be planned for at least three months in advance, and ordered from 'Toko Hennemann,' a Dutch enterprise, in Tarutung.

Visitors from other Mission stations, and occasional travelers, were frequent, for which planning and provisioning was also required. Old missionary hands were aware of the ever present shortages and were apt to bring some supplies along. From across the lake, the last set of visitors brought a few crates. They contained some of the rattan furniture the Weissenbruchs had purchased on Penang, and, at last, the missing stove pipe!

Martha told how "many sick people show up with all kinds of illnesses. They often arrive with injuries which have festered for years, or with age-old chronic problems, like leprosy. Of course, we are unable to help those, but they come again and again, and are unwilling to go to the leper colony at Huta Barat for help. Sometimes, people show up who are already close to death, but still expect to be healed. For days now, an old slave struggles on, hanging around the station. His master and relatives don't bother with him anymore, since he is no longer able to work. Another fellow, whom Hermann cured of his opium smoking habit, is still suffering from boils and keeps showing up for treatment. He is afraid that the villagers will sacrifice him to get him out of this world. One shudders sometimes when one sees all this misery and benightedness.

"The Bataks are a people of beggars and liars," she claimed, "and I am approached daily for a piece of cloth, a jacket, soap, or whatever, because, of course, the *tuan* and the *njonja* are rich. I must remain adamant about not giving in to their requests. If I do it once, I would be asked to do it again and again, and their demands would become ever more impudent. They ask Hermann to lend them some money, which he would surely never see again. Dr. Nommensen, our Mission's leader, has lost hundreds this way. They approach us with such flattering talk, sad and regretful, that one could easily be beguiled. But from what little we have, we don't have a penny to lend. And if we would give them things, we would only teach them to become so-called 'Rice Christians.' Then we would rather have none.

"The people living here show very little interest in the new religion we are teaching. As it is, they did not request a missionary, as is often the case. We have been dispatched to this area, so that Islam will not find entry.

"No one here trusts the other, and they steal from each other, including us, without restraint. They steal our expensive firewood even in broad daylight, which we must obtain from far away. When the women come for medicines, they hang around the house for hours, and then one piece of wood after another disappears in their sacks. I cannot leave a broom, a towel, or a nail lying around, or they will disappear. And all too often these women are dirty. When the women come for Sunday service, they usually gather before or after in front of our house, busying themselves by picking vermin from their hair."

In her letter dated January 1, 1907, Martha expressed to her parents her urgent desire for mail to break her isolation. Mail delivery appeared to be rather insecure, with many letters getting lost. She was delighted when the *prau* arrived bringing some mail and various furniture and clothing items. But most of it was wet, even inside the crates, despite being packed in oil paper. Tropical rain gets through just about everything, and mattresses and clothing items were always in need of drying on the verandah, so that they would not become moldy. However, some crates were still missing, having made an extra trip to somewhere by mistake. They were expected to be in Batu Ras by now, from where they were to be transported by ox cart to Tiga Ras, a trip of five days. There, they would be held until the *prau* picked them up on its next circuit around the lake.

The Weissenbruchs employed three more 'boys,' Manasse, Mitta and Amasalae, in addition to Gayus. Mitta and Amasalae were still pagans. In preparation for a trip to Toba and Silindung, Manasse was exercising Martha's fiery horse, Fritz. Gayus and Manasse were to take the Weissenbruchs two horses around the lake, while Hermann and Martha would cross by boat.

There were often problems with the *prau's* schedule, and, once more, the boat did not arrive. From where they lived, they could see across the length of the lake to Purba, with everything so clear that one thought it not very far. But even the motor boat could take more than five hours to get there, and it would take nine to ten hours if one were able to walk across the lake in a straight line. Samosir, too, looked to be very close, yet it took three hours to get there as the crow flies. This gives an idea of the lake's size. If it is sometimes angry, it may mean, as happened once to Brother Pohlig, three days by motor boat to get from Si Piak to Purba. The boat was trapped in a bay where it could neither land nor continue with its journey.

In a January letter to her parents, written two months after her arrival, Martha reported: "Sister Auguste and I are sitting on the *emper*, the verandah, and write. Around us, all is quiet and there is little sun. It is about seventy degrees Fahrenheit (21 deg. C). Across from our building is the boys' house. Half of it is still serving as the church until the school building is finished. At present, there are several sick people lying inside. They are travelers who have arrived from Si Malungun, and are unable to continue their journey. They are most likely suffering from malaria. All travelers passing through here spend the night at our station, including pagans. They are afraid to stay in one of the villages.

"This morning many people attended our service. Many are afraid that they will be punished by the *begus*, their native ghosts. Some are even still afraid of us white people and run off when one approaches them, especially single women working in the fields. If they are in the company of another woman, they are less fearful. Most people are glad to see us visiting their villages, but others are much less friendly.

"The villages – the closest is only ten minutes away – are hidden in the greenery, and are usually enclosed by a tall wall planted on top with bamboo and trees, with only a small gate for entry, often so low that one must crawl through. They are built like small fortresses. We never enter the houses, which we find too dirty and too dark. It is also very cumbersome to climb the tall 'chicken ladders' serving as access, and then having to crawl through the round entry hole. Usually, four families live in one room, with everyone squatting on the floor.

"There are a few people who regularly attend services, but they are still unable to comprehend what we are actually trying to accomplish. When Hermann and Marinus pray aloud, the people look wonderingly at them and ask afterwards what this was all about; why we fold our hands and close our eyes. It's easy for them to think: 'This is something for white folks, but not for us.' Then there are the threats from their shamans whom they fear in addition to their ghosts. They also believe that Whites eat unclean foods, but don't know what it supposedly is, when they themselves eat just about everything that can be had.

"This morning was market time, which resulted in a lot of traffic at our station. Many who came are simply curious and only want to see what we are doing. They sit openmouthed in the yard and marvel at what is going on. Without saying a word, they watch my activities from beyond the verandah's railing.

"Many also come to hear Hermann pass judgment on their quarrels. It is almost impossible to avoid. All too often the people are very excited and scream and curse, a sight that is both wild and terrible to observe. The object of their quarrels is usually the rice fields which they take away from one another. They attack those working in a field and chase them off. This morning, they attacked a man who is now afraid to return to his village. He will stay here for a while and work for us."

Hermann added a few comments to Martha's letter:

"We also house a couple of ill people here. One is an opium smoker from Samosir, who hopes to get rid of his addiction. The other is a boy, who has abcesses on both legs, from which I removed forty maggots with tweezers. Then came a *Raja*, a chief, with a number of his dependents from the area of Moting and Girsang, and the *tuan* doctor quickly had to change hats to become the *tuan* judge. These people arrived with some unpleasant rice field issues with both parties cursing and lying. Since the constant lying made it impossible to establish who the owner of the rice field was, I decided to turn this case over to the Dutch Controller. Another man, who had come to them to make peace, had been held captive. I will keep him here for his protection."

A month later, Martha wrote that she had not yet missed ice or the European cold. She was little bothered by the heat as the house remained cool, even when the sun was at the zenith. When the sun was at its highest, they usually set their clocks to it. It was surprising how accurately the natives knew time when they did not even know what a clock was.

Some more of the Weissenbruchs' goods finally arrived from Penang, among them ten tins of butter, a treasure. Butter now came from England, Holland, and Bombay, India. Martha expressed her hope of obtaining enough *horbo* milk, water buffalo milk, to make butter herself.

Sitting on the verandah, she wrote, "Hermann sits together with about forty Bataks, most of them *Rajas*, chieftains. At issue is a dispute over a theft. They become very aggravated, wild and raving, with all of them lying, so that one cannot trust a single one. Therefore, it isn't easy for Hermann to elicit the truth. Once a judgment has been made, the punishment is determined by the chieftains according to their customs, their *adat*. Fortunately, these judgments are no longer as cruel as they once were. Ompuhatunggal of Adji Bata, is Hermann's greatest and most powerful opponent. He sits there, making a self-important face, disdainfully chewing his betel – this disgusting stuff – and always screams when he has something to say. These fellows are mostly the *Rajas* who were earlier warring with Hermann."

The Weissenbruchs' planned trip to Toba and Silindung was up in the air, since, at the present time, no one was to leave the station, because of one of the occasional flare-ups of tribal warfare. In addition to the mission station in Lumban, various schools and a government building had been burned. In Lumban na Bolon someone had burned down the mission station, with the youngest child of the Schmieds dying in the fire. In Toba and Uluan, six guards each were ordered posted at every mission

25

station and government building. The government took thirty *Rajas* prisoners from the affected area and brought them to Sibolga. The local Si Piak *Rajas* offered to guard the Si Piak station, not because they were afraid for us, but afraid to suffer the fate of a similar punishment. But then they did not go through with their offer. Governor Westenberg, or rather the Assistant Resident at Si Dolok, sent a troop of soldiers, but the 'trusted protectors,' Bataks, Javanese, and a couple of Dutchmen, used the night to secretly move out and on to Uluan, against their orders. "So, what were we to do?" Martha said. "We had no Christians to guard us, and we were both sick from dysentery with no doctor available. Thus, it turned out that ours was the only station that remained unguarded."

Once more, Martha wrote to her parents for seed stock, to be well-packed in letters. The request was for spinach, lettuce, peas, kohlrabi, savoy and red cabbage, red beets, and lots of flower seeds, but not too much at one time, since the seeds would not keep very long, and the few people at the station could not eat all that can be produced on the large garden plot they had established. The ground of the garden is stoney, and while water is abundant, it is located 66 feet (20 m) below where they live.

Writing from Purba Sariboe in March, she mentioned for the first time the occurrence of a serious headache, but it passed, and they took off across the lake on the 'Tole' to visit a Dutch family, the Guillaumes, in Purba. Their station was located about 660 feet (200 m) above the lake's level, requiring a good half hour in 90 degree Fahrenheit (30 deg. C) heat to ascend. Once there, it was pleasantly cool, the mornings even being cold. From where they lived, one looked down to a beautiful valley with green rice fields, but from their present location, the rugged mountains rose still further. The station was situated on a small plateau, just large enough for the buildings. The Guillaumes had a big telescope with which they could even see the Weissenbruchs' home at Si Piak. She described Mr. Guillaume as a small, happy man, full of humor and very energetic. Their five children ran around barefoot, like all children. Anne Guillaume had two 'girls' employed – Martha emphasized the girls in her letter – since usually only boys were hired. Both girls were bought-off slaves, one nice, the other less

26

pleasant. In the near future, Mr. Guillaume was going to visit the city of Medan, at which time he was going to purchase some shoes for his wife. While he would be at it, Martha asked if he would also bring some for her right away, that is . . . six pairs! Since no one here knew how to repair shoes, they were usually worn down to the bitter end. Concluding her letter, she said, "While I'm writing this, across from me the monkeys (most likely siamangs, lesser apes) are making their 'music' in the forest. The sounds are nice, a mixture of high and low voices, interspersed by the low bass of the larger members."

At Easter, Hermann commented on their festivities. He described being on the verandah and accompanying Martha's singing with his French horn. This always attracted some Bataks who generally liked to hear music. He expressed his hope that their missionary efforts would bear fruit and dispel the 'fog of paganism.' In nearby Parapat, *Raja* Saul performed his pagan sacrificial celebrations in which dancing and singing play a large role. However, these days *Raja* Saul eagerly attended the Christian services and performed his pagan celebrations only as a demonstration of his departure from this heathen way of life. When he visited the station yesterday, he said, "*Tuan*, we want to tell the spirits 'this is our last sacrifice; do not demand more from us, for we want to leave the *ugama na buruk*, the old, worn-out religion, to follow the new and better one.' "

Hermann commented on this statement with, "while, for the time being, I do not expect anything exceptional, I am certain that we are heading for a blessed time." Continuing, he cited another attendee, little *Raja* Ama ni Aba, who, during the services, paid close attention and tried his best to sing along with our foreign melodies. He often prayed with us, not minding the others. The other day, he supposedly told Marinus, the teacher, "I do not keep a *sanggar* at my rice field." A *sanggar* is a superstitious, heathen decoration of green branches, meant to bring plenty of rice. "I hope that God, in his grace, will bless my work without such magic." The little man no longer worked Sundays, and is not afraid, like many others, that this will curtail his supply of food.

Hermann hoped to have all the lumber for the school by the end of April, to gain a better location for his services. He told of his frustration at being unable to express all that he wished to say in the Batak language and found it difficult to convey the thoughts he had about the biblical text. Bemoaning the fact that he was still beholden to his German mental images, he regretted that he still understood Batak lines of thought insufficiently. In order to understand the Batak culture better, he read various Batak fables from which he tried to remember various appropriate adages.

The above comments were followed by an interesting expression. "You can see from the lines I've written that the gospel does enter the mindset of our 'blacks and savages,' " and underlining these terms, he commented in brackets, ("Please note! We never talk like this about our dear Bataks!"). But ever so slowly the gospel, God's powers, which are continually growing, produce strong change. How difficult it must be for a pagan to separate himself from the old, ancestral images and aberrations, is slowly becoming clearer to me."

He described how important health was in missionary work, and mentioned Martha's insufficient blood supply, of which they were already aware in Germany, and her severe headaches, weak legs, and loss of appetite. He blamed it on the daily, unchanging rice diet and their continuing lack of sufficient quantities of vegetables. A few weeks ago, Hermann succeeded in arranging with the Parapat *Raja* to acquire a daily supply of water buffalo milk, supplied in a wine bottle, for Martha to drink every morning. He wrote, however, that there are not many buffalos raised in the area, because of too much opium smoking and the resulting poverty. Also, such an animal gives only about one liter of milk per day; the rest had to be left for the calf. The people are not used to drinking milk, believing that if they do, the calf will die. Around Toba and Silindung many *horbos*, water buffalos, are kept, so that the missionaries get plenty of inexpensive milk, enabling them to make butter and cheese, as well. He described how Brothers Simon and Guillaume experienced the same problem, which is why they purchased some Bengal cows, commonly kept on plantations. Such an animal provided three liters of milk a day, which came close in taste and nutritional value to that of German cows.

However, the Bengal cows were rather expensive and with a calf – or one soon to be born – cost about one hundred dollars, approximately 250 marks. Nevertheless, he and Martha would like to acquire such an animal. "Dear parents," he wrote, "I am sure that Martha's health is important to you, while you are also aware of my financial situation. I had to build the station under severe difficulties, and yet receive the same monetary compensation as every other Brother. Could you, therefore, dear father, instead of some furniture, send us 300 marks? However, when you deposit the money with Mr. Schindler at the Rhenish Mission, state expressly that it is to be paid to me personally, or it will end up in the general pot, whose maw is always wide open. Then we will continue drinking Lake Toba water instead of milk. Today, it is five months since we stood before the altar, and as you can see from our correspondence, 'we do not regret it.' "

Martha then wrote that she was surprised that she had not written home for a long time. However, she was able to explain it by saying that she had frequently been sick with fever, headaches and general weakness. Several times, she had to take quinine. She had a bout of dysentery from which she never fully recovered. It was common for newcomers to this country to suffer much in their first year. She wrote, "Hermann touchingly takes care of me. As much as possible I let Gayus take care of the kitchen, but recently he told us suddenly that he intended to leave. His relatives wanted him to get married, and he had already agreed to follow through with it. But then he decided, without our asking him, to stay instead. However, I'm afraid our four boys won't last too much longer. There's always quarreling among them because Gayus receives a higher wage, eight marks per month and four uniforms per year, while the others get only five, plus the suits. What they don't realize is that they have just come from their village and know little, while Gayus has already worked as a cook for several years and can wash, starch and iron.

"Everything here is very expensive. The natives will do nothing for free, and the *tuan* must pay more than natives for all inland products. And when they steal from him, they do not consider it unjust, for the *tuan* is rich and can replace everything. We are now getting some milk almost every morning. I hand over a bottle with a funnel, and the people milk directly into the bottle. However, a *horbo* frequently has more than one owner, and every four days is moved from one to the other. This results in a different milk supplier every four days, and quite often we don't get any milk at all during a transfer period. Anyway, at home, one would not accept milk from such dirty hands.

"We must spend four-marks-fifty for rice every week, of which the boys need three quarters. We cannot purchase any here and even chickens must come from the village of Toba. We often send our *solu* with others from the village to fetch rice. When they leave at noon, they arrive around 9 p.m. in Si Gumpar. The next day they make their purchases, after which they return on the third day. The Tole sometimes brings us rice from Si Gumpar, but Nommensen Jr. is so forgetful that even a second reminder brings no result. While I'm writing this, *Raja* Saul celebrates his big festivity. Supposedly, for the last time, their invisible *begu*, their spirit, is given sacrifices, and women and girls dance gracefully, each on their own, throughout the night. But whether they will follow the new religion is still very much in question. When they claim that they will, it may sound reassuring, but such things are not taken so seriously here. The people are often unreliable and one cannot trust anybody. *Raja* Saul is one of the best and most helpful. With his own hands he has built a tower for the church bell. It is up on the hill, where the school is to be built."

On April 21, Martha described how Controller Kock arrived unexpectedly and simply installed himself at the station for a number of days. She wrote, "It got busy in our yard, because he had called on many Bataks from a number of villages to come. He had orders from the Governor-General to look for Singamangaraja, the long-sought troublemaker, and to get him to peacefully give up his controversial activities and put himself under the protection of the government. Singamangaraja was to be assured life and freedom. Kock sent letters with delegates to the Singa, but the man has yet to be found, with no one knowing his whereabouts. Dr. Nommensen, who is the only Westerner who has ever seen the Singamangaraja and talked to him, may come tomorrow. This Singa has no permanent place of stay. He is still very much liked and has followers everywhere. We are very interested on how this will be resolved."

All day the Weisenbruchs' yard was occupied by Bataks, who presented their cases to the Controller, who then dictated a fine of from 20 to 40 guilders to the guilty. "Kock is not a Christian; he may even acknowledge some of Muhammad's teachings. He grew up as a child in India and possesses the native's ease of movement and waves his hands like Indians."

A few days later Martha commented that she was glad that everyone had left. Controller Kock did fit well into the house order, going with the flow. However, he talked grandly, and one could sense his inner untruths. He had to wait here for the arrival of the Tole. The Weissenbruchs' next visitors, the Mohris with three children, were expected in two weeks. They would continue their travel to Purba the day following their arrival. Every single traveler heading east or north must do so via Si Piak, which is why there were so many visitors. They always stayed for at least one night.

"I am presently alone with the boys. Gayus cooks rice with chicken and coconut, and a bit of vegetable. Sour pickles, sweet-and-sour pumpkin, sweet *botik*, that is papaya, are served as condiments. Then there is the unavoidable *sambal*, finely chopped fried meat, spiced with Spanish pepper. I am so tired of rice, but there's nothing else. We must always look for vegetables, since rice does not have sufficient nutritional value. Our recently harvested potatoes, no larger than walnuts, had partly rotted. It's almost useless trying to grow them."

A few days ago, the Weissenbruchs' dog killed a 5 foot (1.5 m) long poisonous snake. It was the first one Martha had seen. Snakes, being shy, were rarely visible and were afraid of people. Nevertheless, Hermann had shot three snakes in three weeks, the last one this morning. Tigers were not seen in their area, but were found only on the other side of the lake in the 6,600 foot (2,000 m) high mountains. On their side, the mountains were wooded only on the upper slopes, as the lower part dropped steeply. Referring briefly to her 'tiger experience,' as she called it, Martha thought it a rarity. Some Europeans had been in the country for ten years without ever seeing a tiger. In Bandar, tigers often approached houses, where they would emit a high-pitched, brief scream. Martha reported Hilde Simon's account that she heard tigers calling often in broad daylight, and very close to her home. There were stations, where, at night, tigers snatched dogs from the verandah – all in all, a mixed bag.

At great cost they had seven coconut palm trees shipped in and planted near the shore, about 60 feet (18 m) below the house. Because of a storm's racket during the following night, even their dogs did not hear them being stolen. Hopefully, some friendly chiefs would be able to track down the thieves, who must have come across the lake from Samosir.

"Now, imagine," she wrote soon after the theft, "We did catch the thief who stole our coconut palms in a most peculiar way. A clairvoyant, a Christian from Toba was visiting us. When Hermann told him that our palms had been stolen and asked, 'Might you know something about it?' the man thought about the issue for a moment, looked around, and then said, 'tuan, up there in Huta.' He pointed at a village about two hours distant. 'There are people who will tell you who the thieves are.' He was correct, and the thief was apprehended, after which he was fined to compensate us for the palms and also pay a fine of 60 guilders to the government. Until he finishes paying the Controller, he works as a prisoner under supervision. The clairvoyant did not know the thief's village nor the people there, nor anything of the area. Isn't this odd? He also told another man in Parapat where he could find his stolen horse without even knowing of the theft."

Martha's letter of May 9, described how a Batak tailor happened to travel past Si Piak and was employed by the Weissenbruchs. He even finished a mattress, which he stuffed and padded with beautiful white *kapok,* which they had obtained as a gift from a *Raja. Kapok* is difficult to get here. The Weissenbruchs planted *kapok* trees, which produce their fluffy, cotton-like material in seed pods. In about ten years, there will be plenty of *kapok* available. Hermann planted just about everything that could be planted here. The Weissenbruchs now had 200 *pisang* trees with about 30 bearing fruit. Each 'tree' carried a bunch of bananas up to 30 inches (0.75 m) long, which took approximately six months to ripen. Pineapple, too, took a long time until ready to be harvested. Their stock amounted to about 400-500 pineapple plants with 25 presently ripening. Other plant assets were papayas, lemons, sweet and bitter oranges, and *durian* , but all grew very slowly. There was a time of ripening for each kind of fruit, but there was always something that could be harvested at any given time. Often, there was ripe fruit growing in the lower branches, while blooms sprouted at the top.

A problem arose with Brother Simon in Bandar, another missionary station. He was feverish for months and may also be afflicted with typhoid fever. Several missionary personnel were to travel to Bandar to bring Brother Simon back to health. Hermann was also to go and was expected to be gone for three days. However, he was able to return earlier, having found reliable people to escort the missionary Sisters to Bandar. While Hermann was gone, Martha was concerned about the Singamangaraja's reaction to Controller Kock's invitation, but he neither showed up nor responded in writing. Various fires that burned that evening along the lake might have been signals to him from his followers.

Martha wrote at the beginning of May, "Two weeks from now, Hermann must accompany Sister Zeitter to Lumban Lobu, during which time I will be alone. Then the Mohris with their three children will arrive, the Brinkschmidts from Palipi, and Sister Steinsiek. After that, the Simons are due. There is a continuous coming and going."

Brother Simon's health took a turn for the worse. During the past months, some of the Toba missionaries had reproached him concerning his work. Simon, Guillaume and Theis operated very differently than we in Si Piak, or those in Toba and Silindung. Si Malungun is a huge area, but sparsely populated. Some Brothers thought that the entire Si Malungun work was misplaced and useless and swallowed enormous amounts of money. Only a few yards to the right of the Si Piak station was the dividing line between the areas of Toba and Si Malungun, the Weissenbruchs' area work.

"I'm getting better with the language," Martha wrote, "and also with managing the household, which, with such dependent helpers, is no small task. I am glad to have Gayus, who knows quite a bit, but I'm afraid that he will soon marry. Then, I must teach little Mitta. All Bataks are adept, and they all know how to butcher chickens and other animals and to prepare fish. This spares me from having to eviscerate chickens, which I've always dreaded. And all of them can ride and swim. Day and night, people are fishing on the lake, and we often purchase fish, but only if they are still alive. Fortunately, there are no crocodiles or other dangerous creatures in the lake. This is because the discharge from the lake via the Siguragura Falls, entering into the Assahan river, prevent the entry of such animals.

"At this time, we are experiencing heavy thunderstorms with plenty of lightning every evening. But at the moment, it is oddly quiet. At the beginning of my stay, Sundays seemed to be quieter, more Sunday-like, as if there was a holiday. Earlier this morning, many people attended the service. Often, a lively conversation develops afterwards, either about what has been heard, the new religion the *tuan* is presenting, or about Germany in general. They want to know what grows in Germany and are especially interested in the *eme*, the 'rice,' being grown there. We show them, and let them taste wheat. There are plenty of questions and amazement, all expressed with great liveliness."

On June 2nd, Martha referred to a letter from her mother, telling of her family's shortage of funds. This meant, she wrote, "that our long 'pleading' letter arrived at the wrong time. Of course, we gladly wait for the harmonium and the other things which can come some time later. We have made do until now and can continue doing so. But it looks, father, that you won't be able to send us any 'cow money' either. Milk is becoming scarce, and will shortly run out completely. However, I need clothes and curtains to provide some privacy for our rooms.

"Father, you seem to think that we might have built too luxuriously, which is why we have all this debt, but be aware that Hermann built smaller than the building authorities specified. Our debt amounts to 1,200 guilders, nearly 2,000 marks. A small portion of this has been repaid already, including some of the furniture. The guilders were not for our furniture, but to build our house, the boys' house, the horse stable and chicken coop, and the bath shed. We manage here under much more difficult conditions than most other missionaries. There's hardly ever a subsidy coming from the Mission. We already received a salary advance of 300 guilders from the Mission Headquarters in Barmen and have asked for 800 more to pay off part of the debt. Dr. Nommensen is only permitted to give an advance for up to 1/3 of a salary; if more is asked for, one must request it in Barmen. The Barmen delegates 'wisely' stated that every missionary ought to contribute to the building of his house, so that he gains the feeling that he is living in his own abode. But the missionary does not care for this feeling at all, when, debt-laden, he is transferred to a new station, and must take this debt along without anyone helping to alleviate it.

"When Inspector H. comes next year, some of this may yet be taken care of. The Barmen delegates always figure that the young missionaries, during the two years of their (required) bachelorhood, are able to save some money. But after only nine months here, Hermann had to get the lumber ready in Lumbab Lobu for the boys' house and ship it here and then had to replace his injured horse. We reported all this to Barmen, together with the building plans and expenditures, and are waiting now for their response. Enough of this; it is an unpleasant subject!"

She then bemoaned that Gayus was leaving to get married. Mitta was to take his place, but still needed lots of training. For house cleaning, she employed a poor, little boy by the name of Pangelak, who was happy to get room and board and some clothing, which meant that she would shortly need to sew some more. The little fellow didn't know a thing, and had never handled a broom. A Batak house was never swept. Its floor consisted of bamboo rods, treacherous for Europeans not wanting to get stuck in the gaps, and with refuse dropping through the openings.

"Oh, if no visitors would come for a quarter of a year," Martha kept complaining. "It's just too much. There are too many! When there are so many visitors, and I have no potatoes, no vegetables, no eggs, and maybe no more coffee beans or no flour as well,   maintaining a decent household causes headaches. Ten weeks ago we ordered coffee, and it has still not arrived. No coffee is being grown around here, but sometimes we can get a little from Samosir. We have planted coffee trees in our garden and given plants to Bataks to grow. Hermann is also in the process of having a 'wet' rice field established. To put it in by the lake shore is a major piece of work. In our area, the Bataks grow only dry rice, which doesn't produce as much, although, in general, they are very familiar with how to irrigate fields. Now that the *tuan* is building wet rice fields, our neighbor is also doing it by the lake. The people often say, 'everything grows better with the *tuan*.' Well, nothing grows by itself, and the people simply don't put enough effort into cultivating their grounds. Our Bataks here do not grow fruit, but plant only rice and *gadong*, sweet potatoes. They do not drink coffee and eat only twice a day, mornings at eleven and in the afternoon at five.
"Pangelak arrived yesterday. I handed him right away some soap and sent him to the lake to wash up. A happy, little fellow, he wears only an *ulos*, a loin cloth. He is at most twelve

35

years old and, of course, goes to school. Once again, it's market time, and the lake is full of small and large boats. Many people show up at our doorstep to present their concerns. Some delegates from an outlying area came to ask for a *tuan*, since they had observed that people having a *tuan* were happier. Hermann will travel there, after which a teacher will likely be dispatched for the time being.

"Today, Sunday, the 23rd of June," she wrote, "was a very sad and difficult day. Our carpenter, a Christian, who had been sent to us by Brother Nommensen to help build the school, had been sick for days and died this afternoon. We don't know what he was suffering from, but it must have been something serious, maybe an intestinal obstruction or peritonitis. Now he lies in a coffin which Marinus and the boys put together. The man was to be transported tonight to Si Gumpar, but, unfortunately, our *solu* isn't here, and we can't find one anywhere. The Bataks, the pagans, even more than the Christians, want their dead buried close to where they live, and we would have liked to comply with this custom. None of his relatives or his wife yet know of his death. If our *solu* returns tonight, his body will be taken to his wife during the night; if not, he will be buried here. Well, our *solu* came in time, and one can always get enough oarsmen. However, once again the Bataks' meanness showed at this occasion, when they demanded an excessive 15 ringgit, about 35 marks, when only 4 ringgit sufficed. When Hermann was ready to send them away and suggested that our own boys would take care of it, they relented. One observes again and again, in small ways, the coarseness of these people by how they handled the carpenter's body. They found it unnecessary that we took so much care of the man. The pagan knows nothing of love, except perhaps for himself and his children. Often they have several wives; whoever can afford it, buys himself two. But when worse comes to worst, it happens, as we heard recently, that a man sold his second child to purchase opium. His first had been sold already. To all this, another death was added, that of Brother Mohri, 72 years old. He was in seemingly good health and had just visited us with his family. Now his wife is alone with her three children, the youngest being only one-and-one-half years old!"

Hermann and Martha paid a visit to the Steinsiek mission station in Toba, where she admired the beautiful, tall trees, the palms and the many flowers. The Steinsieks had a garden as one can only have in the tropics. The young Mrs. Nommensen with three children, all of them afflicted with whooping cough, was also visiting. The Steinsieks' children, being older, had already been sent to Germany for further schooling. Nearby the Steinsieks' house was the Sister house, run by Sister Lisette and Sister Steinsiek. They took care of several small Batak orphans and about twenty girls whom they educated. Another Sister ran the girls school. And then there was Sunday school for the little ones, teenagers, adults, and for boys and girls. They all sang very well and loved it, a talent the Bataks seem to possess. The Weissenbruchs visited the leper asylum in Huta Salem. It was located on an airy hill. There was a church, a teacher and several supervisors. The visitors found indescribable misery there, and were very much moved to see the many small children, who still had a long life ahead of them. The people knew not to touch the visitors. "If only the lepers in Parapat would be willing to come here," Martha said.

After a long hiatus, Martha wrote in August from Pangombuan, about a day's trip from Laguboti to Balige. She had made this ride on a very unmanageable horse, tiring her immensely. Subsequently, they continued their ride to Si Gumpar, where the Nommensens were building. The station was in the midst of forest with 130 foot (40 m) tall trees with mighty trunks and crowns. Old Brother Nommensen was still very chipper at 73 years. He was considered indispensable. All requests and complaints ended up with him, and he determined everything. His great love was his power; it shone from his eyes, and everyone meeting him sensed it. The Weissenbruchs continued from Si Gumpar to Si Antar, together with Dr. Schreiber and Sister Lina Zeitter. Unfortunately, the Lombecks they were to visit suffered from dysentery. Their smallest daughter had died a day earlier. Right after the child's burial, they traveled for an hour on the lake to Pangombuan. Hermann and Martha were rowed on very narrow but long boats, barely three feet (90 cm) wide and just as deep. Two of the boats were rigged together and a bench tied to the top. In this way, they crossed some bullrush-overgrown, swampy waters, after which they walked another half hour to their destination. At the station, they found a Batak who understood some German; in Laguboti were two teachers who spoke German quite well, something not very common.

On a September Sunday, service in their finished school was to be held in one hour. Martha wrote, "you ought to hear our school boys sing. A year ago, it was still a muddle with each singing his own tune. Now, however, they can sing even difficult songs with hardly any mistake. Marinus, our teacher, is very musical and plays every melody from memory. Of course, the local Bataks do not as yet observe Sunday, since we have no Christians yet. When our bell rings in the morning, they know it is Sunday and come, but by afternoon they resume their work in the village and the fields, or go fishing on the lake. Often, when we come to the village, they place a clean white mat in the middle of the village square for us to sit on, with everyone else, young and old, surrounding us, sitting on the bare ground. Chickens and pigs, running free, sometimes come alarmingly close. Some of the people don't want to have anything to do with the *tuan*, and simply continue with what they are doing, be it grinding rice or weaving or dying cloth. But such visits are always interesting. We talk with them about their activities and look at the colorful and often artistic decorations of their houses."

By mid-November Martha was already thinking of the coming Christmas, and regretted the Bataks' indifference to this celebration. But she understood their lack of comprehension, and, simultaneously, remarked about the people's apparent loss of trust in their old religion. There was a man who rowed his *solu* every Sunday for three quarters of an hour to come to their service. A nice group of regular church attendees had evolved, and new ones were coming every day, especially women.

The Weissenbruchs were still having trouble with their marriage documents. The Dutch authorities did not recognize them as being married, requiring Hermann to travel again to Si Antar. "The Dutchmen's fussiness and their dawdling are unbelievable!" Martha wrote. "We will use the opportunity to visit Raja, since we have yet to see the Sisters Theis. The Guillaumes and Müllers will also come, and we shall have a little second-wedding celebration. The Müllers were married just two weeks ago in Penang. Although it is the rainy season, and thus not traveling weather, Hermann must get to Si Antar, and I don't care to be alone for six days. So, tomorrow, we will take the rowboat to Tiga Ras, which will take five hours, and then stay overnight with *Pandita* Samuel. A ride of seven hours will take us to Raja, a station lying in the midst of forest, which is always a bit scary. In the evening, no one steps outside anymore with so many tigers around. They have been observed at night walking past the house, so I would rather stay inside."

At the end of November, Hermann reported that his activities were gradually spreading out into the surrounding area. Two months earlier, he had established an outpost in Propa by the lake, and in another five villages the people had expressed interest in building schools. They had concluded a written contract with him for the lumber, which would be ready in two to three months time. If only Nommensen could provide teachers. Despite of two seminars that had been held, there was still a great shortage of teachers.

December had arrived, and the Controller from the east coast had come to Parapat for several days. "It is always disagreeable when these gentlemen are in the area over Sunday. For them, there is no Sunday. They work every day, and in so doing keep the people from our service. During their stay, there's always a big commotion; one of the Bataks wants to be made *Raja*, another a policeman, and this and that. When in the area, these gentlemen usually stop by and sometimes stay for dinner. But there is little, if any, appreciation for our activities. The man from the west coast is even a decided opponent of the missions. In Medan, where there are many Europeans, and on most of the plantations, they do not observe Sunday. On the plantations, every first and fifteenth of a month is a day of rest – Isn't that terrible?" Martha wrote.

"Christmas is approaching quickly, and I have lots to do until then. The boys get white jackets and belts, and I must also keep our teacher's family in mind. One must start thinking about what to give by July, or these presents may not be available by the time they are needed. The school children are eagerly practicing Christmas songs. It sounds very homey coming from the school up on the hill. Sometimes one feels homesick. If our Christmas decorations arrive in time, we will decorate a tree for the service on Christmas eve. But the people still do not understand why we celebrate Christmas. Maybe, little by little, they will get the idea of God's love. It will come, even if we never see or experience it. If one did not know this, one could despair of mission work. And yet, individual people are already quite nice to us, trusting and affectionate, which makes us happy.

"Soon, it will be Christmas, and Sister Weetneeks, a small, sweet person, will come to stay with us for one or two weeks. She is from Latvia and in earlier times was a teacher in Russia. She has visited us before and I like her very much. It appears our station has acquired the reputation of being a vacation place.

"In February, a trip to another conference will become necessary, yet I wish we could stay put for awhile. When we are gone too often, our garden tends to go wild. For months, plenty of roses have bloomed in front of our house. At the next opportunity, we intend to bring some more leafy plants from Silindung. Many of them are plants which, at home, are raised with difficulty in greenhouses. Here, they grow wild." She concluded with the news that Elisabeth Brinkschmidt died in Palipi, a terrible loss for her husband.

Tomorrow is Christmas, Martha wrote. "We, too, will have a tree. Marinus will get it tomorrow, and we have some ornaments for it. Our boys will get some new uniforms which I have made. Unfortunately, I have nothing yet for Marinus's children, since the respective crates did not arrive. I was unable to bake cookies, as I did not have enough butter, nor the necessary forms and sheets, which is why a cake will have to do. Gayus will bake a banana cake in palm oil for the boys, the best treat a Batak can think of. We do not know whether anyone will come for the service, but on the Christmas holiday, Marinus will join us with his family, and maybe a few more." However, when the time came, four teachers with 123 students gathered by their pretty Christmas tree, made of a six-foot-tall *pisang* stalk to which they had attached branches collected in the forest. Probably at total of 350 people pushed into the school building with more trying to get in. The Weissenbruchs spent the evening singing Christmas songs, but had to bundle up sitting on the verandah, since the temperature had dropped to only 62 deg. Fahrenheit (16 deg. C). A storm tossed up big waves on the lake.

Weissenbruchs' House

Settled in

It was now the beginning of January 1908. The mission people in Barmen wanted to expand into Pakpak and transfer the Weissenbruchs there. However, the region's military commander decided that Hermann should stay in Si Piak. The government people in Pakpak were not eager to see too many stations going up in their region, which they did not consider secure yet, and asked only for more Batak teachers for the next two years.

Happily, Hermann and Martha were able to stay in Si Piak. 'Aunt' Nommensen came for a visit. She suffered from bouts of depression, but the visit went well. At the beginning of February, they saw an increase in the attendance at their services, with one to two hundred people showing up, most of them women. Many carried their small children in *ulos*, a cloth-wrapping, on their backs. From time to time one of the children started to cry murderously, interrupting the service.

In February, Martha wrote, "Hermann and Sister Weetneeks had left for a difficult walk into the mountains. I and the boys were all asleep, so that we did not hear the landing of the Tole. Thus, we missed the arrival of the Consular Baron von Bouthelaar from Batavia. He is responsible for all Evangelical Missions in the Netherland East Indies. He is a pleasant Dutchman who speaks very good German. He was going to sleep on the Tole, since the station's guest room was occupied. However, we set up sleeping and washing facilities in the study, where he then stayed. Upon Hermann's return he had many questions for him about our work, and we are now hopeful that the importation of opium will be curtailed."

Another missionary meeting took the couple to Sipoholon. Marinus guarded the station together with the two little boys, Si Pangelak and Si Adong. The older ones came along to carry the luggage. The path to Silindung, part of the travel distance, was not too bad, since everywhere twenty feet (6 m) wide roadways were being established. Soon, cars can be expected to travel all the way to Lake Toba. A third large motor boat was to arrive soon. Not long from now the whole area will be accessible.

Their journey to Sipoholon brought them to a stopover with Dr. Schreiber, where Martha enjoyed musical evenings with two Dutch mission Sisters, the three of them playing a harmonium, a piano, and a violin. Riding from Balige up into the mountains, to an elevation of 4,950 feet (1,500 m), with the horses struggling, provided them with the vista "of a marvelously beautiful piece of Earth, as there are few to be found. From up there the first Europeans must have looked down on Lake Toba. And what must old Brother Nommensen think when he compares 'then' with 'now?' 'Then' he was barely able to save his life, but 'now' he finds many blossoming Christian communities on the lake." Stopping overnight at a guest house, they continued to Pearaja. The trail lead them ever farther down, sometimes along horrible chasms, where deep down a creek rushed. At last, they arrived at the pleasant, very wide Silindung valley, where two rivers pass through. They stopped by the Metzler family. Many other families had already arrived, and were staying in the homes of local missionaries. Hermann could not visit, being busy with the conference nearby. On one day, he and many other *tuans*, traveled south to a place where the first missionaries, Americans, were murdered, and where a memorial stone was to be placed in their honor.

Martha wrote, "There are also two Dutch Sisters visiting, who are traveling Sumatra from the west coast to the east coast. They will probably also come to Si Piak. An English Sister lives in the valley, who talks mostly Batak. Furthermore, an American couple, friends of the Mission, plan to travel around Sumatra. They do not speak a word of German or Batak, and have naively asked whether someone could pick them up on the west coast, then to accompany them to the east coast. A request like this can only be made by Americans or Englishmen! It is incomprehensible to me: how can people consider making such a journey without knowing any local languages?"

On their way home, they made a stop over at the Meisels, where Martha was glad to visit with Mary Meisel, a happy, and satisfied young woman. This mission station is located at a higher elevation, at, what is called the Steppe. It felt too cold for her, but there was fertile ground, with everything growing very well. Theft was virtually nonexistent, but the many tigers kept people in their homes at night. From the Meisels

Martha received, among other things, a bottle of honey, collected in the forest, a large bottle of lemon juice, and a parcel of cinnamon, also from the nearby forest. Afterwards, their travels took them through rugged countryside with many deep canyons, as one would not expect to find on Sumatra. Eventually, they faced the steep descent to Lake Toba, with the horses needing to be led. Home again in Si Piak, they found plenty of letters and gifts from home. From a homeward-bound missionary family they subsequently purchased a harmonium, soon to arrive with the Tole.

Hermann wrote in April: "After an unusually hot day, it is pleasantly cool in the evening. Thousands of crickets and other insects chirp in competition with the croaking frogs, speaking the same language we know from home. The lake is peaceful tonight; when it is angry, as it was yesterday, it threatened to devour our motor boat with its passengers. So, even the Tole can run into danger. At the conference it was decided to station the Tole at Si Piak, which is helpful to my mission work. I now will no longer endanger my life having to use the small Batak canoes, which capsize easily. However, I'm also faced with the responsibility of keeping the Tole in good working order.

"The other day I traveled on the Tole with Brother Fuchs to pick up Brother Brinkschmidt, both going to Pakpak to open up this new territory. The boat's machinist and its helmsman, together with our former cook, Gayus, have moved to Si Piak to man the boat. During the ride, I had an interesting conversation with a Batak I am familiar with from our station at Si Bagandung. He asked me why I wouldn't go to Pakpak, where slaves had until recently been sold at markets. I replied in jest, 'The people there would eat me; you know that, not long ago, the Pakpak folks still butchered people and ate them.' 'Are you afraid to go there?' he asked. 'No,' I responded, 'I have enough to do at Si Piak.' 'But tell me, have you ever eaten human flesh?' 'Yes, *tuan*, I have, because before you *tuans* came to us, we always conducted raids on people. Here, by these shores, and also on Si Piak, we often hid, sometimes 50 to 60 men strong. When a lone fisherman passed by, we rushed him in our boats. On the next market, where we showed up armed with muskets, machetes, or spears, it was announced that we had captured so-and-so from there-and-there. If the relatives bought him back for

50 to 100 guilders, all was well. If not, he was butchered and eaten.' I asked him, 'Did you eat the entire poor fellow?' 'No, only the best flesh; the rest was tossed away.' What is the best flesh of a human?' He pointed at his fingers and said, 'these and a few other pieces.'

"By now, we had traveled some distance. Passing the strait of Si Gaol, I noticed a couple of small woods. When I asked him about them, he replied, 'Up there is a worship place. Look *tuan*, below the woods was a market place, called *Onan Ituk*. This is where our ancestors went to deal with *begus*, the evil spirits. They came in the guise of people and made the market very lively. But once, when the people from Ambarita on Samosir brought dogs to the market, all the *begus* fled, never to return. This is how the *Onan Ituk* market ended.' "

"The Bataks can tell you many interesting stories by which one learns about their mindset. But in the light of truth the gospel is bringing to these people, the honest Batak will realize the web of lies of his ancestral religion. But it is a tough battle, and our enemies attempt to stymy us by telling lies. When I recently asked some attendees to my service to bring their children and friends more often, they told me, '*Tuan*, we are being derided, and asked, how much money we are being paid to come to the service?'

"After more than six hours on the Tole, we arrived in Palipi, to return the next morning to Si Piak. We did not get far, when mighty waves were heading towards us. Soon, we had to vacate the upper deck, since we had difficulty holding on and with spray splattering our faces. Suddenly, the boat's motor went dead, making the Tole a toy of the waves. After some time, our machinist, Wilhelm, got the motor restarted, and a few coughs later it ran smoothly again, and we made it safely back to Si Piak."

In May, Martha wrote to her sister Ria that her fountain pen was defective, which is why she was writing with a quill, an example of how one had to make do here. She was more at ease with the many visitors, except when government people showed up. Some of them tried to cause difficulties for the mission, while others helped wherever they could. On the east coast, moral conditions were quite terrible, which was why the gentlemen were not comfortable having the Mission working there. Many unfamiliar visitors also brought personnel, and she had to count towels, etc., to make certain that everything stayed put.

Some of the missionary families got to go to Germany for vacation and recuperation, where they visited their older children, who had been sent there for their continuing education. Some of the missionary women suffered greatly from not being able to see their older children for years.

Martha told her sister that, at times, she almost despaired from being physically miserable. For some time already she had not been able to eat anything at lunch time. She wrote: "My anemia has become worse. Dr. Schreiber has tested me twice already for malaria without finding anything. Internal tests have not revealed anything either. It is well that we do not have any children, yet. I've now been told to go for four to six weeks to the higher-elevation Steppe, where it is cooler, and where I would be able to drink more milk. The *horbo* we have does not provide any milk yet. Hermann tries everything to get us some cows."

Then, Hermann fell sick with high fever. Being all by themselves and the nearest European six to eight hours away, the Weissenbruchs had to tough it out. Eventually, Dr. Schreiber arrived and determined that Hermann had typhus, with the worst two weeks already past. Hermann was transported by boat and porters to the Schreibers' residence at Pearaja, where Martha continued to take care of him. There, a concerned delegation from Si Piak arrived, mistakenly having been informed that their *tuan*, Hermann, had died. Fortunately, he recovered and they traveled back to Si Piak.

Then came the news that they might be transferred from Si Piak to Pakpak after all. Brother Fuchs was thought to be too young and needed to be replaced by an older, more knowledgeable Brother. The government had requested the simultaneous establishment of three mission stations in the area, with Catholics having asked to enter this area, and Islam also penetrating. Old Dr. Nommensen assigned Brothers Brinkschmidt and Hermann to go there. "If the mission in Barmen agrees, our fate is sealed," she wrote on October 11, and "leaving our Si Piak will be hard. With Pakpak located considerably higher, Nommensen thinks that the colder temperature there will be good for me."

On November 23, Martha mentioned that they had no news yet regarding their transfer to Pakpak. It looked like it was a difficult area to work, with Islam having penetrated so far that entire tribes had converted to it. In addition, the people appeared to be even more suspicious and unfriendly compared to those in other pagan areas. "This is common where Islam has found entry," Martha claimed.

But there was also good news. The Weissenbruchs were able to acquire two cows, one with a calf. For two weeks now, one of the boys milked more than two liters a day. Martha made butter every fourth day, putting the cream into a tightly closing vessel, then shook it mornings or evenings, when it was cooler, until butter solidified. Kneading it afterwards with some water, the butter became so firm that it could be sliced. Every morning Martha drank a glass of uncooked, fresh milk. She told her mother, "if you wonder about how little milk we get, it is because of the poorer grade of cattle here and the less nutritious, course grass we have. The Guillaumes have told me that the cow will provide more milk over time, so that we hope for four liters, eventually. We hope nothing will happen to our animals while we are away. Where the pasture drops off steeply to the lake, we put up a fence. The Guillaumes have lost five cows last year that fell down cliffs. Their area is very mountainous; the animals climb everywhere, and the shepherd boys don't pay enough attention."

After a writing hiatus of over two months, Martha's letter reported at the beginning of February 1909 that their transfer to Pakpak did not go through and that they were delighted about it, and that they were able to stay with the friends they had made in Si Piak. Mentioning one of the Guillaumes' children, Annie, who was twelve years old, she pointed out, that at that age, she should already have returned to Germany for her further education. But she felt that the girl was not behind in learning.

More guests were expected, among them the Controllers from the east and west coast. Martha said: "It really does not matter that I do not speak Dutch; every educated Dutchman speaks German. Only the Semi-Europeans give me trouble. Hermann speaks good Dutch. These days, the 'Sumatra Post,' a newspaper, printed ugly articles about Germans and the Kaiser."

Hermann described very strong rainfalls during one of the recent, regular conferences he attended, causing the Silindung valley to look like a lake. Everything was flooded and bridges were destroyed. It was impossible to bypass the rivers, and so they had to barrel through. On one crossing, only the head of the horse of one of the fellow-travelers, Wagner, and, of course, he himself, remained visible. Hermann wrote, "Some of us swam through, drifting downstream for some distance, while a few non-swimmers had themselves carried across by two strong men. A third, shallower river was crossed by our helpers carrying us. In pouring rain we arrived dripping wet at our night quarters in Paranginan on the Steppe. A two-hour walk the following morning took us to Mara to board the Tole, and, with the lake greatly excited, seasickness made its appearance. Just in time, we reached Nainggolan on Samosir island, where Warneck operated a station for the past one-and-a-half years. Expecting the storm to somehow stop our little boat, we provisioned ourselves in Nainggolan, and, as expected, this is what happened that evening. The five of us bedded down like canned herrings in the small cabin, but by four in the morning we were able to continue.

"God willing, we will be able to baptize our first people this year. One is the wife of our former cook and present helmsman of the Tole, Gayus, who was baptized three years ago. She asked to be baptized together with her small child. It is Martha's task to provide baptism instructions to the woman."

In March, Martha wrote to her sister Ria, "We have now about twenty people, who asked for baptism instructions. Since my knowledge of the Batak language is still very poor, Hermann had to explain the ten commandments to them. The younger ones learn quickly, but it is terribly difficult for the older ones. We often wish that we could enter a Batak soul to understand what drives them to be baptized. Our boys Manasse and Mitta are also among the students. Both plan to marry soon, after which I must teach the new boys. I've got two already, and another is to start soon. Not that we wanted three, but somehow we cannot send one away. One of them has lost his parents and has often begged us to keep him; the other is a Christian from Silindung, who wanted to become a teacher but failed the exam. Since then, he has been wandering the country looking for work. He will be my new cook. The third, Adji Bata, is a neat, quick boy, who I want to have as my room boy. Unfortunately, none of them knows how to milk, this, when we now can get four liters every day. I make butter every three days and have made some hand cheese , which we eat with caraway seeds and salt. Evenings, we often have our homemade cottage cheese and sour milk with bread. We now save quite a bit of money, being able to get our own milk, butter and cheese.

Martha told her sister that despite her lower abdomen problems, her health was now relatively good, but that she was still anemic. Her concern was getting dysentery with its terrible, associated loss of blood. She wrote, "It is now two years since I have had this affliction and have never really recovered from it. I am afraid of being alone during Hermann's frequent two to three day travels. Sometimes, when I am all by myself in the big house, I am gripped by so much fear that I leave our big light burning all night. I'm not a brave missionary's wife!"

Mid-June had come, when they experienced a tragic loss, that of their best and most faithful student, Hudjal, the pride of his father, the *Raja* of Lotung. "We do not know what he suffered from or why he finally died. When we reported his death to his parents, his father's wailing was terrible to hear, a real pagan wailing. And the wife of missionary Theis suddenly died of a pulmonary embolism. They have four children, the oldest five years, the youngest just ten days old." Martha wondered, "Lord, why?" The children found foster parents among the other missionaries; Sister Lina took care of the littlest and left the fourteen-month old Hanna, a weak little girl, with the Weissenbruchs. Hanna's father was now alone at his station in Raja which is located in the midst of the jungle. The people there were suspicious, sinister and uncommunicative. He has worked among these Rajanese for years without any success. She closed her letter with a hint that her own baby would arrive in December.

In August, the entire family, including Hanna and the boys, were hit with colds, one after another. Hanna had developed well, but Martha could not leave the child for even ten minutes in the care of a Batak because they were not clean enough. She had difficulties protecting the little girl from being touched by Batak women who came to see her. Many had scabies and various ugly sores from all the dirt. Brother Theis, Hanna's father, had visited the previous week and was happy to

49

see his little girl coming along so well. Hanna had a little celluloid doll, which greatly aroused the curiosity of the Bataks. They wanted to see the human image and touch it. Martha had to tell them that the doll was for Hanna to play with and not a protection from evil spirits.

"We now have a little pig running around in our yard, a gift from *tuan* Si Polha, who said that he gave it because he did not make the *njonja* a gift upon her arrival. Like most gifts, this one, too, was not pleasant to accept. If one can avoid insulting the donors, one does not accept them. With the Bataks always looking to gain an advantage, many such gifts are intended to make the *tuan* well-disposed towards the donor. Rarely is the gift made from gratitude; sometimes it is, when Hermann has treated someone for his illness. Most people, however, take medicine without giving any thought of expressing their appreciation. Many do not 'request' medicine, they 'demand' it! This is why it is a pleasure, when one finds gratefulness here and there. There's a woman who often comes for medication for her husband, and, when so doing, beams when she hands me some young corn cobs or rice. She is grateful for Hermann treating her man."

A few days ago, old *Ephorus* Nommensen, paid the Weissenbruchs a visit. Sister Nommensen, his wife, who had been frail for a long time, was thought to have died of typhoid fever. Brother Nommensen had become old, and it was good that he had now one of his sons living nearby.

Martha's new cook gave her trouble by making too many mistakes. He lied and was simply unreliable. Hanna's deceased mother suffered much from such behavior and their boys never stayed for long. They cost much, but provided little effective labor, always demanding more money and clothing than was due them. They were all true pagans, wanting nothing more than lots of money.

Now, in August, Hermann mentioned in a letter to Martha's mother that it had been one year since he had recovered from a serious illness and was able to return with Martha to Si Piak. "Since then we have both been healthy and Martha feels wonderfully strong. Being able to travel now more easily, I recently brought along the old chairman, Dr. Nommensen, who will travel with missionary Theis to Si Antar. It is not easy for this 78-year old man to inspect his large diocese very often. From Si Gumpar, his *Ephorat*, his bishopric, extends in the four cardinal directions, requiring three to five day trips to cover the area. Within this expanse lie 40 main stations with about 400 substations, on which live 90,000 Christians. Two weeks ago, Sister Nommensen went to her 'higher home,' the heavens. Brother Nommensen now lives with his seven year old daughter and his married son, Jonathan. The young man has been for eight years the parish commissioner of Si Gumpar."

Commenting about children and their plenitude, Hermann described how a Batak woman with many children carries the two youngest in a cloth on her back, while leading the two others by the hand. "This looks most delightful. The Bataks love their children very much, unfortunately, all too often the wrong way. They are afraid to punish their offspring, fearing that, suddenly, its *tondi*, its spirit, might flee. The child would then fall ill, maybe even die. If a six year old boy is to go to school, the parents may ask him first, whether he wants to. If the little rascal says 'no,' they tell the *tuan*, 'The boy doesn't want to.' Then there's nothing that can be done. I think, however, that something could still be done," he wrote, "but the time for the nine-tailed whip hasn't arrived yet, and at home, it is gone from the schools."

Adding to a letter to Martha's parents, Hermann wrote from Purba about the station manned by Brother Theis. "The station is located halfway up the mountain, about a thousand feet (300 m) above Lake Toba. On the narrow ledge is only space for the station itself, which, from the lake, looks like a swallow's nest, stuck to the mountain side. In the many nearby canyons and rugged area live large numbers of wild pigs, which even visit the station by night. Tomorrow morning at four o'clock, I'll lie in wait in the moonshine for the brazen fellows, and see if I can shoot one. Brother Theis recently killed a stag, and we preserved one of its haunches."

A month later, in September, Martha told her parents that their new cook, Pondia, was in the shade pushing Hanna around in her little baby carriage. The baptism students were a delight for Hermann, but were frequently derided by other tribal members. One of his participants, Ama ni Aba, a *Raja*, was recently asked by his ruler, *Tuan* Dolok, to attend a 'bone celebration.' Oftentimes, Bataks kept the bones of their parents buried in the floor of their house. After some time these bones were disinterred, and in the course of various pagan customs, reburied. The more they honor the spirits of their ancestors, the more they believe they would be blessed by them. The celebration was accompanied by a great feast, with the butchered animals dedicated to the spirits. It had been quite a temptation for Ama ni Aba to attend. Such celebrations exert magical powers upon the Bataks, but he told his ruler that he no longer could participate in the spirit worship, nor eat any more of the sacrificial meat. Following Batak law, he had to donate a *horbo*, a water buffalo, which he did willingly.

The wife of Dr. Schreiber stayed about four weeks at quiet Si Piak to recover from the restlessness in the village of Pearaja, where they lived. She came without her five children, and looked very pale when she arrived. For months she had been unable to sleep properly and was afraid that she would need to go to Germany for recuperation.

In the following letter, Martha alluded again to being pregnant – the condition never being mentioned openly – by writing, "I feel very good and am always hungry. At the same time, I'm as fit as I rarely have been before. Oddly, even my headaches have disappeared. We hope that everything will turn out well and happen on time. Dr. Schreiber paid us a visit and Sister Lina will be around when the time comes. The Millers will also be here. They are worried about a premature birth. The previous year they themselves had a stillborn baby having been alone and without help."

Hermann wrote to Max and Ria, in mid-December, "I sometimes wish I could introduce our baptism applicants to you! 'These dirty Bataks,' one sometimes hears from certain people. Oh, I can say, they have become much cleaner externally, and I wonder if their hearts are not purer than many a heart of unbelieving Europeans? 'Where are those planters and settlers,' our *Ompu* Taini asked seriously and sorrowful, 'who aren't too sinful and evil to ask for God's forgiveness.'

"Later, next January, we expect Duke Johann Albrecht von Mecklenburg-Braunschweig to visit Sumatra. At first, it was planned to have him spend a night with us in Si Piak, but this has been changed. The gentleman will travel only to Toba, there to get an impression of the Mission's success. The German colonial administration should follow the Dutch government's example, which supports the Mission very differently. Once a school has twenty-five students, a station receives a subsidy of 200 marks and for its first furnishings 630 marks. These subsidies increase with the number of students. Vocational schools receive 850 marks annually. For Huta Salem, where there are now more than 200 lepers, the government pays 8.50 marks per person per month. In addition, all missionaries receive annually a large supply of medicines and dressing material, supplemented by scales, mortars, etc. This is done by a government with experience in colonial matters!"

Just prior to Christmas 1909, Martha, wrote to her parents, "The attendance at our service increases more and more. Today, our schoolroom was full to the hilt with 125 children, among them forty-five girls. They enthusiastically practice Christmas songs. Many such songs have been translated into the Batak language. We also have a hymn book with 277 songs."

She continued describing how her 'Weck' food preservation kit was working full steam. They had butchered their piglet the previous week, enough for preserving four pig roasts, twelve small jars of liver sausage, made following Sister Steinsiek's recipe, and four jars of headcheese. The butchering went well enough, but they were glad when it was over. Their larder included also three jars of venison roast, seven of kohlrabi, and four jars of beans. Now they enjoyed looking at their store of victuals. They salted the piglet's ribs and ate them with pea, bean or lentil soup.

Brother Gabriel from Purba came by to bring, in addition to many rose cuttings, 3,000 guilders school subsidy money in silver. He didn't dare keep it in Purba, since he was alone there, and had to travel often. At Si Piak a strongbox was available, which he did not have.

"Tomorrow is baptism day," Martha wrote. "Among the people is a couple, a *Raja* of a noble family with his wife. Both are very smart people, who have entered their new faith most thoroughly. He's actually only deputy *Raja* . His older brother, the actual *Raja*, lost his voice through the use of opium. It is touching to observe, when he brings his mute brother along for the services, telling him every time: 'Even if you can't talk, you can hear and let God's word enter your heart.' We had such a wonderful Christmas; yesterday evening many *solus* from the

53

outlying substations came rowing in moonlight across the lake. Even our enlarged school turns out to be too small now every Sunday. Last night, at least 200 people stood outside. We appreciate seeing the people to be baptized appearing in their best dress. They say that they purchase new dresses, since they do not want to be baptized in their 'heathen' jackets. The *Raja's* wife, I mentioned above, brought a very precious jacket of black silk with red and golden cords and fine silver chains, and asked whether she could wear this as a Christian. Of course, she could, for the jacket has no connection with paganism. She suggested, however, that the people would claim that it would be the *badjudipelebegu*, the jacket within which she had sacrificed the *begus*, the old spirits. Every museum would pay good money for this jacket, which is truly beautiful, a true Batak work of art. We often admire the good taste of these people, who display such harmony and delicacy in their color combinations without them being overbearing."

Batak Family

The Year 1910 with the larger Family

"On December 31, 1909, at four in the morning, dear parents and grandparents, God's mercy gave us a healthy daughter, Elisabeth, in short Else!" Martha reported home.

Three weeks later, she wrote about the Bataks' reaction to their little daughter: "The Bataks were happy, but some probably regretted secretly that it wasn't a boy. The wives of the teachers and the Christian women came right away to see the baby. They were proud when they were allowed to take it in their arms. How often Hermann had to bring his little daughter onto the verandah to show it to the people. My cook made every effort to make my life easier, I must truly say. My preserves came in handy, in that I can simply warm them and need not be concerned with cooking. Yesterday was Hermann's birthday. I put his little daughter in her white dress on the birthday table and surrounded her with roses."

Meanwhile, the duke and duchess have come and gone. The couple visited Laguboti on Sunday, where everyone was delighted by the pair. They dined at Pohligs with their entourage, an aide-de-camp with his wife, a professor, a doctor, and several of the local Dutch officials. When they landed on the beach at Toba they were greeted by a Batak band of trombonists with 'Deutschland, Deutschland über alles.' The young duchess, only twenty-five years of age, was thought to be very charming. When the table was set at Pohligs, she said, "I would love to help, but it probably isn't befitting." Here at Si Piak, we had set up a cannon, and the Bataks had concocted some powder. Its first shot thundered loudly across the lake when the dignitaries passed by, but upon the second shot, the barrel exploded and iron pieces flew over the people's heads. Fortunately no one was injured. After this, the Bataks said," *Tuan*, God protected us," after which they gathered around the blasted cannon to thank Him for it. The boat landed on Samosir, where the couple visited a true pagan village with it residents. Unfortunately, Hermann had tonsillitis, preventing him from going to Samosir. Our teachers went across, but were disappointed that the duke did not wear a chest-full of medals, but wore only a simple khaki suit. It was also told, that their lordships were so tired that, at a later dinner in Sari

Budolok, he fell asleep sitting at the table. "But enough of the duke's visit," Martha concluded.

The coming year will see a lot of visitors, and Martha thought that she was slowly getting used to it and took it easy. Often guests brought their own attendants, making life somewhat easier for the hosts. Among the visitors would also be director Spieker from Barmen. The Mission there expected the Weissenbruchs to pay off the building costs from their salary. However, at this year's conference, the singular request was for Barmen to assume the cost for the main building's construction as well as the annex buildings. Inspector Wagner had expressed the opinion that the recent salary increase would enable the Weissenbruchs to gradually free themselves from the building's debt load, but they found this impossible. The Barmen Mission provided the same amount of funds for every station, never mind that construction lumber was more expensive at some places and cheaper at others. The conference protocol listed the Weissenbruchs as a prime example of what was an unreasonable expectation of the Mission authorities.

Another such expectation by the Barmen headquarters was to ask old man Nommensen to travel all by himself to inspect missions on Java, Engano and Mentawai.

Martha, writing to her mother, explained why the missionaries did not train girls for household help. It is done in Silindung where there are many mission children, but these girls did not provide much help. Any missionary wife who could take care herself of her children, would do so. And there was always the problem of where to accommodate the girls. Another reason was the concern about the girls' long hair, which, all too often was 'populated.' The Christian girls in Silindung have become cleaner already. It is also not customary for girls to enter into some service, since most of them marry very early.

In March, Hermann wrote to his father-in-law from Si Piak: "I returned this afternoon from my two-hour distant missionary branch, which I established in November of last year. The young teacher, only recently arrived from the seminary, has had a difficult time at the station where crass paganism is still the rule and hardly anyone comes for the service. It was therefore most pleasant to experience the welcome by the local village chief, who had asked for my visit. He expressed his desire to abandon paganism and to accept God's word. When I entered the village, I noticed immediately that it was his pleasure to welcome me. Grass had been cut for my horse, and a rice shed had been furnished with mats where our meal was to be taken. The little black pig, intended to become our food, lay already lifeless on the ground and to my surprise, had become white. Following European custom, the people had scalded it to remove the bristles. Had they followed their own custom, they would have held the killed piglet over a straw fire to scorch off all that is inedible to a Batak's stomach. While waiting for the meal to be readied, I had an opportunity to chat with the men about their customs. They told me that, when a young wife enters her husband's house for the first time with her left foot first, she'll bring an evil spirit into the house; if she does it with the right foot, it will bring good fortune. If this pagan belief were correct, then my good Martha must have entered my house with her right foot first, for she has brought me plenty of fortune."

In May, Martha wrote to her parents, "my letters became fewer." Her excuse for the delay was because of the many visitors they had had. One of the guests was a Dutchman on a journey around the world, a nice gentleman with a great interest for everything. Then, a family with four children arrived for a week, joined by a Sister on her way to Russia. She is traveling through China and then, in two weeks on the Trans-Siberian Railroad, goes all the way to St. Petersburg. And plenty of other visitors showed up, as well. With the large verandahs and large rooms one notices the many people only when they gather at the dinner table, but with *ristafel*, it doesn't matter whether there are six or eight people, or more. Little Hanna's father with his two boys stayed for almost three weeks."

July passed, and Martha reported that her little Else was coming along fine, but was scared of the Batak women, even when they just looked at her, a behavior Martha wanted to maintain.

Then, a planter's wife inquired whether she could come to board at the mission station in Si Piak for her recovery. She was very adamant, and it was unpleasant having to deny the request. Another cook needed to be trained. Whenever one had become proficient, he left, and the entire lot, once they had earned a bit of money, didn't care for regular work any more. Her currently departing cook wanted to become a trader. And then there were the people gathering the timber for the church building. This all happened with lots of shouting and screaming and one could hear them already when they were still high up in the mountains. It was actually surprising how well one could hear every sound coming from across the lake. A comet made its appearance in 1910, and she wrote about how clearly visible it was. The Bataks believed that it was an omen for a great die-off among humans across the world, but most of them just didn't worry about it, as was their way. It had become very dry, and they had to take their cows up into the hills, where they had to be stabled every night because of tigers. On Samosir, three tigers had established themselves and were scaring the people. Although the land bridge connecting Samosir island with the mainland had been broken, dryness, and the resulting lower water level, shrunk the break, making it easy for tigers to swim across. In closing, Martha listed her request for seed stock, which was for parsley, celery, leak, carrots, kohlrabi, Swiss chard, lettuce, onions, and red beets.

A month later, Martha wrote that Hermann took the Tole to Toba to pick up a shipload of rice which Nommensen had purchased for them. She said, "if one leaves such a task to Bataks too much is stolen." Cholera threatened the area again, and the people were much afraid. The illness was spread because of the Bataks' disastrous custom of transporting people suffering from it, and carrying the bodies of the deceased to their home village, which passed the illness on. It was unbearable for Bataks to die and to be buried in a foreign place, but most caught the illness on plantations or on one of their trading trips. While the government had establish rulings to control this transport of the sick and dead, it took time for them to take hold.

Much 'ghosting' went through people's heads. The Singamangaraja, who was killed by government forces three years ago, was supposed to be still alive, and was gaining supporters once again. According to the people's belief, this man was actually invulnerable. Now, they had found a plant on a field in the neighborhood, from which they believed a human would grow and worshipped it. Our Christians asked, "*Tuan*, can that be true?" In Si Malungun, to the plantations there, a number of assistants have come from Berlin's high society, often sons who had to depart because of debt they had incurred. They included a personal friend of the crown prince, and a brother of prelate W. He had gone totally to seed, drinks and leads a rotten life.

In a letter he wrote in August, Hermann bemoaned his solitude in Si Piak, because Martha was vacationing in Purba. He found the house cold and empty without his wife, despite having plenty to do. He commiserated with his father-in-law that it felt as if his wife had left for Germany. For company, Hermann made do with Minta, now, as a Christian called Hendrik. Their former cook, now married, lived in a nearby village. And, not to forget, he congratulated his father-in-law on the honor he received upon his resignation from his post as county school inspector.

"Let me tell you something about my work here," he wrote. "My main focus is the building of a church. The chiefs of the Parapat and Adji Bata area, for which the church is to serve, have agreed to supply the required lumber before the end of this year. This is something that doesn't just fall on the Christians, for, if they had to do this all by themselves, they would have to wait another ten to fifteen years yet. No, school and church are common property, to which friend and foe must contribute. This is an age-old custom, and once the chiefs thought the issue worthwhile, it was followed. After that, their subjects are put to the task. The mission must respect this custom, for without the chiefs' agreement, nothing would happen. I must admit that the church project is none of my doing. It came to pass because of the chiefs of the two areas and the tribes, still good pagans, agreeing to this project. I only wanted to build a house for the teachers and enlarge the school building, but my first Christians and among them my *Raja* Israel, jumped ahead. '*Tuan*,' they said, 'let's also build a church right away; that makes it one task, and the teacher's house will get done on the side.' I had to laugh about their daring plan, telling them that they had no understanding of the size and difficulty of the project. 'Come along to Toba, so that I can first show you what a church looks like.' So, one day, horses were saddled, we took off, and inspected the church in the seven-hour distant Lumbun Lobu. There, the quantity of lumber needed was right away established. From Lumbun Lobu, my people went on to the stations at Si Toran and Pongombusan, where they were heartily welcomed by the local missionaries and their people, thinking them to be the first Christians from Si Piak, strangers to each other. Afterwards, my people praised the hospitality of the Christians, and felt the warmth of their community for the first time in their lives. In earlier times only a tribal member was considered a friend; all others were enemies. Now, belief in the new religion connects also those that earlier were foreign and standing apart.

"The plans for the church building went back and forth, and in April, a second conference with the chiefs took place. I was afraid they would be scared off by the large quantity of timber required. After they had assembled in a large semicircle in the yard, I joined them. In order to promote some comfort, I had a box of cigars passed around. It was quickly emptied. Everyone listened peacefully to what I presented, and half an hour later everything had been cleared up and accepted. It was more than I had dared to expect! Another box of rather cheap cigars was sacrificed, the harmonium was rolled out onto the *emper* and was played together with my French horn."

Hermann entered into a description of the timber the 140 families had to supply. The quantities were absolutely amazing. Some of the 300 feet (9 m) by 3 feet dia. (30 cm) columns had to be cut in the mountains 3,000 feet (900 m) above Lake Toba and required 70-80 men to pull them down. And this was by far not all! None of the people were rich.

In addition to the earlier mentioned, human-like plant, another, more ingrained superstition had raised its head. There was talk that shortly a great man would come, stronger than anyone before, even stronger than the Dutch. He would smash all those who did not surrender to him and would not wear the little piece of lead, a symbol of their submission to him. These small lead pieces played a large role in the lives of the heathen Batak. Shamans inscribed them with various sayings. They were hung around children's necks or kept in a house to protect people from illnesses. Upon Hermann's question who the soon-to-arrive, mighty man was, he was told that this was a secret. It appeared the toxicity of lead was as yet unknown at this time.

Hermann wrote: "I soon realized that the subject wasn't as innocent as I had first assumed. The priest-king Singamangaraja , who had been pursued and finally killed by the government, was supposed to be still alive, and anyone accepting this piece of lead would put himself under his rule; those refusing would be ground to dust. It was revealing that the

Christians and baptism applicants were kept uninformed, so that they would not pass this information on to the missionaries and the government. So, before I took off for Purba, I dispatched some reliable people to try to shed some light on these ongoings. I also reported the problem to the Dutch official in Siantar. When I returned from Purba, an official had arrived and with the help of my teacher and two smart Christians, they had been able to track the plotters down. The two Christians masqueraded, as if wanting to put themselves under the protection of the Mighty One. This was how they soon found someone willing to sell them a piece of soft lead for two guilders. This man was arrested, and following it, about 120 people in three areas were identified who had purchased this lead. Where had this 'lead story' originated? We were told that on the plateau at Toba lived a *Raja* by name of Nasiatbagi, who was distributing the softened lead. Many people from our area had supposedly visited him to learn from this chief the art of how to soften lead by the application of oil and lemon juice, then to sell it as his agents across the land. The result was that the people kept their children from attending school and services, all this, eventually, resulting in an insurrection against Dutch rule. Thus the Dutch official required all those who had sold or purchased lead to head for Siantar, there to answer to the Controller. I, too, had a serious word with the chiefs, which left an impression, so that they agreed to send their children back to school and the service again, and even to come themselves. I was pleased to learn that only four people in Parapat had bought lead, and that none of the Christians and applicants had bothered with it."

In October, Martha wrote from Si Piak that, God willing, they could expect a little boy in April, and that she hoped to gain some more strength for this event and the forthcoming additional work.

Except for a letter in October, it took until February 20, 1911, for Martha to report that the Batak Bible was to be revised and readied for printing, also that a training session for native preachers had been started. From the more than 600 teachers and assistant teachers, the ten best had been selected, and would now move with their families to Sipoholon, where they would ready themselves in the course of two years to become preachers. With the large number of auxiliary stations, the missions had to work to get more native fellow-workers.

Now it was Hermann's turn to add to Martha's letter, "I just received word from Dr. Nommensen that the young missionary Brockhaus drowned together with four Nias men when their boat capsized in their attempt to reach an outlying steamship. The young man's widow, a teacher, married only recently, will return to Germany in July. With the dearth of workers here in the Dutch East Indies, his death is especially painful."

In April, Hermann fell ill with dysentery, putting him to bed for a week. Unfortunately, despite every effort to prevent contamination, their little girl, Else, also became sick.

Their friends, the Steinsieks, would shortly travel to Germany for a stay of eight months, which they sorely needed. Missionary Steinsiek had recently lost his memory on various occasions, and, when riding off in the morning to a subsidiary station under the best of conditions, could not recall where he was and what he wanted when he arrived there. He had to be brought home by the local teacher. Illustrating the hard life these missionaries had, Martha described that Sister Lina had been called for a sudden visit to Mentawai Island. And what misery she found with the two missionary families residing there! One family expected a birth the next day. The husband of the other family lay unconscious for six days with blackwater fever, while his wife with high a fever, lay in bed in an adjoining room. The couple was immediately transported to Sumatra-proper. "How lucky we are with the climate here in Si Piak," Martha commented.

Now, she waited for Sister Lina, a trained midwife, to come and stay with her for four to five weeks. Martha felt stressed by her pregnancy, having had already some contractions. "I hope she comes tomorrow, or it may be too late."

The growing family

Gertrud, their second Child, is born

On April 26, 1911 Hermann informed Martha's parents that at 11:30 A.M. Martha gave birth to an eight pound girl they named Gertrud. Both mother and child were in good health. Their teacher Kenan visited and said that it ought to have been a boy. The Bataks love to have many sons, not so unusual for Germans either. To the Metzlers, six daughters were born. After the sixth, the Bataks came to express their condolences to the *tuan* and the *njonja*.

A month later, Martha told about Bataks being unable to comprehend that her child did not turn out to be a boy. She wrote, "I believe they felt sorry for us from the depth of their hearts. Our boy, Ortas, kept asking me whether the *njonja* is truly happy with her child."

Their little foster child, Hanna, contracted malaria, resulting in terrible cramps. They eventually subsided, and the family hoped that this terrible affliction was over. But the little girl had to go through a quinine treatment. Good news came from Hanna's father, who had become engaged to Sister Langemann. This meant that, once married, Hanna would return to her father and his new wife.

Cholera broke out every year, but it was particularly rampant in April of 1911. Si Piak Station was especially endangered, since they had no other water than that from the lake. Si Piak was also the stopover for all Tobanese and Silindung people. Everyone who was infected, ill, dying, or already dead, traveling, being carried or transported from plantations on the east coast, passed through there. It was a disgrace for Bataks, not to be buried at home, which was why they even transported the dead. "At one time, a corpse lay for hours in the grass in front of our house, and my husband was unable to get the people to bury the man. No, the man had to get back to his village. Finally, for much money, four men were found to transport the body by paddling through the night. They returned the following evening, but by next morning all four were dead from unknown reasons."

The Weissenbruchs took various measures, like total isolation, and asked their God for help. There was little help beyond that. Their teacher, Marinus, was also sick with cholera.

Martha was glad that her 'boys' did not run away and could take care of their little three year old foster child, Hanna. Martha had to nurse six-week-old Gertrud and take care of her husband, who had also fallen ill with cholera. "What if he dies? How would I get a coffin?" were the thoughts tormenting her. But a family source said that Martha's down-to-earth remedy, schnapps, the dry German kind, not the sweet American stuff, was good against cholera! Eventually, these dire times passed.

In August, the little family headed to Pakpak for a vacation. To get there took seven hours of riding. But the cooler climate was very attractive. The children were carried, Gertrud in a little bed with a cover against the sun, and Else in their largest cloth hamper, of course also with a cover. For Martha a *tandu*, a sedan chair, was provided halfway through the journey. "Unknowingly," she wrote, "we hired opium smokers for porters, who weren't up to the task. Hermann had to get a new group of men. We had to climb a 2,330 foot (700 m) high mountain. Together with our two boys, who carried Gertrud, I was way ahead on my sturdy pony along the switch backs. Only the last, steepest part, I had to climb on foot. Arriving on top, a cool, refreshing wind greeted us, and it was a joy to breathe. For three quarters of an hour, we waited for Hermann at the edge of the timber forest to catch up with the two other children. I took the time to nurse our little one. The trail was gorgeous and, at times, wildly romantic with its rushing mountain streams. The children were also happy, being able to move about in their baskets as they liked, at times falling asleep. At one time we had to follow a wild river downstream for about 500 feet (150 m), then cross it on a rattan suspension bridge built without a single nail. By five in the afternoon we arrived at our destination, happily and very tired. But we were glad that we had dared making the trip despite the warnings we had received. For much of the distance, the trail passed through forest, which supposedly held many tigers and game.

"A Dutch settlement was nearby the missionary station with an officer, a lieutenant and a doctor, all married. It seemed the area wasn't considered quite peaceful yet, which is why guards were posted through the night. A man called Bande aud Atji, who the government had been after for some time, and his gang, all fanatical Muslims, were making the area unsafe. Most of the people around here are opium smokers, including women.

They even blow opium up babies' noses when their mothers go to the market and want their child to sleep for a few hours. Most of the Bataks up here are therefore pale, weak-willed people. Not too long ago, these Pakpak folks were still cannibals. Even today they continue a horrible   practice. When a woman dies in childbirth, they bury the living child with her." Hermann adding to Martha's letter, wrote, "My colleague Brinkschmidt has a difficult time here with the Muslims who eagerly push their religion, even with fire and sword. Ten days ago, they tried to burn down the *huta*, the home of a Christian chief. Although they poured petroleum onto the flammable roof made of sugar palm fibers, the house didn't burn down. The perpetrators are now on the run, with their wives imprisoned. Here, the government works closely with the missions like nowhere else, which is why the most respected chiefs are already Christians. A beautiful church has been built, and a trade school offers young men the opportunity to become proficient in construction and carpentry."

"Soon after our return from Pakpak," Martha wrote in October, "*Ephorus* Nommensen with several *tuans* arrived to evaluate the location for the new station on Samosir suggested by Hermann. This means that we would gain neighbors a little more than an hour's ride on the Tole   across the lake. Nommensen brought one of his sons along, a real globetrotter. He has made millions in Brazil and now travels constantly, at times living in New York, then in Paris. He visited his father twice in the past three years." Martha could not comprehend how the young man could stand it without an occupation. He had just transferred 3,000 marks to his father, so that the old man could once more visit his younger children in Germany. The old *Ephorus* Nommensen recently celebrated his fiftieth anniversary and was honored greatly by Europeans and Bataks alike. The Bataks really loved their old *ompu*, their grandfather, as they called him. Nommensen also exerted great power over them, and his word was always final. He had his own ways of dealing with the people. The story went that when some sinner was unwilling to admit to his wrongdoing, he had him touch an electric battery. The terror and fear this induced made him admit his wrongdoing very quickly."

At the beginning of October, the Weissenbruchs held their first mission festivities, and just about everyone living in the area showed up, about 1,500 people, all gathering in and around their yard. A *Raja* donated a substantial amount of money for the church construction, and several water buffaloes and a ram were given for the festivities.

In November, Martha wrote, "we were able to baptize 89 people, adults and children. But the Bataks are an uncommunicative people and one never knows how deeply they have taken in what they have learned. The chiefs of Parapat are all Christians now, but in the neighboring Adji Bata, the people still conduct their Bone Celebrations. For this they disinter the bones of the *ompus*, the grandfathers, from places inside houses, then bury them again with much noise and music outside the village. Mediums perform magic, through which the spirit of the deceased talks. Such festivities are very tempting for Christians, especially if the bones are of relatives. But they are strongly forbidden to attend these celebrations. One of the baptized women went there, just to watch, and today admitted publicly to her mistake. This pagan spectacle has been going on for days, but, today, on Sunday, even the heathen won't dare any more to make such noise."

The Weissenbruchs' young parish began to flower, and with a growing number of people showing interest, the small school building became way too small. They decided to split their activities – Hermann taught the adults, their teacher took the boys, and Martha, the women and girls. Furthermore, outlying substations were established. Hermann had started construction of the church, to which everyone was made to contribute, even the heathen, it being a community project. They also had to pay for the lumber and transport it, too.

But then she wrote again: "Hermann is not well. He had much to do and is presently without help from our teacher, Kenan, who is attending a seminar. Hermann is feverish and suffers from headaches and intestinal problems. We hope that it is only residue from dysentery and nothing more serious. Soon, by early December, little Hanna Theis will be picked up and returned to her father with his new wife."

In the years to come Hermann's 'intestinal problems' were diagnosed as being Tropical Sprue.

By now, February 1912 had come along. Martha wrote from Si Piak, "Gertrud is doing very well, and is always happy, while Else is more delicate and causes us to worry since she had dysentery. However, she keeps busy all day. Both girls love animals. We presently keep a stag in an enclosure; when he is called he comes to be hand-fed. We also have three dogs and some rabbits. Unfortunately, it has turned out that, due to a lack of personnel, the new mission station at Ambarita on Samosir Island, just across from us, will not be established. The Fries's visited from Nias Island to recuperate at Si Piak, with its better climate. They lost two daughters in one day from dysentery. How much better do we have it on Sumatra proper than the Nias folks!" Martha concluded.

In her book, '*Seine Gehülfin,*' 'His Helper,' its subtitle being,'*Working and Proving their worth; German Missionary Wives in Indonesia 1865–1930,*' Annemarie Töpperwien vividly described the contributions missionary women made to the success of the Mission. She also described the privations these women experienced, especially on the island of Nias, off the west coast of Sumatra, where the Rhenish Mission was also strongly engaged in introducing Lutheran Christianity. The climate on Nias was unhealthy, with medical assistance nonexistent. Töpperwien's book's emphasis lies in describing how the wives of missionaries were expected to provide various missionary services to their husbands without receiving any monetary compensation. The Rhenish Mission Society simply expected these women to follow their husbands in all endeavors, with many suffering until 'death did part them.' In addition, if they did not lose their husbands through illness, it was their children's deaths they had to mourn.

Hermann came down again with dysentery around Pentecost, and had to stay in bed. Martha, too, for months, felt weak and miserable. She had trouble with her lungs, and it was hoped that her affliction would not become chronic.

Again and again, it is amazing to read in Martha's letters how much in clothing, seeds and other materials was supplied by her parents in Germany. And, that most of these supplies made it to Sumatra!

In September, she wrote about a guest, a Catholic man from Luxembourg, a globetrotter, who, for six years was traveling the world on foot. He had an agreement with a newspaper which he supplied with reports and pictures, for which he would receive a payment of 65,000 franks upon his return. He was going to travel to Java, Australia, and North America. He traveled without any weapons, and hired a new guide for every day of travel. On the way from Si Antar to Si Piak, he spotted a tiger crouched nearby in the grass. The creature only raised its head and let them pass. Martha concluded this story with, "one meets all kinds of people here!"

The Weissenbruchs, too, kept traveling a lot, however only locally, and the number and kinds of people they met was astounding. By now, traveling had become easier with cars available, and long horseback rides were no longer required. A reliable Batak of the Steinsieks gave them a four-and-one-half hour ride to Butas, and from there, Dr. Schreiber took them on another two hours' ride to Pea Raja. "Our days with the Schreibers were very nice and interesting. The Resident of Sumatra's west coast was also present, living with his family next door. Evenings, we dined grandly on several courses, served by two attendants, a Javanese and a Batak, both dressed entirely in white. The Resident's wife is a very fine person, while he is less so. He is part Indian, and I have the impression that she has some trouble with this. She inquired of the Schreibers whether they would be welcome, in order to recuperate from the fever they were suffering from. As the Resident later admitted, it was, however, mainly to get to know the mission. He is a believer, and is thus a blessing for the country. But the couple has children who misbehave and are poorly educated, causing their mother great pains. Here, again, his Indian blood may come through. Their nanny, a German, is a most unhappy being. She had engaged herself to a planter who was visiting Germany; then, happily and innocently, she journeyed to Sumatra. After she arrived and was able to look behind the facade, she became aware of her fiancé's past life. She broke off the engagement, even refused his offer to pay for her return to Germany. After a stint with other missionaries, she found the position with the Resident."

The Schreibers kept an open house, not just for visitors, but for the ill and often deathly sick as well. For years now, they had paid much out of their own pocket, never asking for payment. Sure, they were rich, but they also had to take care of their six children.

Martha wrote in November of 1912 that they soon hoped to get better mail service. A wide road was to be built between Si

Antar and Toba, which would bring mail every week, and they no longer needed to find all kinds of ways to get mail out from Si Piak. But this would mean also that more travelers of various kind would show up, which was less pleasant to look forward to. The station planned to be built next year at Ambarita, across from us, would be run by a Dutchman. He was ordained by a free Dutch church, but accepted by the Barmen Mission. "Unfortunately, he is Dutch," Martha said. She would have preferred a German. "Maybe he will take a German wife, as most Dutchmen do who join the Rhenish Mission Society." The Guillaumes returned from their eight-month visit to Germany, but did not find their home in Purba any more. It had burned down. The station will be relocated, since it was not well-placed for mission work. The old place was now occupied by a plantation owner, who intended to build a vacation home there. Unfortunately, more and more plantations were being established, encroaching ever closer on Si Piak. The Bataks' more miserable elements gathered on the plantations, joining the rabble from Java, which made up the majority of the workers.

"Else and Gertrud play with their small nanny, Maria, in the yard. Else will soon be three years old and seems to resemble me, while Gertrud in figure and nature, as well as in cheerfulness, takes more after her father. It is presently the nicest time of the year, and we are often outside," Martha wrote. "In the morning, my first walk outside with the children, is to feed the seventy chicks and the almost one hundred chickens and roosters we keep. We must have that many in order to get enough eggs and meat. The chickens prefer to lay their eggs in the tall rice grass, where they are hard to find, which is why we are often short of them. This is how the chicks come along without me having to do anything about it."

Else asked her father the night before he left in her German-Batak mishmash – with Gertrud using the same lingo – about his forthcoming trip. On his way to a conference in Raja, Hermann took the Tole to Purba, and so that he did not have to walk for six hours, he took his horse, Hector, on board as well. He was happy to report that in three weeks the church would go up, 730 feet (22 m) long, 415 feet (12.5 m) wide, with 100 feet (3 m) high galleries along its inside, opposite the altar. The apse was going to have seven corners and the tower a height of 90 feet (27 m). It will be the tallest tower in Batak land.

In November, Martha wrote that, while their old home, Germany, remained always on their minds, they now had two 'home' countries – one of which is in Si Piak, on Sumatra. Missionary children did not develop a similar feeling for their German home country. In their later lives, they were not at home anywhere, and their hearts were anchored nowhere. "But these are sentimental thoughts. Away with them!" she wrote. "I think that Gertrud, with her happy disposition, will make it well in the world."

"Hermann is away again, and I do not care to be alone, although it is safer here than in Germany. It is amazing how much has changed in the six years of my being here. The Batak men have cut their long hair, in which, in earlier times, lived some kind of spirit, among many other living entities. Shorter hair makes them look much cleaner. Rarely does one hear the old pagan spirit music anymore which was meant to expel evil ghosts. Even the most hardened heathen say that, since the *tuan* introduced the new teachings, magicians and shamans have lost their power. We still experience, that people going on a trip, ask us for a protective talisman, or for one against some illness – of course, in vain. The shamans have lost quite a bit of income this way, but oddly enough, they have remained friendly towards us. '*Hauhaou*,' the Batak thinks, 'What can be done about it anyway? Typical Batak fatalism."

Finally, after having received a new camera – their old one had failed – they are able again to send some pictures to Germany. Their latest photos were taken by a Chinese in Pea Raja. The *Tuan* Purba, the Resident at Purba, came by car to Raja to greet his former *Tuan*. He kindly rented the car of *Tuan Raja*, the Resident of Raja, to take the entire group of the Theisens, Guillaumes, Brother Gabriel and Hermann, to Purba. However, with all their kindness, both the *Tuan* Purba and the *Tuan Raja*, were enemies of the Mission.

This was just an example of how car traffic was increasing. It was said that there were now about 500 automobiles operated on the east coast.

At the beginning of 1913, Martha expressed her regret that many Christmas parcels and mail did not make it in time. Everything took at least four weeks to make it from Germany.

Hermann had come down with tonsillitis once more. For days he was unable to speak a word, requiring communication via slate board and stylus. Recently, Hermann had to fight with his teachers, who asked that the chief of Adji Bata, the Big Man, their *Raja*, appointed to this position by the government, ought not to have to wait for his baptism. But he will likely have to wait and study some more, since he is not yet ready! By mid-February the man resigned. It turned out that he was going to conduct a pagan death ceremony for his still living mother, with the attendant heathen racket. Of course, baptism applicants and those baptized already are not allowed to do this. These Bone Celebrations are thought to be a conclusion of life, and often the reason for pushing to become a Christian in the future. His old mother was a true heathen and, according to Batak belief, her *tondi*, her spirit, would be low and despised if her son did not conduct this celebration. In addition to the *gondang*, the pagan music, the *Raja* wanted to get Christian trombonists for his festivities, but this was not permitted. The two beliefs must be kept separate. Evil spirits were thought to be present while this music was performed. This is why a Christian who participated in these celebrations had to publicly confess his aberration before the entire parish, and might even be expelled from it.

The cost of living was getting ever higher, and soon a general increase in salaries for the missionaries must be requested from Barmen. For one guilder, one now got only a third of the rice than a little over a year ago. And despite having cows, they must sometimes buy milk and butter for months at a time, as well as other preserves. They tried to get *horbo* milk from the Bataks, but once they had learned to milk them, they also wanted good money for it. The Bataks learned to drink milk from us Europeans. Batak children grew up without cow's or *horbo* milk, and were nursed by their mothers for two to three years. However, one could still see many poorly nourished children.

In a letter written at Pentecost, Martha told her parents that she required an operation. Her letter did not mention what kind, but referred to an unknown, probably lost letter of Hermann's, describing it. The operation, done by a Swiss doctor, was successful. As was customary for this Swiss and his Russian doctor wife, missionaries were not charged anything.

In June, Hermann had to attend another Mission conference and returned with bad news. The Weissenbruchs were to transfer to another station at Balige, on the southern shore of Lake Toba. The station was presently not manned, and Brother Pilgram, who started it thirty years ago and lived through warlike times there, now lay bedridden and near death in Laguboti. He visited Germany last year and left there in good health, but then arrived ill in Sumatra. Balige Station was maintained by neighboring stations, as far as this was possible with the lack of personnel. The parish moneys and books had been kept for more than a year by Bataks, and the situation had become very tenuous. Hermann wrote, "I will have my work cut out to get everything back in good order." There were over 6,000 Christians living in Balige, but with much conflict among them. The mission house there was old and decrepit, small and unhealthy. A search was on to find a new location for the station. The old one was lying amidst the dust, smoke and fumes of the village. Hermann wrote, "this meant that I must build again and, for a second time, must go through all the troubles of establishing a station. There will be renewed cost, without us being compensated for the expenses we incurred at Si Piak. Fortunately, building a house is now much easier, so that one does not have to pay quite so much out of one's own pocket. I fought the transfer as best I could, being in the midst of building the church in Si Piak. Also for Martha's benefit, for the air in Balige is by far less clean than in our Si Piak. To all of my objections, Brother Nommensen had only one response: 'I don't see another solution, as much as I would want to keep you in Si Piak.' Brother Pilgram had his own ways of working the mission, being a bit outside accepted practices. In a conversation on the Tole, on our way to the conference, everyone agreed that it would not be easy to become Pilgram's successor. Balige is a port town on the lake with all kinds of people and lots of trading and traffic. One native store butts against the next, and two European companies have offices there. Balige has a mail and telegraph station and a prison, always full of natives. A government official and a veterinarian reside there with their families. The Balige residents are real traders. They build their European-like boats themselves, using them to travel Lake Toba from market to market.

"When our people in Si Piak heard of our transfer, of which they had learned before my return, they were very sad and wanted to travel to *ompu* Nommensen to try to change his mind. This also means that Martha's operation will have to wait. Now I must hurry; twenty chiefs with whom I must discuss the construction of the Si Piak church and the money for it are sitting outside."

"By July, Brother Pilgram had died, and his widow asked whether she could stay with us in Balige until her return to Germany next year. We agreed." In her July letter, Martha reminded her father of his words to her at her departure to Sumatra, seven years ago: "I will not see you again!" "Well, sometimes I think it will not take that long any more until we can come for a visit to Germany. Nommensen has designated *Tuan* Brückner from Muara to succeed us in Si Piak. But things aren't going well there. Supposedly, *Tuan* Brückner had the superior chief of Muara deposed earlier by the government. We do not know whether he was correct in doing this. It gained him many enemies in the parish, which is why he is to be transferred. However, our parish people in Si Piak, having heard a few things about this issue from market people in Muara, positively resist accepting *Tuan* Brückner. We now hope that Nommensen will not transfer Brückner, but keep him in Muara, and send someone else to Si Piak. There's also upheaval concerning the Ambarita station on Samosir, where there are now 17,000 people. They have built a school over there, and Hermann sent one of his best teachers across. Nommensen, however, takes his time making a decision."

In August, Martha stayed with Drs. Senn for a checkup. Both he and his wife are doctors in Si Antar. There may be a benign tumor near the kidneys, and an appendix operation may become necessary. She observed that this town was very busy with people from just about every nation. Mrs. Senn, a very fine lady from a Russian officer's family, had just been operated on by her husband because of appendicitis. Her six brothers are all officers. "She's very kind and not at all 'emancipated,' " Martha remarked: "The lady is still not feeling well, but her household keeps on humming along. People like the Senns have very different help than we missionaries. Their Chinese cook is as good as any in Europe and cooks complex dishes which people like us know only from a cook book. Their 'boy's' only task is to keep the living rooms in order and to serve at the dinner table. For their bedrooms, they employ *babus*, Javanese women."

Martha commented, "I wouldn't want all that help, but it sure makes life easier. It looks like our transfer is certain, although Inspector Spieker is not comfortable with it and would prefer Missionary Lombek to go to Balige. But Nommensen is totally committed to his plan. He even wants us to make the move to Balige quickly, and for me to have the operation afterwards. With Nommensen, one must defend oneself vigorously; he has no consideration for others, especially women. We are willing to make the move, but we don't like to be pushed."

In September, Martha wrote to her mother from Si Antar: "I just came back with the children from Sariboe Dolok from two weeks' vacation. What a difference there is between Si Antar and Sariboe Dolok. The former lies 1,230 feet (370 m) above sea level, the latter 5,000 feet (1,500 m), and mornings and evenings has a temperature of only 55 degrees Fahrenheit (13 deg. C). During the first days, I longed for sun and warmth, but then I really enjoyed the coolness and freshness up there. I left Sariboe Dolok on Thursday, leaving the children with 'aunt' Guillaume. Else had a bad fever during the first days of our stay, but Gertrud is getting rounder and stronger every day. When Toko Hennemann arrived with his car to pick me up, they wanted to come along, of course, but resigned themselves to staying with aunt Guillaume. These car rides are wonderful. Without them, I wouldn't have been able to make the trip in one day. The 41 miles (66 km) took about three hours by automobile. I stopped only briefly in Raja with the Thiessens, because smallpox is widespread there. We aren't quite sure yet whether to have the children inoculated."

Martha's tumor seemed to be shrinking and not require surgical removal, but her appendix, according to Dr. Senn, must have given her trouble for the past five years and contributed to her misery. Her lungs had also suffered. She wrote: "If I don't recuperate well after the operation, I will go to Germany. I would do well in Si Piak, but it is doubtful it will work in Balige. Nommensen is holding to our transfer, even if it takes place without me, and I don't even have to return to Si Piak following the operation. He just doesn't care for sick women! He even left his first wife, ill, alone with their children in Germany. She died after seven years without ever seeing him again. We missionaries out here think less of what he has accomplished in Sumatra, and more about how his wife suffered through the bitter

76

years alone. This makes us ask: 'Was that God's will?' We will leave our beloved Si Piak to go to Balige. If only we would be left in peace until my surgery is past and I'm back on my feet. The pressure demonstrates such a lack of mercy and makes us feel very bitter. We also find no support in Barmen. Inspector Spieker doesn't mean a thing to us, and the entire mission community here holds him in low esteem. Dr. Schreiber wrote us recently that the mood in Germany is the same. It is a sad situation, hovering like a curse over the Mission."

Martha mentioned to her parents that they found it unjust that she and Hermann would not be compensated for their expenses in setting up the station in Si Piak. For new stations the Mission Society paid not only for the house and its painting, but also for all annexes, like the boys' house, the storage building, and the horse stable, all enclosed by a barbed wire fence. In earlier times, new missionaries received only 2,000 marks and whatever cost more had to be paid by the new station keepers. Barmen had finally realized that it was impossible nowadays to set up a station for less than 5,000 marks. Life was becoming ever more expensive, and yet salaries were still at the level of fifty years ago. And if someone wasn't in good health and needed more hired help, it was impossible to make do.

"None of our helpers will move with us to Balige, so we must start afresh. Only someone who has worked with Batak help knows what that means. Why Nommensen picked us, is a mystery. It isn't practical, since as soon as Hermann has set up everything and established himself there, we will take off for Germany anyway. Then another person will have to take over the finished nest, and the parish will face another change."

On September 9, 1913, Hermann wrote from Si Antar to Martha's mother that his wife, after only six days, was doing very well after her surgery. It had entailed the removal of her deformed appendix. She had also enjoyed the fancier life style at Drs. Senn. He also asked to have several nice dresses sent, for which he offered to pay.

HKBP Church in Balige, built By Hermann Weissenbruch

The Transfer to Balige

In October, Martha and the children headed for Laguboti, while Hermann moved from Si Piak, establishing himself in Balige. Another week, and she would also head for Balige. She delighted in telling her mother how well she felt staying for four weeks with the Senns, that they were the most kind people, yet not Christians in the Weissenbruchs' sense. She said, "We never dared judge them. They did not charge us a penny for the operation and the time I spent with them. I enjoyed drinking good wine and had to drink a bottle of Vichy water every day – all this in addition to the excellent cuisine. I think I wasn't a cheap patient."

Once Martha was fully recovered, Hermann picked her up and they passed through Si Piak where the people welcomed them with a celebration. They then headed for Balige, where another one took place.

Two days after their arrival in Balige, a letter from the Rhenish Mission in Barmen arrived, saying that, under all circumstances, they were to remain in Si Piak. All Nommensen said when he heard about it was, "Well, it's good that you are already there."

The years now following were riven with difficulties and battles, so that they asked themselves whether they were the right people to deal with this place. The fractious locals were fighting continuously. In addition, serious accusations had been raised against the Balige *Pandita* . Nommensen's judgment of Hermann was that he was, "mild but firm."

The time before Christmas was not very pleasant because the teacher of every subsidiary station arrived with the village elders for the settlement of accounts for the past year. Statistics had to be prepared, bills of income and expenditure filed, and subsidies and medicine requests to the government for the coming year also had to be prepared. With all that, the Balige folks were so high-handed: they wanted to codetermine and rule as well, so that Hermann had to keep a tight rein, all the while remaining kind. Aunt Pilgram, who was living with them, turned out to be a helpful person. She was going to return to Germany next April. Nommensen had arrived in order to welcome Count von Limburg-Styrum, who had visited Balige thirty years ago and had been staying with the Pilgrams. With regard to visitors – it was like Grand Central Station, with one visitor relieving the previous one.

The new year had come, and on the 18th of January 1914, Martha wrote to her mother that all of them had come down with colds. For weeks now, Else wasn't eating well and looked pale, most of which they attributed to the unhealthy living conditions of their new home. No one believed Nommensen, who declared the old Balige station to be healthy, and everyone knew that, in order to push through his plans, he firmly called black white. He had become like a Batak in this way. She said, "when I told him recently that I was mad at him, he laughed and responded, 'I'd be that, too, in your place.' "

"These days, we are often looking at the building plans for the new house, which we can modify within certain limits. Construction is to start the beginning of February. The house will be very nice and airy. Once Aunt Pilgram has left, one of the Laguboti Sisters will come here. I, myself, will no longer do parish work; it is too much for me with two children now."

February had come, but the house construction had not been started. It was to be built by the students of the vocational school who have had no time for it yet. Martha and Hermann were afraid that they would have to stay in the old house through another rainy season. She wrote that, "in addition to the organizational work for the large Balige parish, Hermann must also take care of the Mission's Tole boat which had been transferred to the Balige Station. As of this year, Balige Station, the area's hub, has become the center where medicines are distributed to the areas of Toba, Uluan and Samosir. Hermann is in charge of recording and reporting these matters to the government. In addition, there are other problems, such as a teacher in an outlying station, who for years has embezzled parish money. And there are still more problems, all of which cause us to be very unhappy. And, lo and behold, our *Ephorus* Nommensen recently celebrated his 80th birthday. He is still full of vim and vigor which makes one wonder."

Hermann added to this communication that three Dutch officials joined Nommensen's birthday celebrations, and that the old man did not feel any lessening of his strength. He could still travel with whatever transportation was available, be it a horse, a boat, or a car. Should he tire, he would lie down anywhere – on a hard board, or, on the boat, between crates and equipment; there he was asleep in a minute. A few months ago, he became a full-fledged vegetarian and attributed his well-being to it. Now, he wanted to convert everybody to his newfound mode of life, but he was often told, "for seventy years you drank coffee and ate meat. When we get to be as old as you are, we may do it, too." Certainly, one can do without meat, but in the tropics the substitutes for good vegetables and butter, etc., were often amiss. When they left Si Piak, they also had to leave their cows behind, since the pasture in the Balige area was poor. Now they missed their daily fresh milk. Milk was available, but a boy had to walk for half an hour to another village to fetch it. They had sold half of their fifteen cows, large and small, to their successor at Si Piak for 800 marks; the other half remained theirs. This sale meant that they experienced no loss, and soon intended to send the money to their parents in Germany to invest it on behalf of their children. To take care of the 10,000 Christians of the Balige parish was sometimes overwhelming. "Oh, it is wonderful to do missionary work," Hermann exclaimed, "but having to fight again and again with a lack of physical strength can become depressing and cripples the joy one so desperately needs for mission work."

Troubles arose over the plot where the new station was to be built. One of the plot owners withdrew his permission, thinking that what he intended to give to the Mission he might be able to sell for more money a few years down the road. Finally, one *Raja* provided the best possible location as a gift. Now, only water was needed by sinking a well. It had not been decided when the new house would be finished – maybe in October, when their third child was due, a most unsuitable time. However, they looked forward to, eventually, moving away from Balige, since they were taking more quinine in half a year there than in one year in Si Piak. And in Silindung cholera was rampant, so that the forthcoming conference would most likely be relocated. "I shall spend the week of the conference with the Steinsieks in Laguboti," Martha wrote, "since I feel relatively well, considering my condition. But Balige is a difficult station, simply because of the many visitors. For lunch today, we were eleven people, and for the afternoon coffee, fifteen. This is much too much; it happens too often and is exhausting me."

Martha commented in August of 1914 that she hoped "our dear fatherland will be victorious, without too many lives being lost." World War I had begun. Fortunately, Germany had not invaded Holland, so that the Germans in the Dutch East Indies were not that much affected. It was terrible that England had entered the war against Germany. Some German reservists who tried to get to China to report there for service had been held in Singapore. Sumatran newspapers circulating in the Malay language were not permitted to print smear articles, yet it was interesting how well teachers and educated people were informed about geography and the world's situation. All foodstuffs had risen considerably in price, and they had stocked up, since they did not expect to receive any more merchandise from Europe. The *tokos*, the merchants, were already sold out of canned milk, matches, flour, etc. The building of the new house was making slow progress, and it did not appear as if they could move in before the baby arrived. Martha wrote that she was sometimes worried about giving birth, especially since they had no trained midwife available. She was comforted by the thought that old *Ompu* Nommensen lived not that far away. He had frequently helped European women as well as uncounted numbers of Batak women to give birth.

It was now October, and Hermann wrote, since Martha wasn't doing so well: "Our little girl is already two weeks old. Else and Gertrud are delighted about their little sister." He discussed the events of the war in Europe, adding patriotic wishes for his fatherland. And the mood in Holland – as they read in those German newspapers that finally made it through – was not favorable towards Germany. "I often itch to take part in the fight."

In November, Hermann continued another of Martha's letters with patriotic comments. "The 'Emden,' a small German cruiser, detached from the German Pacific Fleet, performed a daring feat by steaming into the port of Penang. When a French torpedo boat, a guard ship, demanded from the 'Emden,' sporting a fourth fake funnel typical of this size British warship, to identify itself as to its nationality, her commander signaled 'British.' The 'Emden' steamed close to a Russian cruiser, whose captain was spending time with his wife in a hotel, fired 13 shots and a torpedo, sinking the Russian ship in a few minutes. When the French ship entered the fray, it was sunk, too. The 'Emden' launched boats to rescue the shipwrecked, then left the harbor as if being on home turf. This was reported in the Sumatra 'Post.'

Shortly thereafter, a Japanese cruiser suffered the same fate; it was sunk, too. People here were highly surprised about the 'duitsche sprokschip,' the 'Flying German,' as they called it. Penang was terrorized, and the English newspapers were not allowed to report the incident. The 'Times' wrote that nine German cruisers were operating in the Indian Ocean, but that 70 battleships had been dispatched to catch the nine enemy ships! "What an honor for us!" Hermann commented. The British have arrested all Germans in Penang, including their families. They were afraid that the 'Emden' received wireless information from them.

Hermann concluded that their first year in Balige had come to a close, it having been the most difficult one so far. There had been much opposition and anger in the parish. And to make matters worse, letters from home via Amsterdam now took six weeks.

In November, Martha commented on the misinformation spread by Indian, Malay, and Batak newspapers, reporting only German defeats and atrocities, the desperation in the German army, things every German knew were lies. The Europeans knew it, but the natives were not supposed to learn the truth. The Mission tried to set things straight in its occasional newsletters. But they heard comments now like, "*Tuan*, since Christianity has arrived, warring has stopped among ourselves; we thought you people did not fight any more either." It is not easy to properly respond to such questions. "But," she stated, "we are very proud of being German and remain confident of our victory and in our dealings with the neutral, but mostly England-friendly Dutch. However, we are glad to be in a Dutch colony and not an English one. We are now unable to get certain foodstuffs like flour, milk, butter and sugar. Soon, we will have to bake bread from corn and rice meal. Our worst problem is whether we will receive salaries for the next quarter. Our little Hanna is a very healthy, strong baby, and is developing well. Else already helps in the care of her sister. Gertrud is a real little imp, always giving us something to laugh about. Both girls' German is terrible. They appear to think in Batak, then translate it into German."

On December 11, they happily moved into their new house and immediately felt much better. From up there, they could admire the beautiful environment around Balige. And their new house had been very well built.

In an April letter in 1915, Hermann talked about the many relatives and friends engaged, wounded, or lost in the ongoing war and, together with the Nommensen, still expected Germany to be victorious. Martha delighted in her new home with wonderful meadows behind and the various trees Hermann had planted. The old house was now used for the distribution of medicines, sewing and religious studies on the *emper.* "And the parish troubles we encountered have been resolved," she wrote. "There was an important hearing with all *tuans* from Toba being present, as well as *Pandita* Friedrich, and the teachers. The two old gentlemen, Nommensen and Meerwaldt, finally dismissed them, since things just couldn't be worked out because of envy and ill will among them. Now, new people will be appointed. One of the dismissed elders was close to taking a second wife, and when warned not to, he argued that Abraham had had four wives and yet was the father of the faithful. There is plenty of deep-seated Christianity in the Balige area, but the station's parish is particularly difficult. It goes back to old enmity between two tribes, with hatreds acting against better knowledge. We now have a government school in Balige for the sons and daughters of chiefs. Lessons are given in Malay, with religious studies only once a week. Lessons are given by two Batak males and a Batak female teacher, she, with red ribbons in her hair, dresses in a white, embroidered European dress, and gold jewelry galore. Well, these are modern times. However, few girls attend this school. Most mothers know better and send their daughters to the mission school."

May came along, and Martha, writing to her sister Ria, described the fine connections they had with other missionary people in the area surrounding Balige. However, relations with the Dutch had their limits. It was peculiar to observe the fissure between Dutch and Germans, even in the Mission, which included some Dutch people. Particularly now, in war times, the nationalities drew apart; the Germans banded together, suffering and hoping the best for their fatherland.

There's more cholera going around. A neighbor, Her de Boer, had put up a three-tiered fence of barbed wire around his abode and would not let any native come close to him. The infected villages were immediately closed off and open markets were forbidden in the hope of halting the spread by this means. There had also been horrendous thunderstorms and an earthquake almost every week. A large part of the current harvest had been destroyed by floods.

It was now August 1915, and it appeared that correspondence was slowing down even more due to the war, although the delivery system as such still worked quite well. The land was in the grip of a dry spell, and their attempts to grow food were stymied despite repeated seeding. Martha asked for more seeds, if they could be sent during these times. If they would not arrive in time to be sown by October, they expected to eat few vegetables in the coming year. Martha expressed her concern about how much would have changed and look foreign, once they would be able to visit Germany. And, surprisingly, in closing, Martha asked her mother for hers and her father's birth dates, saying, "I don't even know exactly how old you are."

In October, a letter from home arrived after taking ten weeks. A ship with 300 sacks of mail had burned recently. Karl, Martha's brother, had died recently from war injuries. A pair of interesting visitors showed up; two Syrian pastors, as they called themselves, who were collecting donations for a Syrian orphanage in Niniveh. They presented all kinds of documents, including one from Nommensen. The conversation was laboriously conducted in English. The older one of the two had two sons in the Turkish army, and the younger one, two brothers. They had already been traveling for eighteen months, thus had left before the war's outbreak. Martha regretted needing most of her remaining eyesight for sewing – an explanation for the reduction in correspondence – and said that Hanna's birthday was yesterday, with the little tike already chasing through the house.

February 1916 had come. Hermann required that no small children be allowed to join their mothers at the service, which resulted in a wonderfully quiet and peaceful sermon. Despite the increased cost in materials, the parish was going to pay for the building of a boys' school. A house for Sisters was in the process of being built. For some time now, they had observed Chinese and Japanese flooding Batak country. The Japanese especially were everywhere, buying zinc wherever they could get it. One of them wanted to buy the roof of the old church, made of zinc sheeting, and was going to supply some nice corrugated sheet metal in its place. Of course, Hermann did not go along with this. Afterwards we heard that bullets were to be produced from the zinc. A Japanese hotel had sprung up and there was suspicion of something else being behind it.

Almost five months passed before Martha wrote again. That could also mean that letters written in the intervening time were lost. However, Martha admitted on June 29th that, except for postcards, she had not written for a long time, yet had also not received any mail from home. She literally begged her parents to write more often. Before long, they expected to take a three- to four-week vacation at a recuperation place in the mountains. "We will need to bring various foods along, but rice, chickens, cucumbers, and milk can be purchased there. It is situated in wonderfully fresh air with a marvelous vista of Lake Toba, and what is more important to us Baligers," she wrote, "is its solitude. We have such a busy house. There's not a week when we do not have different visitors for two or three days at a time. It is tiring, and costs more than we can afford. We butchered a forty to fifty pound pig the other day, and I was able to make twenty-four sausages in the pig skins, and preserve bacon, smoked meat, and headcheese in jars. These preserves keep for months."

In a letter dated July 9th, 1916, Martha confirmed the receipt of a letter from her parents dated January 30th! Martha wrote: "At the moment, I'm alone with the children. There's another conference in Sipoholon, and all *tuans* from Toba, Samosir and Si Malungun went there on a freight truck. Inspector Warneck is supposed to come to Sumatra after the war to take Nommensen's position. We are all looking forward to it."

There was also some success. In 1916, the new home for Sisters was finished and dedicated. This was Sister Anna Alfs' new location. The hospital and school building were completed shortly thereafter.

However, the Batak mission was entering a critical period. Many government officials were friendly to Muslims. The smart Bataks, especially those in government positions, were watching this battle between the government and the mission with disdain. It was most apparent with schools that the government and mission stood in opposition. The government schools were non-religious; they fearfully avoided everything that could somehow further Christianity. In addition, they tried to draw the best, most able children into their schools. And there were various government rulings and laws which were directed against the Mission, something the Mission could not tolerate. It appeared that higher government circles were opposed to this, but local, individual officials had too much power and were operating against it. Nommensen had written harsh letters to the Governor General in Batavia, threatening that he would go all the way to the Dutch Queen if these problems were not taken care of. A crisis had to occur in order to set things straight.

Once again, the family made it up to the vacation home, the 'Jungborn,' in the mountains, only to find tragedy there. "On April 17, 1917, little Hanna died!" Martha wrote. "She somehow discovered the quinine tablets in our absence. We found quinine in her vomit, and in the span of an hour she fell asleep on my lap, never to awake again!" Once more, their faith carried them through this loss. On December 4, 1917, Martha's father died in Germany without her ever seeing him again.

Martha appeared to have also suffered a miscarriage in November of 1916, and felt depressed since then. Mornings, she was giving school lessons to Else and Gertrud for two hours, and requested to have books sent from Germany for the second and third school year. Having applied to Barmen for a vacation to Germany two years hence, they considered sending Else, in the company of Sister Anna, Mrs. Alf's daughter, earlier than that, if at all possible. This raised the question with whom Else was going to stay in Germany, and they hoped it to be with Mrs. Alf and Aunt Anna.

Half a year passed, and letters from home seemed to have become scarce, since Martha was again literally begging for more. Other missionaries received plenty of mail. She was still dealing with the loss of Hanna, and her health had worsened, with heartbeats missing frequently. She had to stay in bed as much as possible, considering the many visitors and guests. Martha commented that the Batak Mission was facing hard times. "Culture' is coming in giant steps to the Bataks, who are not ready for it. To make money is their top priority, and God's word falls by the wayside. In order to escape the church's regimen, entire families convert to Islam. But God rules and he will find ways to bring our Bataks to Him," she wrote.

Writing again from the 'Jungborn' facility in late December of 1917, she confirmed that she had learned from her sister Ria's letter, that her father has died. Two months before his death, Martha had dreamed of his passing.

Then, April 1918 brought more trouble for the Mission which Hermann had to deal with. A month later, Martha, wrote about her mother's admittance to a hospital, hoping that it was nothing serious. "Since Hanna's death," she said, "I do not have a servant girl any more. It is not good to have a Batak girl in the house, because it causes my girls to pick up bad Batak habits, plus the Batak girls will talk with mine about things that are not for children's ears. But I will try to get one of my previous servant girls for mending of clothing to work by the hour. I'm feeling much better and the missing heartbeats are a thing of the past. When I hold our daily school lessons, I must watch that they do not stress Else too much; Gertrud is much stronger. The two have their own garden and do their own planting of flowers, sugarcane and corn. We have now decided not to send Else before we can make it to Germany, and who knows when such travel becomes possible. We are doing fine here in Sumatra and notice little of the war shortages you experience, except that everything has become more expensive, including flour from Australia, but we have stocked up well."

In September, Martha explained that now was the transition from the dry to the wet season which usually brought an increase in illnesses. This time it was the Spanish flu that affected Europeans as well as the natives. The Mission people were trying to get ready for a visit to Germany, but without a successor or substitute for a vacant, or temporarily vacant position, Barmen's 'okay' meant nothing. Because of the war, there were just too many whose visit home was overdue. The Sisters from Nias Island were coming to Sumatra to find respite here. It was a real emigration from Nias, and they didn't know where to put them, since all housekeepers needed their own domiciles. And on the 'Jungborn' it was too cold for the Nias people.

A month later, Martha, in a letter to her mother, wrote, "it is wonderful that you are feeling better, my dear mother. You must get well, so that I can see you once more. It is my dearest wish and my prayer. Tomorrow, the Dietzolds are coming. They lost their only child two weeks ago. He is a merchant, who earlier lived in Balige. His wife is utterly distraught, and I'm a little afraid of their coming. But if I, who have gone through the same ordeal, can help her, I shall be glad to do so. They inquired about this yesterday, and we sent our agreement by telegraph. There is much misery here due to the war. Many have died, since they were unable to get to Germany in time for recuperation. The long idleness is most difficult for the crews of German ships which lie idle waiting here, and many Germans working on the plantations have lost their jobs. If the plantation owners do not discharge their German employees, they are no longer supplied rice. Sumatra is now unable to produce sufficient rice for the plantation workers; it has to be imported from English areas. If only peace would come! We also notice the effects of the war among the natives. They have become rebellious and radical, pure Social Democrats. And the government assigns the blame to the Mission, which has become the scapegoat for everything that has gone wrong. More and more Europeans are arriving in Balige to open hotels, guest houses, or whatever. This is not at all pleasant. Fortunately, we live away from all this hubbub. At our Si Piak, one small villa is being built close to the next, all vacation homes of rich people who spend a few months of the year there."

By December 1918 the Weissenbruchs were desperately waiting for news from their 'dear fatherland,' hoping to learn what was to become of it. Martha feared that they were headed for the worst of all times. In Balige they had one to two deaths daily, especially among children. "We cooked porridge every day, and people came three times a day from nearby to pick up some for their sick children. God be thanked," she wrote, "so far, our children have been spared illness. On Christmas Eve, we had fourteen adults and six children around our Christmas tree. I would have preferred not to have that many people this year, but we saw how happy folks were to come, and it turned into a really nice evening. Two German plantation owners from Deli joined us that evening. They were staying in one of the hotels and had gone out on Christmas Eve for a walk, passing several churches where Holy Night was celebrated. They were so taken by it all that they asked whether they could join us. They hadn't seen a Christmas tree for a decade, and it seemed our celebration awakened something in them. One of them, a Bavarian, had tears in his eyes. In his colleague one could recognize a former military officer."

The year 1919 had arrived, and Martha expressed her sorrow as to when "our poor fatherland will find peace from its enemies? And what will be this winter's situation with food? We hope that mail delivery will soon be operating again, and that ship travel will become possible for Germans. God willing, we shall come in the spring of 1920. However, at this time there is still no replacement for us. Could you, please, send us the school books for the fourth year? We need them desperately. Should you have difficulties shipping them, do it through J. H. Meerwalt in Utrecht; sending something via Holland is still the safest way."

Hermann added: "Mission work has come to a stop; the number of Christians may even be declining. At this time, the lukewarm and the indolent are dropping out, while the more serious band together. And why are Mission workers not permitted to travel home? Many wives of missionaries are so sick that they may never see Europe again. But we keep working confidently, and hoping, praying and believing that our work will not be in vain. We also hope and pray for our poor people at home."

It was now February 1919, and Martha, in a letter to her mother, expressed her continued concern for her situation in Germany, and Germany's situation in general; and whether they will make it through to the fall harvest in Germany with the dearth of foodstuffs. "And we have it so good here that we are almost ashamed of it. For the past week, I'm here in Palipe with the Sisters Fuchs, while Hermann remains alone in Balige. Palipe is an exceptionally beautiful Station, located right by the lake, an idyllic spot. The children swim in the lake and catch little fish. A few days from now, Hermann will come, after which we will travel to a few places, among them Si Piak, to visit our former people. Then it is back to Balige."

By March, mail seemed to travel faster. Martha implored her mother to let her know what she was actually suffering from as she had never written about it. On Sumatra, they were still receiving contradictory information about the conditions in Germany and wondered, for instance, whether there would now be a separation between Church and State. Mission work had fallen on hard times, with revolutionary ideas rampant among the

Bataks. "What is happening here, we would not have thought possible two years ago. We really do not know how the Batak Mission will develop. The Bataks strive for independence and many would love to shake us off. However, the more knowledgeable elements are very well aware that they aren't ready for it yet. To all this, add the suspicions cast upon us by some Europeans, who write libelous articles about us in the newspapers. They sow suspicions among the populace, claiming that the missionary families live mostly on the parish purse. These people, who spend in one month as much money as we do in a year, cannot comprehend how we can make it in these expensive times. Our Bataks read these articles, and the poorer elements believe every word. It will be our task to lead the growing and already grown generation, who were baptized as children to true Christianity, so that it will take root in their hearts. It may well be that God will lead our Bataks through hard times in order to win them for Himself. We are waiting very much for Warneck to take over. Since Nommensen's death we are without a leader. Our present *Ephorus* Kessel's wife is totally incapacitated by gout and both are old. Many of our children have become 13 to 14 years old without ever having attended a real school. And yet, we are doing well and only wish we could share some of our good fortunes with you."

To the death of a small child in Martha's family in Germany, she commented, "that every time of suffering holds also a blessing. God surely does not make mistakes. Upon Hanna's passing, a woman who had lost two children told me that one even learns to be grateful for it – and so it is. God does not send that for which He does not also provide the strength to cope with." Martha asked in her letter whether the masses in Germany had turned more to God during these hard years, or whether the opposite held true? "It is a peculiar time we live in, and it looks as if we are headed for the end of time, though it may take a few more generations. We have experienced such a change in the past two to three years that the Sisters returning from their extended, war-induced stay in Europe will be surprised as to what they will find here. Two years ago, a so-called 'Christian Alliance' arose from within the people without any assistance from the Mission. Its representatives were even received by the Governor General. Now, the Alliance, steered by dubious elements, has assumed a position in direct opposition to the Mission. It has turned into a social-democratic party, casting suspicion upon the Mission. Its leader is a Batak Methodist who spent years in Singapore and has started an English school here in Balige. The Mission Consul suggested that the Mission needed to get in touch with the Alliance, even if it would mean relinquishing old, proven principles. We do not know how things will work out."

Hermann added to the letter that his work among the heathen in Si Piak had been considerably easier, more ideal and rewarding, than here in Balige among Christians with 'Bolchevick' ideas.

Something of a Revival must have taken place on Nias Island, and they wished the movement would catch on in Batakland. Martha saw the Nias people as being more feeling-oriented, while Bataks were pure materialists and intellectuals.

June 1919 had come, and Martha was delighted for some mail from home she had received after months of waiting. Sumatra was experiencing a month-long dry spell, not a drop of rain having fallen, and dust, dust, everywhere, with vegetables being very dear and rice barely affordable. There had been a major volcanic eruption on Java with thousands dead. There were many Germans wandering the local area who were without employment. A few days ago, a stoker and a deck hand from a German ship passed through, looking for work on the plantations. The Dutch government was now helping such people and provided free travel and accommodation when they were looking for work. Many of these men had not had any news from home for years. The Mission had been expelled from China, and Martha wondered how things stood in Africa.

In mid-August Martha expressed her joy that it was no longer necessary to send letters through Dutch intermediaries, as they had been forced to do through the past years. She was also wondering whether their parcel with coffee and tea had been received in Germany. Her mother had still not revealed what she was actually suffering from, although she wrote that she had to see doctors in Wiesbaden again. For three weeks the family was once more in the mountains at the 'Jungborn' vacation home, enjoying the quiet and fresh air. She wrote, "Aunt Anna, who desperately needs to get home, is with us. However, the British Consul does not permit Germans, even ill people, to travel. The sick and those with 12-14 year old children will be able to travel next spring, which means we will not get away until the spring of 1921. Even if we could, we would not want to send Else and Gertrud on their own to Germany. We shall keep them here, even if this means that they will be held back a year in their education. There's also the question of where they can stay in Germany. It would certainly be better to find a place with relatives versus accommodation at an institutional home. But it is difficult to find someone who will assume such a responsibility. Added to all this is that the Barmen Mission has insufficient replacements for all the people who want to or need to travel home after being stuck here for many years."

Hermann continued this letter by writing, "Everything here is now 200-300% more expensive, with European merchandise unaffordable. As a result of our last conference in Sipoholon, a unanimous request was forwarded to Barmen to increase our salaries, which are still stuck where they were fifty years ago. Recently, I told *Ephorus* Kessel that, if I did not receive an increase, considering Balige's expensiveness, I would have to request a transfer. That helped, and I now get 200 marks more, but Martha still does not know how to make ends meet." Other Europeans think, and say so openly, that missionaries must have secret sources or commit some dubious deeds, because it must be impossible to live on the money they get. And the people, especially the Bataks, believe it."

"Much has changed during the war, especially the people's attitude towards Europeans," Martha wrote. "As a result of this, the Batak people's development advances in great strides. It shows already in their appearance. In earlier times, they were dirty and wore rarely-washed blue sarongs. Now the laundry and ironing folks at the *pasar* have lots to do to keep those white dresses clean. 'Our' Bataks are a most intelligent, educable people and demand more and more schools for higher education. In Balige alone are five schools, a Dutch, an English, a government school, as well as our boys and girls Mission schools. All kinds of people have found their way here. There are Europeans, people of mixed race, Japanese, Javanese, Indians, Chinese, Malays and, of course, Bataks. A big hotel is to be built in Balige, since the town has become a hub between the east and west coast. Yesterday, a German machinist from the 'Kleist' who could not afford an expensive hotel stayed with us. The German ships, including their cargo, will soon be picked up by the English. The crews will not receive pay, only free transportation home, but most say, 'what am I to do in Germany without work or bread?' So they try to find work here. We help as much as is possible, but there aren't many plantations accepting Germans. Because they control the capital, the English rule everywhere, and here in the Dutch East Indies it isn't the Dutch but the English Consul. This man recently expressed his indignation when he learned how many German missionaries were working on Sumatra."

September had come, and Martha told of her joy for the school books she had received from Germany. The Bataks asked for and got more high schools from the government, but they had to pay high fees, which they did gladly. The result was that their children can become government officials, doctors, veterinarians, mail officials, railroad officials, and more. It was regrettable that the Mission started too late with high school education. The government schools alienated children from Christianity. However, the Mission teacher, Anna Alfs, managed a girls' school with 525 girls, together with two full time male teachers and six women teachers, and several assistant teachers. It was a joy to see this operation, where attendance was voluntary.

In November, a number of people passed through who had spent the war years in Germany. From them, the Weissenbruchs learned in greater detail of what had happened in Germany, quite different from the Indian and Dutch newspaper reports they had had to rely on.

The problem of when and how to send Gertrud and Else to Germany remained foremost on their minds prior to Christmas 1919. The girls were falling behind in their studies, and there was no response yet from the Alfs in Germany, as to whether the two would be accepted at their small educational institute. "Well, if they can't get passage in the spring of 1920, they will simply have to wait until 1921 when we will be able to return." Hermann added that a returnee from Germany advised not to send the girls now; conditions in Germany were so bad, it would be like murder.

The Barmen Mission had to dispense enormous sums of money for its many travelers. Those coming from Germany told that the Mission was close to bankruptcy, and salaries might come only for a quarter of a year longer. "We don't know what will happen then, but we would not have enough to live for even one month.

"We get together with other Europeans on a casual basis; no invitations, no big events, just for an hour with a cup of tea. We did not issue invitations for Christmas Eve – it's just too much. But families with children love to come, for we are the only ones with a Christmas tree. If any come, they will be welcome."

In February of 1920, they received news that Martha's sister, Ria, and her husband, Max, in Miehlen, in the state of Hesse, would be willing to take the girls, once they made it back. For unknown reasons these plans came to naught, and when the girls came to spend their years in Germany, it was in the Mission's children home in Mettmann and Kaiserswerth in the care of Sisters Anna and Millie Alfs. Their passage was paid for by the Barmen Mission, but no date for their passage had been advised yet.

Then, in 1920, the time came to say goodbye to their two girls, ten year old Else and nine year old Gertrud. Eight missionary families with a total of 23 children were able to travel to Germany. The separation at Medan's harbor, Belawan, when the children boarded the ship, was heartbreaking, with Gertrud repeatedly crying from the railing, "Mother, you must come, too!" It was a relief when the ship finally weighed anchor and steamed away, for what they thought to be, at most, two to four years of separation. It became seven years, and the children returned to Germany at the worst possible time – years of shortages and malnutrition. In June of 1920, Martha's mother died.

In October 1922 Martha wrote, "Work among the Batak has become ever more difficult; there is a real Bolshevik streak running through them. It is a people going through its awkward age. Everything has gone too fast for these people, and they are now possessed by arrogance and delusions of grandeur. They obtain their negative information about us Germans from Indian newspapers, and the Batak papers, run by discharged *panditas* and teachers. So it happened that our forthcoming Mission director, Warneck, was recently compared with Judas, after he had denied their request for self-administration of certain Mission moneys. We also see a rise in sects organized by Bataks who have been trained by Methodists in Singapore, and the Catholics are also entering the fray."

Way past midnight on February 10, 1923, Hermann penned a letter to Martha in Balige in which he expressed his deep religious feelings, and his concern for his health and continued well-being. He gave her instructions about some locally invested personal moneys and how and where to get to them. Problems with the building of a church and with the people had mounted, all this a tremendous pain to him. Expressing his doubts, he said: "After more than nine years of work in Balige, I ask myself: Why did I have to come here, I, who did not feel up to this difficult task? I have had a continuous battle with this twin parish which is so little connected. Each part has its own favorite pursuit. We human beings simply work differently than the Lord. Never before has my heart felt so tight as this night, but by now it has calmed down somewhat. Good night, now, my Dear. Sleep well in Pangoeroeran. May God protect you and the children, bless our parish, and bring peace to all those living outside it. This is my prayer."

Martha then exulted about the years of peace and fruitful results that followed. Good things happened, and "in 1924 the most beautiful church in the Dutch East Indies was dedicated in Balige ," as Martha joyfully recorded in her diary. Many people were impressed by the church's beauty. However, during the first services, they had to place some Elders at the entrance who required the women to spit out their wad of betel before entering. In addition, the women were no longer allowed to bring their small children to the service in order to maintain quiet.

In a 1926 December letter, Hermann wrote to the Mission in Barmen that they expected to return to Germany on March 11, on the steamship 'Derfflinger.' Alas, another year would pass until they were able to take this very same ship.

Eventually, the 12th of March 1927 arrived. Upon their departure from Balige they appreciated the care and love of their parish. Even Hermann's worst foe, *Raja* Titus, approached him with tears in his eyes, telling him, "*Tuan*, we have made your life difficult whenever we could, but we realize now that we were wrong and thank you for remaining firm with us."

At last they were able to board the 'Derfflinger' with a number of other missionary families. By now, their children had been 'on their own' in Germany for seven years. The couple arrived in Genoa on April 5. Their train journey from Italy to Germany was not without troubles. Hermann's coat was forgotten somewhere, luggage was misrouted, and, to top it off – despite having purchased tickets for 3rd class, they were pushed into a 4th class coach on one of the trip's legs. Martha felt that their fellow travelers saw them as strangers in what she called "their dear German motherland", and that is how they felt themselves – like strangers – a feeling that never quite left them during their subsequent two year stay in Germany.

But the joy was great, when they found their girls waiting at the railway station in Tübingen with friends from the Mission welcoming them, as well.

They were able to spend a week at the Tropics Recuperation Center. The medical report from the institute on the family stated:

"Between the fall of 1904 to spring of 1927, Hermann Weissenbruch spent twenty-two and a-half years without interruption on Sumatra. There, he suffered from dysentery, typhus, and cholera. He has reported tiredness, migraines and stomach upsets. He is well-nourished and has a normal blood supply. He shows heart irregularities, myocarditis, and requires three months of total rest. His eyesight needs corrective glasses. It was high time for his return, since a continued stay on Sumatra would have increased the danger of Tropical Sprue. His stomach troubles must be attributed to the various illnesses he suffered. It is likely that he will recover fully. His wife Martha, suffers from the consequences of chronic pleurisy and lung inflammation, and a moving kidney on her right side. Gertrud W., who has lived in Germany since 1920, has been checked now for the first time. She suffers from worms, that is, ankylastomiasis, with resulting anemia. Else W. suffered from dysentery as a child and suffers from anemia."

Upon their arrival in Wiesbaden, they were welcomed by members of their family, Martha's siblings, nephews, nieces, and sisters-in-law, and, except for the siblings, all unknown to them. Afterwards, the entire group met for a welcome party. The following days were filled with seeing friends.

Eventually, and for the next two years, Martha and Hermann were able to settle down in the Reichsstraße in Barmen to be joined by Else and Gertrud. At the beginning, they were very much aware of the distance that had developed between them but soon rediscovered each other.

And then came the requests of Brothers to perform this or that service. Hermann had to attend many Sunday festivities, which meant that he was rarely home on this day. During the two years of their parent's visit, the girls finished their *Gymnasium* education, Else the *Obertertia*, the 11th grade, and Gertrud, the *Untersekunda*, the 9th grade.

Hermann had been diagnosed as suffering from Tropical Sprue, a malabsorbtion disease characterized by inflammation of the small intestine. It manifests itself by diarrhea, fever, and could become chronic, resulting in weight loss and fatigue. This required frequent trips to a physician in Holland, but also necessitated that he come home from the pastoral duties he had assumed for his midday, dietary meal. On May 14, 1928, Hermann spent another week at the Leiden Clinics for Tropical Illnesses in Holland. No signs of Sprue were detected at that time, and the doctors thought him to be 'tropics-ready' once more, although another year in Germany was thought to be good for him.

Separated from his family, Hermann spent several months at the university in Hamburg, where he took courses in linguistics, especially Malay and Dutch, but also psychology. He felt distant from the university activities and the 5,000 much younger male and female students thronging the university grounds, but especially from the women's pageboy hair cuts and their smoking of cigarettes. "I don't think I will ever get used to it," he concluded.

In communications with Inspector Warneck in Sumatra, the inspector described the increasing troubles the Mission was encountering as being caused by rabble-rousers. He properly interpreted these occurrences as being concealed attacks on the Dutch colonial government, saying, "What these troublemakers want in the parishes, they want even more so politically. Since they cannot confront the government directly, they try it on us. The troublemakers are communist-oriented and incited by Indian and Russian rabble-rousers. What the Mission experiences now foreshadows what will sooner or later have to be faced by the government," he wrote in December of 1928.

When Hermann and Martha's return to Sumatra approached, Else traveled to Ria, Martha's sister, on Easter 1929, where she was to help in the household for a year. Gertrud stayed with a foster parent in Barmen.

Weissenbruchs' second Departure to Sumatra

Soon enough, the day of their departure and their return to Sumatra arrived. It was celebrated by a farewell party at the Mission's facilities in Barmen on July 9, 1929. After some stopovers with relatives, they traveled by train via Basel to Genoa, where they boarded the 'Coblenz' on July 23. Unfortunately, their train journey from Basel to Genoa was at night, but with a full moon, they were able to admire the Alps by moonlight.

With their ship delayed by a day, they took the opportunity to take a day trip with Mr. & Mrs. Dahlhäuser, the manager of the seaman's home, where they stayed overnight, and their travel companion, Dr. Werdermann. The party traveled to Nervi, where they spent a few pleasant hours on the beach. Martha enjoyed the wonderful beach, framed by high mountains, the flowering gardens and whitewashed villas, and before them the deep-blue sea – all and all, a beautiful composition. In the evening, they took the train back to Genoa. Late that night, the ship weighed anchor, and they had one last look at the city with its thousands of lights.

"We crept into our beds; Hermann had to climb to the upper bunk, and I had to watch not to bang my head on the mattress springs above me. In the coming days, we enjoyed some nice dinners at our table. The company on board is very mixed, and one can observe the beginnings of equality among people; aside from Germans, there are Englishmen, Hollanders, Spaniards, Japanese, Chinese, and other hard-to-identify characters. This would have been impossible in previous years; nowadays it is taken for granted. The Chinese yakyaking around us is sometimes terrible. One could conduct ethnic studies in this environment."

They passed Elba, Corsica, and the Stromboli volcano, then the Strait of Messina, the Scilla and Charybdis of classical lore, to enter the open Mediterranean Sea, steaming past Crete to arrive in Port Said. On the 10th of August, 1929, they celebrated Hermann's 25th anniversary in Mission work, and on the 16th of August arrived in Belawan, on Sumatra. The following morning took them to Sitorang together with *Ephorus* Nommensen Jr. for a celebration of their return. A trumpet orchestra played the German song, *"Es blickt so still der Mond mich an, es fließt so ruhig der Rhein ."* Martha jested that, while she was half a daughter of this river, being born nearby, she was surprised by this performance and had difficulty suppressing her laughter. "This melody was followed by a number of other songs, one worse than the other," she commented.

On September 1, they moved into their new home in Sitorang. Their predecessor had written: "In Sitorang everything is as in Parsambilan," meaning there is no worse place in all of Batakland. But Martha corrected this viewpoint – somewhat, by saying, "Thank God, this judgment was not quite correct, even if things looked dreadful." About 65% of the baptized population stayed away from God's word. Couples were not married, the youth were not confirmed and the children were not baptized. It was a large area, requiring Hermann to make long trips into the nearby mountains, into the 'kingdom of the tiger,' where four people had been eaten by them in the past year. In Lumban Pinaradrung a tiger even entered a Batak house. A man had walked his dog, who ran away into a house with the tiger following. The people sitting inside literally froze. The tiger tripped on a matt on the floor on which two girls were sleeping. The beast must have been totally disoriented and frightened and, not knowing where the door was, took one leap, crashed through the rickety wall and escaped. A year ago, one of the Mission's Elders was torn apart by a tiger not far from Porsoburan Station. The man had been working by moonlight in his garden. The people don't dare call a tiger by its name, *babiat* in Batak, but rather talk about 'grandfather' or 'the strong one.'

Two months after their arrival, Hermann wrote, "The situation in Sitorang is unpleasant and difficult when looking at the great mass of people. But there is also a desire to hear the Lord's word. On September 8, when visiting Balige, our old parish, I gave three services, in the morning, at noon and in the evening, for about a thousand people. After one of the services, a man followed us and said: *"Tuan,* forgive me for those times when I was often so impudent and unkind to you; I'm sorry!"
Sitorang managed twelve widely dispersed branches, the territory of three earlier missionaries which must now be covered by Hermann, with many areas accessible only by difficult trails.

"The earlier pillars of missionary work had gone to seed and live in bigamy. My husband will soon have the 'pleasure' of expelling them," Martha wrote in her memoirs. "We conduct nightly meetings on village squares and visit also individual families. Whoever stays away from services, is expelled. This has caused a salutary stir in the community, with many now coming to put their affairs in order. They are then required to attend lectures three times a week for nine months, after which they are, in front of the parish, ceremonially welcomed back into the community. After the first year, sixty have returned, with the same number of pagans having been baptized. There is a peculiar mishmash of Christians and pagans in our community," she wrote, "and apparently insufficient attention was paid in earlier times to keep the two separate. This becomes especially noticeable at burials, even among our elders. At these heathen burials, a terrible racket of howling, screaming and dancing ensues, as if there were no resurrection."

Martha delighted in her work with the women, especially a very old woman, who, when coming to her lectures, sat sunk in herself before her, mumbling the same words over and over. On their visits through the villages, they tried to tell the people why they had come to Sumatra. They received responses like, "Oh, because you felt too cold over there," or, when Hermann asked a previously baptized man why he no longer attended service, was told, "You just go on praying to the Holy Spirit to come and urge us on." A Batak is rarely at a loss for a reply.

In a report Hermann typed in November 1929, in Sitorang, he described his missionary excursions into the mountains surrounding the village.

To prepare for this trip of several days, and because it was the rainy season, he had to pack his provisions in two petroleum cans that could be closed tightly. He was limited to a total of about 35 quarts, which he had to stow intelligently. His little Batak horse wasn't the sturdiest, and his 'boy,' accompanying him, was not used to climbing while carrying the two cans. Thus, from time to time, the young fellow was allowed to put his load onto the saddle. They happened to come across a former Elder, Abraham by name, and his wife Rebecca, who permitted their son to help the two travelers reach the mountain ridge. From there they could see the Mission station way down in the valley with the magnificent lake reflecting the light of the sun.

Two-and-a-half hours later they reached the first Mission branch, Siriaria, at the foot of the like-named mountain.

When he entered their school, he wrote, "forty black, shining pairs of eyes looked at me curiously and a bit fearfully, since they did not know this new *tuan* yet. He found the group wanting in cleanliness and knowledge, compared to his former parish in Balige. Outside, an old pagan, *Raja* Hurangan, known to be a medium for evil spirits, sat with his white-haired wife on a reed mat. She was working some flax from which, in earlier times, Bataks had made clothing. Hermann wrote: "I joined them on the mat and struck up a conversation by referring to the man's name, saying that *Raja* Hurangan means actually 'The chief who suffers from a shortcoming.' And see, you do suffer from a shortcoming, the word of life, the living God, which is why you sacrifice to the *begus*, the evil spirits. So, why do you keep away from school? 'Yes, *tuan*,' he said, 'I have often tried, but there's always something that keeps me from coming. Sometimes I have forgotten to bring my slendang, my shoulder cloth, then it is something else.' Yes, I believe you," I responded. "The devil does not want you to come.' " He promised to join our gathering that very evening, but did not show up.

The villagers had butchered a piglet in Hermann's honor and had roasted it over the fire. After a highly spiced meal of rice, he was able to brew himself (from his provisions) a good cup of coffee for dessert. At six o'clock the bell rang for service. Afterwards, he had a serious talk with the village chiefs concerning the fact that girls were getting married much too early, frequently at the age of 13 or 14. This resulted in more divorces and other troubles. Furthermore, boys were sent to school, but few, if any girls. Hermann told the elders that this must be because parents loved only their sons and not their daughters. If they continued this practice, they would never become independent in a hundred years. Therefore, it was most important that their daughters, the mothers-to-be, be educated as well. They seemed to understand this and promised to do so. "But let's see if they will keep their word," Hermann commented. "The Bataks have an appropriate saying, '*Molo soada roha, godang sidalian*,' meaning, that 'When one has no mind for something, one has many empty excuses.' They'll get to hear this from me many times yet."

Later, his nightly accommodation was readied, which consisted of a kind of hammock, made of canvas with sewn-in,

103

folded edges, into which two poles were inserted, the ends of which rested on a couple of school benches. Despite his blankets and a heavy coat, he got quite cold at the 4,300 feet (1,300 m) elevation.

After the weather cleared the next morning, his journey continued through valleys and rivers, mostly on muddy, slippery loam trails, and only occasionally was he able to ride his horse. Eventually, the sun broke through the clouds and he enjoyed an incredible vista of giant mountains, canyons, and a high plateau with villages. Among them was Maranti, where he and his companions were headed. But he was still separated from it by deep gorges. Sometimes, the trail led along barely three foot (1 m) wide ridges with a yawning chasm on both sides. A single misstep of horse or man, and the depths would have taken them. Then came a descent, where the Elder who was guiding them suggested that Hermann inspect it before attempting the fourteen steps that had been chiseled into the mountainside. Steep drop-offs beckoned on both sides. "I climbed the steps on all fours," he wrote, and the horse had to be taken on a long detour before they were able to meet again at the bottom of a canyon. Of course, there they had to cross a torrential creek, which his companions said was impossible to cross after strong rains.

Maranti consisted of twelve small Batak villages with about 150 families. Hermann wrote that, when he dismounted by the school, "I was immediately surrounded by about forty men, who gaped at me. I recognized them as still true pagans, some of them members of the peculiar sect of Pormalims, a mixture of various religions, that is, Batak paganism, Islamic and Christian beliefs. They are fanatics and unreceptive to missionary work. They even look like the Toba people and are largely untouched by culture." He quickly became engaged in conversations with them, at which time one of them commented that Hermann had to be an opium smoker because of his pale complexion. Here, too, only 43 boys gathered from far outlying villages to attend school.

Hermann also recounted the following experience: "While I was still occupied in the school building, I could hear, close-by, heathen drum music, accompanied by clarinets. Some gun salutes arose, all-in-all an ear-shattering din, mixed with the wailing of the bereaved. The teacher told me that a six-year-old boy had died, and that this 'racket' had already gone on for several days. When I was finished at the school, I walked over to the village square, where a colorful picture presented itself. I wished I had a camera so I could have taken a photograph. Hundreds of villagers sat on mats or stood near the dead boy's home. In front of the house stood a coffin, made from the trunk of a sugar palm, which the Bataks like to use for this purpose. The trunk had been split lengthwise in half, with the two halves tied together with some rope. On one side sat the Batak orchestra, making its ear-shattering noise. This was, however, surpassed by the screaming, wailing shouts of the men and women. They were holding large pieces of cloth over their heads together with the dead boy's few possessions, including a blackboard.

"I stood there silently and deeply moved for several minutes, and studied the pain-distorted faces. I saw the blood that was dripping from the women's scratched cheeks, and the terrible hopelessness of this paganism, so far from God, and my heart was deeply shaken. The dead boy's grandfather, whom I knew, noticed me standing there, and approached, asking me if I wanted to see the boy's corpse. I asked him whether he would be able to arrange for a few minutes of quiet. With some effort he succeeded. I then told the people that we Christians have a word from God, which says 'to weep with the weeping.' That I felt the parents' pain having lost their only boy so early in life, and that I mourned with them. But, I continued, I was even more sad that they mourned without the hope of ever seeing their boy again. We Christians, I told them, even speak at the burial of seeing each other again. We believe that He, who has taken away the power of death, has said, 'I am the resurrection and life; whoever believes in Me, shall live, though he would die.' They listened silently, but while I spoke in Batak, my words were of a different world, words coming from Eternity and the transience of Man and the hopelessness of the heathen. I do not know whether they understood, but, maybe, just maybe, I had put a sense of Christian hope into the one or the other's heart.

"Not far away lay the body of a water buffalo in its blood. His life had been sacrificed for this occasion. Next to the coffin lay something, which appeared indefinable to me. It looked like a small coffin, and when the women moved its cover a bit aside, I recognized a bundled-up skull and skeleton, the remains of an ancestor, which had been kept buried in the house. These remains were to be re-interred together with the boy's body, his grandchild. This seemed to be an act of desperation, since the boy's father had no other son; he was *punu*, childless, without a male descendant.

"Once everyone had received their share of meat, the boy's little body was taken away to be buried in some hidden corner. When I asked why that was done so secretly, I was told that I would not see any graves in the entire Maranti community. All had been leveled. In earlier times grave robbers had sometimes, in a blood feud, disinterred the corpses' heads if they had not been able to obtain them from the living. I was told that the government had required the dead to be buried in proper graves, but although such graveyards existed now, no bodies would be found there."

Hermann paid visits to several other villages, then was accompanied by chief Omoe Sidomdom to the district chief, Porduaan, who had previously visited Hermann in Sitorang. The trail they took was most interesting and panoramic. Hermann had visited there twelve years ago with some colleagues to see the two magnificent waterfalls at Tangga, the Siguragura Falls, where Lake Toba's waters drop 200 feet (60 m) and then 990 feet (300 m) with a mighty noise into a large basin. The roar and dripping water made it impossible to understand the spoken word. From there, the river was called Arek Arimo, the Tiger River, which emptied into the Asahan River, and eventually into the ocean on Sumatra's east coast.

While Hermann took the chief and elders there, he took them to task for letting the school shack deteriorate so badly that the children had to flee when it rained. Going on and getting to a government building, where the Dutch representative stayed when visiting, Hermann had the local teacher take the protocol, which recorded the requirements for building a proper school, and had the mostly illiterate men affix their thumbprints to the document. They were impressed. Leaving there, he was told that tigers had killed three people this very year, including a chief.

Visiting several more villages, he found the people living there to be either still pagans or poor Christians. While Christianity had found acceptance in the Toba districts, it had not done so in this more remote area. Hermann concluded his observations by saying, "I can travel my path happily and gratefully, because I meet people I can advise, who realized their failures and want to begin a new life." Then he thought of the millions of people in his native Germany, who could not be persuaded to return to their parish, the church, and to Christ. "Oh, how great is my people's misery."

By now 1931 had come, and something was astir in Lumban Silondet, where people gathered on Sunday evenings for religious studies. They asked that, from time to time, a teacher be sent to them. But among the locals was a *porbaringin*, a lieutenant of Singamangaraja, the dead warrior-king. These lieutenants maintained the king's poisonous legacy among the people. They were usually smart fellows, astute speakers, who posed difficulties in discourse. One of these lieutenants had recently died in Silomba, and two were installed in place of the one, a manifestation of the endurance of paganism.

Martha's comment on the state of the world was sorrowful. She said that the people lived only for the present, not knowing what would come tomorrow. She was also bothered by disagreements in the Mission's organization.

On the date of their Silver Anniversary, the 31st of October 1931, Martha mentioned her girls, thinking that Else would take awhile to find her proper path. Gertrud, who had become engaged in Germany on the date of the Weissenbruchs' anniversary to Alfred Rutkowsky, had found her way into the Mission and would find her life's work in Sumatra, her home country. Her entering the Mission was taken by Martha as proof that God steered his disciples. She referred to an ancestor whose son wanted to enter the Mission but was not permitted to follow his wish. The father, supposedly bothered by his conscience, prayed that many of his descendants would yet enter the Mission. Martha now claimed that she was the 36th and Gertrud would be the 37th family member! Thinking that this ancestor was still praying in the Heavens for more descendants to follow this route, she expected his wish to be granted by the Lord. Alas – none did!

The Mission in Germany was not doing well. Contacts with Dutch organizations attempted to find support and means to assist the Barmen Mission. The personnel had their salaries cut by 40%, the foreign missionaries by 20%, but by December 1932 they were able to rescind the cuts and resume full payment. The political and economic conditions in Germany were less than helpful. The National Socialist Party was refusing to join the government and insisted on full power for itself. The Mission's director explained how difficult it was to maintain 508 Mission employees, not counting those at the Mission headquarters. To help limit expenses, Barmen had stopped working in New Guinea and turned missionary work there over to American organizations.

In September of 1932, Alfred Rutkowsky, their future son-in-law, came to Sumatra for missionary work. He was followed by Gertrud in April of 1933, who stayed with her parents until the 9th of November 1933, the date of her wedding. This reduced the Mission's official waiting time to be allowed to marry, substantially, to which the Mission's Director expressed his displeasure in a letter to Hermann in January of 1934. It did not take long for the newlyweds and their parents to welcome their first child and grandchild, Christa, on October 17, 1934.

Else had also found the man of her life in Heinz Otto, a businessman, employed with a German Import-Export company in Wuppertal. Married on February 22, 1936, the company sent them to Borneo, where they arrived on April 19. The Weissenbruchs regretted that they had been unable to meet with them on their way to Borneo. Some time later, Else was able to pay her parents a three-week visit.

In January of 1934, Director Warneck mentioned that the year 1933 brought a 'magnificent change' to Germany, unfortunately, also great confusion to the Church. Unfortunately, the Reichs-Bishop abandoned the evangelical youth organization, and against everybody's wish, incorporated it into the Hitler-Youth, a political organization.

Half a year later, Warneck referred to information according to which the native population wanted to become independent from Europeans, saying, "This is a serious development to which we must pay attention. It requires that parishes we deem ready should be given their independence. A letter to this extent will shortly go out to all Mission stations. With the dire situation concerning our school subsidies, it means that parishes must learn to fend for themselves. This will require some effort on our part, and will also lead to some disappointments."

Martha's recollections now skip several years to 1936.

A Mission correspondence in midyear of 1936 discussed the worsening health of Hermann, and his resulting inability to stay in touch with the more remote and difficult to reach Mission branches. It was suggested that he return to Germany, although the return of every older Brother meant a severe loss to the Mission's activities. Warneck's communication concluded with, "It may be that your son-in-law, Rutkowsky, ought to calm down a bit. I cannot say that his letters are very pleasant to read. He seems to be one of those people who believe that only with their coming, true light begins to shine. According to him, whatever has been done so far is of no value. We old ones know the Mission's shortcomings and are receptive to reasonable critique, but a little modesty and patience until things are better understood would be appropriate for the young man. I'm writing this confidentially; maybe you can exert some influence on him. It is very much desired that his capabilities will be of benefit to the Mission and the Mission's Sisters."

"Our parish has grown and has shrunk; it has moved like waves," as Martha described it. "There have been times when the Balige church has been full, and when it has been empty. Times of emptiness and indifference. Is it our own fault? Are we not drawing sufficiently from the springs of life ourselves?" she wondered and questioned. But in Nonna br. Hasiboean, the wife of their medical assistant, Andreas, they had found great help. This woman was very active when it came to visiting the sick in the villages and stirring up the lazies. Many of their Batak helpers were, however, still not fully ready for mission work.

The 'independents' were becoming more numerous. They were basically a national movement, as was happening all over the world these days. They did not have enough power – yet – to move against the Dutch government, which was why the Mission served as the anvil that's being hit upon. "Away with European management! We Bataks can do it ourselves!" They elected their own *ephorus*, who had been dismissed because of embezzlement. But they found teachers and established their own small parishes and schools across the land. Bad things were happening: they baptized without previous studies and without the authority to do so. Much conflict and confusion had thus entered their parishes. The Mission's Sinta Jonathan had been seduced to become their leader, despite Hermann's warning, "Beware that you won't be a Judas!" He replied: "It's for the money!" Since his wife did not follow him, he eventually told his 'independent' congregation that what they were doing was wrong – until they threw him out.

Even worse were the Catholics with their subversive actions, their propaganda, their numbers – and their full purses. They had established themselves at key points, from which they also proselytized in the outlying areas. They established their own schools and told the people: "Everyone bringing us their child will get 20 guilders." This was the way they operated, and it is no wonder that many Bataks fell for it. As Martha put it, "The Catholic Sisters wipe the kids noses on the streets and offer various sweets, all means of attracting women and children." One of the Mission's best speakers, a highly gifted man, who had been dismissed because of sex offenses, was now an eager propagandist for the Catholics. However, in an hour of contemplation, the man admitted: "I know I have taken the wrong path, if it were not for the money." Other dishonest characters use the Catholics' showing as a weapon, saying: "If you don't do as we wish, we'll get the Catholics!"

Samaria was one of the girls from Martha's women's circle. She had married, but was widowed a year later. Following Batak custom, she became the property of her deceased husband's tribe and was to marry his brother, who was studying to become a teacher. Until he was finished, Samaria lived with her parents. Then, the planned marriage to the brother fell apart, and the two parental parties began fighting over the inheritance and the repayment of the dowry. There was much back and forth; however, she became a valuable asset for the Mission in her village. The parents kept litigating and Samaria was pulled hither and yon, so that, eventually, her wish for another marriage became ever more burning. It would have resulted in the replacement of the dowry and the end of the parental quarrels.

She prayed for another suitor, and – lo and behold – only a few days later, she received a letter from a widower with four children. She was terrified, for she had not prayed for a widower with children. But soon, she realized that this was God's answer to her request, and that she could not say "no" to it. She bid farewell to her women's group and traveled to the city of Medan, where she now lived among Muslims.

In October of 1936, Martha continued with her recollections, describing the joy, when her daughter, Else, came to visit from Borneo for three weeks. Hermann's illness had become a constantly variable problem; at times he felt better, only to get worse again. Earlier, in August, they had vacationed with the Nommensens in Parapat, the village close to Si Piak. Actually, Si Piak had been incorporated into Parapat. Hermann was able to preach once more to his former parish, and was able to return the aged widow of *Raja* Israel to the church's fold, together with her sons and daughters-in-law. Because of some bitter experiences, they had left the church and joined one of the independent congregations. Then Martha told the story of *Raja* Israel, known also by his original name, Ama ni Gane, and his wife Emma:

"Emma, as her Christian name was to become, was a tall, strong woman, who exerted great power in her village. Her husband had shown interest in the new teachings and in addition to the gatherings, joined Hermann in his study to ask him questions. He had a good head and was interested also in conditions in Europe. His wife quarreled with him and warned: 'You will see what will happen, if you associate with this 'Whiteeye;' misfortune will befall our sons and our livestock will perish.' When one of her children died, she was beyond herself and screamed at her husband to stay away from the Mission. For a short time she was successful. But God had put his hand onto this couple to open them in order to be one of the first to accept the new teachings.

"Emma broke through a weak spot in the floor of their house and hurt herself seriously. The leg swelled and soon festered. To alleviate her pain, a shaman was called, who applied lime and tar to the wound. But before he administered help, he required that a buffalo and a pig had to be sacrificed to appease the evil spirit, which had caused the accident. But despite their hope for improvement, the wound festered. The pair was aware that the white man had good medicines and was willing to help, but when her husband suggested she see him, her eyes flared from hatred. She would not let Hermann get close to her. Weeks passed and the pain got worse. Finally, she permitted my husband to come with his sharp little knife and after a prayer, made a deep incision into the wound. A large quantity of pus escaped. Afterward, her pain was soon gone and her condition improved. A few weeks later she was able to walk again. Now, the leaf turned, and she urged her husband to go to the gatherings and listen to the new teachings.

"It took a couple of years, but they became the first to join the baptism studies. And they did not rest until several relatives joined and a large number of their villagers, eventually, totaling 38 people. Ama ni Gane chose as his Christian name, *Raja* Israel, and his wife, Emma. Now, *Raja* Israel has long entered Eternity."

However, while they stayed at Parapat, bad news were reported. Dr. Güß, his wife and a visitor from Germany, visiting some nearby sulfur springs, had been asphyxiated by the gases. In addition, two Brothers, one of them younger, whom they had expected to work for many years, had died suddenly.

But life was renewed. A grandchild, Ute, was born to Rutkowskys, in Tarutung, Sumatra, on November 10, 1936, and Renate, to Ottos, on Borneo.

In November 1937, Hermann reported to the Barmen Mission Director that his health had very much deteriorated, and that he did not wish Mission work to suffer from his frailty. Recounting his service to the Mission, of which the last eight and a half years had been spent in Sitorang with seven parishes in the lowlands and twenty-three in the mountains. He declared himself ready to return to Germany, although he felt that he and his wife had become estranged from their country of birth.

Lastly, in a letter dated December 1937 to Barmen, Hermann described his ideas of how he might have been able to stay awhile longer. If he had been able to find someone to work the mountain parishes, he could have taken care of the lowland ones. Then, the thought of retiring on Sumatra surfaced, since the mild Toba climate was more amenable to the couple. However, problems with the transfer of pension payments were thought to be too troublesome. Doctors recommended that they retire to the milder climate of the Wiesbaden area, where some of Martha's relatives lived. Their problem was, however, that they did not think they would be able to afford an apartment there.

Finally, he advised of his and Martha's return from the port of Belawan at Medan on the steamship 'Scharnhorst,' sailing on April 4, 1938. But, then, on February 6, it turned out that their departure had been postponed to May 2nd, on the 'Potsdam.'

The delay enabled Hermann to better prepare for proper transfer of his responsibilities. Unfortunately, no replacement had been found for him, and it would take at least four months to find a Brother to take over.

This meant that his neighbor, Brother Nommensen Jr., would, in addition to his 30,000 Christians, have also to assume responsibility for the 15,000 baptized people and the 32 parishes in Hermann's territory. He recalled when the Mission had 14 missionaries at the stations, excluding the *Ephorus* and teachers. Now, there were only 4!

And the questions as to where in Germany to retire was in constant flux, and was complicated by a request from Batak parish elders to the local *Ephorus* to keep Hermann in the Toba area. Eventually, a decision was made to retire to the city of Bad Honnef, in Hesse. But their plans continued to change.

Hermann and Martha in retirement

The Weissenbruchs' Retirement in Germany

On May 18, 1938, Hermann and Martha arrived in Wiesbaden, where they stayed with relatives. Homeward bound, onboard ship, dysentery struck him again, and at home the doctors told him to avoid going into mountains. On August 4, he received a medical report, advising him of his hypertension with an initial systolic pressure of 255. Four weeks of treatment reduced it to 215. He was to maintain complete physical and mental rest for at least a year. Thereafter, he would be fully capable of resuming service. But doctors had also diagnosed him with kidney atrophy and arteriosclerosis.

Finally, they succeeded in finding a three-room apartment in Wiesbaden-Biebrich, Schlageterstraße 52. Falling ill again, and fearing an outbreak of the Sprue, he was bed-bound for two weeks, and had to leave most of the work of getting established in the new home to Martha. But having to stay put, Martha was able to feed him a proper diet. In November, he was contemplating becoming active in church work in the new year, 1939, and by July of that year was already engaged in some activities.

On September 1, 1939, Germany invaded Poland and W.W.II began. Hermann mentioned heavy bombers flying over their house after their takeoff at the nearby Erbenheim air base. In January of 1940 Hermann was advised that he had been put on *Wartegeld*, semiretirement, since full retirement was not permitted during war times.

The Rhenish Mission Society was run in a patriachalic fashion, where women were considered secondary, whether they were the wives of missionaries or Sisters. If salaries for the men were low, there was only 'pocket money' for the Sisters, and only in 1988 was the amount raised to the level of a pension!

At the time, restrictions were placed on some pastors, such as being forbidden to speak anywhere in Germany, another being required to relocate to another area. Hermann felt unsettled in the Wiesbaden area, having grown up in and around Barmen, whereas Martha, her relatives nearby, was comfortable. She had told him, however, that wherever he went, she would follow. While in the past they often had to wait for weeks for mail to arrive, airmail had since come into service. Nevertheless, a letter from Gertrud from Sumatra or Else from Borneo to Germany could still take three weeks.

On May 10, 1940 Germany invaded Holland, and with the Dutch East Indies being a Dutch colony, the members of the Rhenish Mission on Sumatra became enemy personnel and were interned.

In a letter dated August 16, 1940, Hermann wrote to his wife his instructions for the time after his 'departure,' accompanied by some sentiments. One was, how and where to find his final resting place. After some soul searching, he had decided it to be in Wiesbaden. He regretted that he could not be buried on Sumatra, in his beloved Batakland, where he felt at home. He spelled out what he would like to have said in this eulogy and what melodies he would like sung. His gold watch, given to him by the Balige congregation upon their departure, was to go to Alfred Rutkowsky, his son-in-law, but, as he said, "It is not suited for daily use, because of its fragility." A few other items he wanted to be given to Heinz Otto, his other son-in-law, Else's husband. "All in all, unimportant items," as he called them. His wish that their children and grandchildren would remain God's children, came true only for the next generation, his children. Most members of the subsequent generation decided on clean breaks from what their grandparents had believed in and had worked so tirelessly for in a foreign land.

On September 10, 1941, Hermann referred to a wire received from the Japanese ship, Asamamaru, that his daughter Else with her two daughters, several Sisters and other Germans had arrived in Kobe, Japan, after having been released from internment in Blitar on East Java by the invading Japanese and the Dutch authorities.

In late fall of 1941, both Hermann and Martha were sick, but especially Martha. The long years in the tropics were catching up. They were now suffering from amebic dysentery, for which they were treated at a couple of locations. Afterwards, the couple returned to their apartment in W.-Biebrich, where they lived past the end of W.W.II.

Rutkowsky family lore tells that grandfather Weissenbruch had promised his wife that he would remain with her to the end of the war. Germany capitulated on May 8, 1945, and Hermann Weissenbruch died on July 21, 1945, a little more than two months later, at the age of 68. He passed away peacefully while sitting at a table with his wife.

Martha Weissenbruch was able to stay in the apartment – not easy at this time with housing widely destroyed – until her son-in-law, Alfred Rutkowsky, came to Germany in 1946 from six years internment in India. His family arrived the following year, 1947, from Sumatra and joined the two, meaning that six people lived in the three-room apartment. Eventually, Alfred returned to Sumatra in 1955. Gertrud and their daughter, Dorothea, born in 1949, followed him in 1957. The Wiesbaden household was dissolved and Martha retired to the home 'Heimatfreude' for missionaries, where she knew many former colleagues and missionary wives. There she passed away on April 16, 1962, at the age of 79.

Irmgard, Else, and Renate Otto

2. Heinz & Elisabeth Otto, née Weissenbruch
and their Children

Elisabeth Weissenbruch, called Else, was born on December 31, 1909, in Si Piak on Sumatra. She met her future husband, Heinz Otto, in 1929 at the Rhenish Mission Headquarters in Wuppertal-Barmen.

Karl Heinz Otto was born in Wuppertal on March 31, 1909. Following his graduation, his Abitur, he became a business apprentice at the '*Rheinisch-Bornesische-Handelsverein.*' Upon completion of his apprenticeship permanent employment was extended.

Heinz wrote: "I was a lively 21 years old when, one morning, on the 13th of August 1930, I was called in to see the director of the company in Barmen. At such times several questions cross one's mind: 'How-where-when might I have failed? Could I have done something wrong? Be prepared for whatever comes and remain calm!'

"Upon entering the director's sanctum sanctorum, I attempted to read from Director Bader's facial expressions whether I was facing a problem or pleasant news. But it was a smile that greeted me and the question: 'If you want to go to the Dutch East Indies, you must be gone four weeks from now!'

"At lunch time I hurried to see my parents, who owned a laundry business, to bring the good news. To my folks, sitting at the lunch table, I said, as if it were unimportant, 'In four weeks I'm going to travel to India!' One could hear some silverware being dropped. Then the questions came, and some tears of joy were wiped off. It meant that my employment was secure, something not self-evident after New York's 'Black Friday' in 1929, and the subsequent worldwide economic crisis."

Thus, on September 18, 1930 Heinz left for Borneo, the southern part of the island today known as Indonesia's Kalimantan, as the trade representative of '*R.A.G. Hennemann & Co.*,' a division of the '*Rheinisch-Bornesiche-Handelsverein.*' Hennemann & Co. traded in lumber, palm oil, hevea latex, spices, and various raw materials.

He worked there for five years until his first vacation in Germany in 1936, where he met Else again, with whom he had maintained contact through correspondence. The two married on February 22, 1936. In April of 1936, ship's passage on the 'Potsdam,' departing from Genoa, took them to their future home, the village of Bandjermasin on the southeast coast of Borneo. *Bandjer* means 'high water' and '*masin*' salty. They arrived there in May with Heinz continuing his work as a trader.

Heinz's description of the Borneo of his time was that it had been under Dutch colonial rule from 1606 until 1946, the end of W.W. II. Borneo is twenty times the size of Holland. The Dutch had established some settlements along the coast, but had barely entered the interior. The island was thinly populated by at most three million people, most of them living along the coast, with few spread across its vast interior. Malays and Chinese had established small villages along its coastline. The frugal, venturesome Chinese especially conducted business upriver with even the smallest settlements. Without the Chinese presence no trade, even limited, would have been possible, as Heinz claims. Dayaks, native people, constituting the majority of the population, lived along the rivers where they farmed rice, complementing their nutrition with forest products. It must be understood that rivers were, more or less, the only means for travel and transportation, since the jungle and the topography were simply too troublesome to cross.

Plentiful rainfall produced a broad spectrum of plant growth with several types of palm trees growing along the island's shores and many valuable tropical hardwoods inland. There were 800 species of orchids. Tree sap, rattan, and sago palms, the latter's heart being edible, were other products for sale, together with numerous other edible plants and fruits. Heinz mentioned also durian, whose smell was so powerful that it was not permitted on board ships. Borneo's rivers teamed with fish, just as the surrounding sea did, and snakes, turtles and crocodiles populated the estuaries and rivers. Varans, 'flying' reptiles, were found inland. On Borneo and Sumatra grew approximately 450 species of trees, many reaching diameters in excess of two-and-a-half feet (75 cm), and numerous ferns. Hanging in the trees were the black nests of honey bees, their honey highly desired, but their nests difficult and dangerous to access.

The village of Bandjermasin was located by a river, 12 miles (20 km) from where it entered the sea. Only flat-bottomed ships coming from Singapore or Surabaya were able to make it all the way to Bandjermasin, and then only at high tide. The land by the river was so low that it experienced daily inundation by the tides. The Ottos lived in a house, which, like all others in the area, stood on 7 ft (2 meter) high stilts. At noon the thermometer climbed to 120 degrees Fahrenheit (50 deg. Celsius), calling for several showers a day. The swampy environment did not allow for a piped water supply, requiring the residents to procure their own water by collecting rain run-off from the roofs of their buildings in huge containers during the rainy season from October to April.

Between their large wooden house and the about 120 ft (35 meter) distant service buildings, containing the kitchen, shower, and toilet, two giant tanks of 600 cubic feet (20 cubic meter), held the collected water. Tapping into the tanks' water, colored brownish from the roof's shingles, required its filtration through pumice rocks, each process producing only a single bucket of clean water, which still needed to be boiled before use. For drinking the family used imported bottled mineral water. Electric power was only available between six o'clock in the evening and six o'clock in the morning.

Else gave birth to their first child, Renate, on January 26, 1937, followed by Irmgard on July 7, 1938, and Rolf Dieter on May 7, 1940. The little boy died of encephalitis on October 17, 1940, with his father never having seen him.

Following Germany's invasion of Holland, Heinz, being German, was in May of 1940 placed in 'Protective Internment,' as it was called. Prior to the Japanese invasion of the Dutch East Indies he was, together with other German Internees, transferred by the Dutch to Dheradun in India, where he met his brother-in-law, Alfred Rutkowsky. Together, Heinz and Alfred were repatriated to Germany in 1946.

Else and the children experienced similar internment in November of 1940 in Blitar on Java, spending a year there, until 'liberated' by the Japanese. The German government had made arrangements with the Japanese government to repatriate the women and children under Red Cross auspices via Japan and the Trans-Siberian Railroad to Germany, and Else opted for this opportunity. However, Germany's invasion of the Soviet Union put a stop to this, and the family was stranded in Japan for the remainder of the war.

In September 1941 they boarded the Japanese passenger liner Asama Maru in Batavia for Kobe in Japan. Upon leaving, they encountered terrible conditions at customs in Batavia: their suitcases were broken open and many items were confiscated. A number of German women and children disembarked in Shanghai.

Renate, due to poor nutrition, had become very ill on board and upon their arrival in Kobe had to be hospitalized for two weeks. The German evacuees were received by the German consulate staff and found accommodation at the nice Tor Hotel near Yokohama. Irmgard and Renate still recall the beautiful Japanese garden surrounding the hotel. The crews of German raiders and U-boats came visiting their stranded compatriots and brought the children little presents of drawing paper and coloring pencils. More relocations followed, the first to the Nara Hotel, which had a beautiful garden with deer grazing on its lawn, then to the village of Atami, which was located by the ocean. On February 11, 1943, another move followed, this time to Yokohama, where the children were able to attend the 'International School' which, due to the war, stood vacant. Mothers provided the teaching.

In 1944, bombing of Tokyo and Yokohama by the U.S. Air Force began, which affected also the German U-boat detachment in the port of Yokohama. Else helped with the treatment of the injured. Following the bombing, Else and the children were once more relocated, this time, on April 16, 1944, to Funatsu, to the Bekkan Hotel, at Lake Kawaguchi, close to Mount Fujiyama. The hotel lay amidst a large garden with carp ponds and small hidden bowers among the volcanic rocks. It was a 'summer retreat' with tatami floors, that is, they were made of tightly woven raffia, framed in man-size wooden lattices. Each frame made for a sleeping place. Of course, the rooms could be entered only with shoes off! At first, they had to sleep on futons; later, they received beds that had been removed from the 'Gneisenau,' a new German cruise ship that had not made it back to Germany prior to the outbreak of the war. The Japanese took over the 20,000 ton ship, and, according to Renate's later information, converted it to an aircraft carrier.

Else wrote that the hotel's floors had many cracks, and because of the building's light construction for use as a summer retreat, it was totally unsuited as a winter quarter, causing them to suffer very much from the cold. Only some rooms had hearths, which were so poor that only by sitting close to them did they provided some warmth. The snow was so deep that they sank into it up to their knees in their light tropical shoes. The hotel's water pipes had frozen and some had burst. The lake, too, was frozen. To get water they had to hack a hole, after which water was transferred to the hotel via a bucket chain.

At the Bekkan Hotel Renate had found a friend, an elderly gentleman by the name of Walther Marr, whom, as she recalls, "I nicknamed 'Fairytales.' He lived in a little house adjacent to the hotel and took care that all went well for the women and children lodging at the Bekkan. He dealt with Japanese officials and distributed foodstuffs, such as flour, sugar, and other scarce items our mothers received through private means. I sometimes helped him sort items or, sitting there, simply enjoyed his company."

'Fairytales' put together a 'memory album' for Renate, herewith as an excerpt: "The Bekkan lies directly on the shore of Lake Kawaguchi and is built on cooled lava flows which once emptied here into the lake. They had formed many small bays and coves and promontories reaching far into the lake, which, on three sides, is enclosed by high mountains. Enclosing the landscape in the south, rises majestic 'Fuji' to 13,300 ft. The lake is deep and its shores drop steeply."

Sustenance consisted mainly of potatoes, of which the Japanese provided plenty. Occasionally, carrots and cabbage complemented their diet. There was little, if any meat. They never got to see any fresh meat through the entire six-and-a-half years of their stay in Japan. Corned beef and canned tuna were turned into hash or *Frikadellen*, a kind of German hamburger. Butter always arrived rancid and the squishy white bread was all too often moldy. They received the canned fish and corned beef through the German consulate, supposedly retrieved from captured and sunk enemy freighters. The women were also issued cigarettes, which could be traded on farmsteads for eggs. Otherwise, they had little contact with Japanese. Adults, as well as children, learned only the most important Japanese terms for communication.

Funatsu was a small village, built on lava rocks, located at Lake Kawaguchi, and featured a number of very pleasant hotels. Irmgard recalls the lake as being very deep with innumerable small bays. The children loved to jump from the high rocks into the lake and enjoyed the bathing beach, from which they tossed some of the birchwood furniture into the lake, and, using it as floats swam far out. It was a children's paradise. Once Renate swam straight across the lake. Of course, this was followed by her mother's rebuke. According to Renate, Irmgard got often into trouble, because of the mischief she produced.

'Fairytales' wrote about Irmgard: "She was one of the 'wildest' children. Wherever something was going on or was about to happen, she was for certain a part of it. She climbed high up into trees to swing on branches that one thought she'd fall down at any moment. She climbed onto the roof, from which she leaped to the next, a 14 ft drop between. One day she talked Renate into doing it. Once was enough for her, while Irmgard kept leaping back and forth. With two pigtails in back, and a face as wide as it was high, she countered all reproaches with an impish smile. At first, I found Renate uninteresting. Only when my son Horst mentioned her repeatedly, and I heard of her being well-liked among the children, did I listen up. Because of her activity as the community nurse their '*Mami*,' their mother Else, was often absent. On these occasions the childless Mrs. Vobis took over care of Renate and Irmgard and reported on how well behaved the two Otto children were and even went readily to sleep when '*Mami*' had been called away."

Every fall they observed groups of monks who, holding torches, climbed Mount Fuji. And there were many temples in the neighborhood where festivities took place, such as the Cherry Blossom Celebration, the Lantern Celebration, and the Carp Celebration. Irmgard recalls them as being "excitingly beautiful." However, the girls were afraid of the eerie masks the celebrants wore, and the large, noisy drums with the attendant foreign, and to them, weird music.

The glassed-in verandah was used as a school room, and the oldest children received their first lessons there. With more and more German families moving to the area by Lake Kawaguchi, their children came to their hotel and four elementary classes were set up, taught by two German female and two male teachers.

Here, by Lake Kawaguchi, the families experienced little of the war, although Mount Fuji seemed to have been the landmark for air raids on Yokohama and Tokyo. At times, the children could observe some of the attackers being shot down by Japanese antiaircraft fire. However, the women and children were never in danger. When Tokyo and Yokohama were fire-bombed and burned brightly, they could see the glowing sky from their location.

Towards the end of the Pacific campaign German nationals experienced some resentment from the Japanese. Much later, Renate read that the Japanese had felt militarily abandoned after Germany had capitulated.

The American occupation troops discovered Lake Kawaguchi, and some of the German Embassy personnel who occupied the most beautiful hotel by the lake were relocated to free this prime area for the victors. Irmgard recalls the first sweets the children enjoyed, something unknown to them until then. The mothers were invited to barbecue parties. Jeep trips arranged by American soldiers took the women and children to the ice caves at Mount Fuji. The time spent at Lake Kawaguchi was a wonderful period for the children, as Renate and Irmgard recall.

Upon the war's end, the German women became impatient to be repatriated to Germany. When the German embassy personnel was to be repatriated a couple of years later, with no mention of the other German expatriates from the Dutch East Indies, several women turned to American officials, informing them that they were refugees from the Dutch East Indies, and, wasn't it known that their husbands were interned in Dheradun in India? This came as a surprise to the Americans, and the women and children were promised passage on the lower deck of the military vessel 'General Blake,' a troop transporter.

On August 17, 1947, their enforced stay in Japan came to an end, when they boarded the 'General Blake,' sailing from Yokohama to Shanghai, where an additional 514 German expatriates from the Dutch East Indies came on board. For a few days, the ship lay in port, giving the children the opportunity to observe the colorful life on shore and on the Yangtse River, also called the Yellow River, with its many junks and houseboats. At sea, food remains had been tossed overboard. Being children, they now tossed eggs, bread, cake, and food remains to the boats below and 'enjoyed' watching the people fight for them. But soon they were forbidden to continue this kind of 'entertainment.'

Continuing their journey, they experienced a serious typhoon, which tossed big fish on board. Passage through the Suez Canal took several days, delayed by the many wrecks. For a few days, the ship anchored at Port Said which time the women used to buy clothing and school satchels for the children with the dollars they had saved. However, no one was permitted to disembark. All purchases were conducted by tossing ropes to the traders in their boats below, after which merchandise as well as payments went up or down.

The ship passed Gibraltar on its way to Bremerhaven in Germany, where it arrived on October 1, 1947. Everyone took fright when they saw the destruction wrought by the war, and people, some in prisoner garb, were engaged in the cleanup of piles of rubble. They had to disembark right away. A train took them to a camp in Ludwigsburg. It became a long ride with many stops, often on open tracks. At train stations they were supplied with soup, tea, and some biscuits. Arriving at the camp, they had to get their own bedding from an attic to spend the next two nights there, and recall still today that they had never been so cold before.

Three days later their father arrived, who had already been repatriated from Dheradun in December of 1946, to pick them up and take them to Wiesbaden in the American Zone, where he lived with Martha Weissenbruch's sister, Ria Conradi and her husband, Max.

The ride to Wiesbaden looked like it would be an 'adventure.' People hung like grapes even on the outside of carriages. Heinz suggested riding the train's buffers, which Else vetoed in a passionate fight. Then, as Irmgard recalls, their mother remembered the cigarettes she had bought on the ship, and had the idea of offering these to the train personnel. Quickly, the family was assigned space in a compartment; the girls, however, rode on the lap of strangers. And their luck held: their luggage made it, too, on their parents' laps. They arrived at 5 A.M. at the Wiesbaden railroad station, from where they had to walk, carrying their luggage, to Adelheidstraße 17, to the Conradis, to find shelter together with Gustav and aunt Elisabeth. For ten years Else and Heinz occupied one room with the use of the kitchen, taking meals communally in the living room. Renate's and Irmgard's beds stood in aunt Li's (Elisabeth) room. The shortage of living space in postwar Germany was so great that it took the Ottos until 1956 to be able to move into their own apartment on Knausstraße in Wiesbaden.

In 1958 Irmgard made the acquaintance of Robert Sponer at a sports facility. The couple married on October 13, 1959, finding accommodation in a two-family house Robert had built in Schlangenbad-Georgenborn, right next to the forest. His parents occupied the ground floor.

Daughter Sabine saw the light of the world on March 7, 1963. A son, Robert, born on May 12, 1964, died quickly on the following day from complications at birth. He was followed by the birth of Ulrike on August 31, 1965 and Mathias on October 27, 1968.

On May 25,1979 Irmgard and Robert divorced. Irmgard moved with her children to Idstein-Dasbach, where she married Helmut Seifert in August of 1988. Helmut died in December of 1996. Sabine commented much, much later that, "Helmut Seifert took the children in order to get the woman."

In 1993, Irmgard, having learned a bit of Japanese, ventured back to Japan with her husband, Helmut. They traveled in the company of a couple, the Schulzes; Else Otto had met the wife under peculiar circumstances. Waiting at the check-out of a supermarket in Niedernhausen in Germany, she noticed a woman standing next to her, wearing a Japanese brooch, like one she owned. Of course, Else asked where the stranger had obtained this piece of jewelry. They introduced each other, and it turned out that the woman, Ingeborg Schulze, had been one of the German expatriates in Japan, and had been a frequent playmate of Renate and Irmgard. Ingeborg Schulze's father had been the German ambassador and had lived with his family not far from the Ottos.

But Irmgard found the 'old' Japan, she had recalled so vividly, gone. The cities had become what she called 'Americanized.' All the old, nice hotels at Lake Kawaguchi had been torn down; a bridge had been built across the lake, and huge parking lots ruined the landscape.

Irmgard continues living in her house in Idstein-Dasbach. She gives piano lessons to a couple of dozen students and takes lessons herself. For 30 years she has been singing in a local chorus and has sung most great choral works. Her daughter Sabine, wheelchair-bound since age 30, occupies the lower floor of her house. There, she has written her life's story, the account of her incapacitation, which has since been self-published in German and English, with her aunt Renate working on a Danish translation.

Renate, after finishing elementary school, entered into a three year apprenticeship as a seamstress. Following her journeyman's year, she worked at the fashion school in Frankfurt, where she obtained her master's degree in the profession. She then worked as a freelance textile restorer at the Historical Museum in Frankfurt.

In 1960 she met Ib Rohde, a Dane, son of her piano teacher Gerda Schreiber, also Danish. He had just returned from Cairo in Egypt, where he had played the viola in the Cairo Symphony Orchestra. Once he had found a new position at the *Philharmonia-Hungarica* Orchestra in Marl, Germany, the couple married a year later on August 11, 1961. Renate gave birth to daughter Kirsten on December 20, 1961, in Wiesbaden, and daughter Birgit on February 28, 1963 in Marl. In July of 1968 the family moved to Aarhus in Denmark, where Annette was born on November 2, 1968, followed by Jens on April 18, 1970 in Holsterbro. In 1971 the family moved to Viborg, where Ib had been offered the position of director of the local music school.

While Ib was a good musician and teacher, he had an alcohol problem which prevented him from realizing his full potential in the musical world. Since his addiction weighed heavily on his family and his professional work, Renate divorced Ib on April 14, 1976, receiving custody of the children. Since her occupation as a seamstress would not support the family, she learned to become a nurse and subsequently worked for twelve years in intensive care at the Viborg hospital. She became a Danish citizen on March 30, 1977.

In 1988 Renate 'lost her bearings' in Viborg, as she described it. Since her children had 'left the nest,' with the exception of Jens, she decided to leave Viborg and move back to Germany, where she worked as a domestic, then as a nurse in a retirement home. However, she no longer felt comfortable in

Germany and, missing her children, returned in 1991 to Denmark, where she married Kjeld Weber Carlsen on January 11, 1992, a marriage that was not to last. The couple separated on December 7, 1994. Since then, Renate lives in Aarhus.

Both sisters retained their connection with the Lutheran faith of their forebears. Irmgard is the first chairperson of her local church council in Dasbach, while Renate is the second chairperson of the church council in Aarhus.

Elisabeth Otto died on July 20, 1986 from complications of cancer in Idstein-Dasbach, where she was taken care of by her daughters. Heinz Otto died in Wuppertal, where he had moved to in 1989, on February 14, 1991.

Alfred Rutkowsky

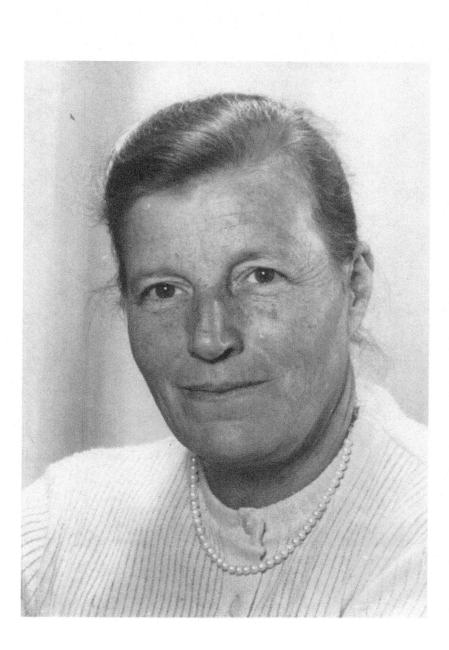

Gertrud Rutkowsky

Gertrud and Alfred's wedding

3. Alfred and Gertrud Rutkowsky, née Weissenbruch

The Rutkowskys' Journey to Sumatra

Gertrud Weissenbruch was born on April 26, 1911, in Si Piak on Sumatra. She met her future husband, Karl Alfred Rutkowsky, in 1931, at the Rhenish Mission Headquarters in Wuppertal-Barmen.

Karl Alfred Rutkowsky was born on July 28, 1908 in Lütgendortmund, Germany. His father was a miner who had migrated westward from East Prussia. His mother Auguste, née Joswig, gave birth to seven children, of which Alfred was the sixth.

His curriculum vitae is 'insubstantial,' in that it does not tell much of the man, and as he himself claims, "nothing much is to be reported about my (early) life, except that it was directly determined by my parents." From 1914 to 1922, he attended elementary school in Lütgendortmund, then a religious seminary in Holzwickede. In 1925 he joined the Rhenish Missionary Society. While a member of the Society, he attended a number of semesters at the universities of Heidelberg in 1929, Leiden in 1930/31, Hamburg in 1931, and Bethel in 1931/32. He mentioned various teachers he encountered: "Some had an immediate influence, assisting me in the direction I was to take, others were a warning to me."

Mr. Hannig, the director of the mission seminary Alfred attended, corresponded in various letters with Mr. Oestereicher in Heidelberg about Alfred. Mentioning him in a 1928 letter, he said that Alfred was presently in the final year of his studies, stating: "Alfred is a talented, diligent young man, hungry to learn, but seems still too young for dispatch abroad on missionary work. He will conclude his studies by the end of this year. We have the following plans for the young man: Inspector Warneck urgently desires to have a specialist on Islam available for Sumatra, which Rutkowsky is supposed to become. This is why he is to immerse himself thoroughly in the Arabic language.

"Would it therefore be possible to send the young man to you to Heidelberg, where he could assist you in various church matters, while you could teach him Arabic at the same time? It might also be possible for him to attend some classes at the university. I am certain that you would enjoy educating this capable young man. After he has stayed with you until October of 1929, we would put him for half a year into the hands of superintendent Simon, and after that have him study for a year at the university in Hamburg or another suitable location. Might Cairo be such a place? Thereafter he could depart for mission work."

Alfred also had to learn Dutch. For this, a trip to Holland was planned in the winter of 1929/1930. His studies at the university in Hamburg took Alfred into 1931. Then, in August and September, he participated in a course on tropical medicine in Tübingen.

By end of October 1931, Mr. Hannig, writing once more to Professor Oestereicher, indicated, "Brother Rutkowsky will probably travel abroad in the coming spring. The mission's financial situation has made his departure this fall impossible. Rutkowsky will spend the winter at the candidate seminary, this being a stopgap solution. Brother Rutkowsky has found a young girl with whom he would like to become engaged, a sweet and fine human being, she is the daughter of one of our Sumatran missionaries."

Gertrud Weissenbruch was born in 1911 in Sipiak, Sumatra, the daughter of Hermann and Martha Weissenbruch. In 1920, in a traumatic separation from her parents at the age of nine, she traveled with her older sister, Else, and a gaggle of other missionary children and adults to Germany for her further education. Her parents had expected to follow their daughters two to three years later, to be reunited at least for the duration of the parents' visit to Germany. However, this separation turned into seven years, possibly because the Mission found itself, as was frequently the case, in financially dire straights and could not make the funds available for a home visit.

After a one year stay with relatives, Max and Ria (Martha's sister), Gertrud went to a Mission school in Mettmann. During her parents' two-year visit to Germany in 1927-1929, she lived with them in Barmen, where she completed her high school diploma. From Easter 1930 on, she lived at another school for missionary daughters in Kaiserswerth, where she acquired practical knowledge, sang in the church choir, and assisted in church services for children.

She was able to follow her heart's desire to study music, however, the general economic malaise in Germany at the time forced her to abandon the conservatory, and to consider nursing. While she was still vacillating, she wrote, "God gave me clarity," and entered the Mission. Shortly after becoming engaged to Alfred Rutkowsky in 1931, she broke off her conservatory studies to engage in housekeeping studies and practice. In the summer of 1932 she spent four months in Holland with her teacher, Mr. Gdans, to learn the basics of the Dutch language.

Alfred Rutkowsky met his future wife, Gertrud Weissenbruch, when she was 21, at Mission Headquarters in Barmen. On July 18, 1931, in a letter to the Mission's Director, Alfred requested the Directorate's permission for his engagement with Gertrud and, as he wrote, "so that I can undertake the respective steps for the realization of my intention." With the same letter, Alfred also requested information about the date of his departure for Sumatra.

In response to Alfred's request, Mission Headquarters sent a letter to Gertrud on September 28 requesting, in addition to her curriculum vitae and medical testimony, the results of a quinine test, as well as a pastoral testimony. The letter further stated, "Since you are presenting these documents belatedly, it will, unfortunately, not be possible to discuss the subject in today's Deputation meeting. A personal testimony of Sister Anna Alfs would be desirable." The letter concluded expressing the hope that the few weeks delay until October would not matter that much and that the Deputation's agreement could be issued at its next meeting.

Sister Anna, responding to the Mission's Inspector, supplied the requested testimony for Gertrud, by writing: "Gertrud grew up under my eyes in Balige and has always been dear to me. It was with much joy that I learned from her of her decision to become engaged to Alfred Rutkowsky. She is aware of the difficult side of Mission service, and knows that one cannot walk this path solely by one's own strength. She may still be young, but always engages in the task she faces with all her strength and does nothing halfway. As far as I can determine, she has very much matured during the past years in the service of the local children's Sunday school. I think her to be a truly sincere and upright human being. To those not close to her, she may appear at times somewhat austere, but a deep nature is hidden beneath. We have often talked about the tasks awaiting her abroad. I hope she will be a faithful wife to her husband."

The testimony of the Evangelical Church Congregation in Kaiserswerth read as follows: "Gertrud Weissenbruch is personally and in official matters known to me for several years. The conspicuous characteristic of her nature is the sober clarity of her speaking and her actions. She is simultaneously distant, removing herself from the world, life and people, just as she can lose herself in these. I always had in her a reliable assistant in Sunday school and singer in the church choir. It is my impression that she was always deeply involved, but never tried to stand out, and I always appreciated her friendly nature. Her judgments have been cautious and restrained, far from romanticism, but appropriate and rational. It is difficult for me to judge her position in matters of belief, but I can say with assurance that behind her chaste restraint in statements about her inner life dwells a sincere connection with the Lord, making her humble and obedient. All in all: I think Gertrud Weissenbruch will make an outstanding pastor's or missionary's wife."

On October 6, 1931, in a follow-up letter to the Mission, Alfred asked whether the Deputation would give its approval for his engagement at the October meeting. Explaining that the forthcoming Reformation celebration was the Silver anniversary of Gertrud's parents, they would like to enter into their engagement on that day.

In a statement dated November 25, 1931, the Mission advised that the Mission candidate Alfred Rutkowsky's request could not be presented to the Deputation at the October meeting, but that the director subsequently obtained the chairman's permission for the engagement on October 31. The Deputation, in its meeting on November 23, gave its consent to this engagement.

The months of waiting for the permission for the couple's engagement and Alfred's eventual dispatch to Sumatra were filled with various studies in preparation for Alfred's mission activities.

Gertrud's letter in January of 1932 described her frustration about the delay in Alfred's departure due to the lack of Mission funds. She no longer felt at home at the Mission facilities, where all too often she was demanded to do this or that, and said, "I am no longer a child, and won't let myself be treated as a child anymore. I'm Alfred's fiancée, no more and no less." Her long letter to her father made clear that Gertrud was more than ready to leave the confining Mission environment and to get back to her roots and her parents.

Not long thereafter, Director Warneck advised that Alfred's departure to Sumatra had been agreed upon at their last meeting in Barmen, and that he could take a Dutch ship traveling 3rd class. Of course, once there, he had to begin his work and complete his Batak language exam, as well as the required two year wait to marry. Warneck suggested that Alfred work for several years with Brother Kappner in an area where he could apply his knowledge of Islam, and where he, with his young legs, could walk to the remote mountain branches of the Mission. On August 27, 1932, Alfred left Germany for Sumatra, arriving there on September 16, to stay with the Nommensens in Si Gumpar to learn the Batak language.

On January 27, 1933, Inspector Warneck wrote to Alfred: "At the recent Deputation meeting it was decided that your fiancée will be permitted to depart. Personally, I am very much for a betrothed to travel abroad months before the wedding, so she can settle in. It will be much easier for your Gertrud, since she can live with her parents. I must not remind you again that meetings with her are to be restricted to rare occasions. It would be best if you would not see each other at all. In this context you must consider Batak custom which finds contact between the engaged totally inappropriate. Of course, every kind of affection, even the most innocent, must be omitted. But you are aware of this. The time of your wedding will then be decided in one of our meetings.

"By now, you have been in the country for some time and will have seen and heard things which may trigger your critique. In a church that has grown as quickly as ours and with the number of its European workers so quickly needing to be reduced, everything is, of course, not as it ought to be. This makes it easy to look for mistakes and talk big. I hope you will be cautious in this matter. However, I have heard rumors that you are quick with plenty of critical comments. This is not appropriate for a young man like you. Before acquiring the right to criticize, one must truly get to know and understand the situation. Every one of our young Brothers now entering the field is ignorant of the conditions from which the Batak people developed with tremendous speed in just a few decades. Whoever objects to still finding pagan ideas among Christian Batak will not understand the corrupting inheritance with which the present generation is burdened, maybe without being aware of it. That this heritage cannot disappear in one fell swoop ought to be obvious.

"Whoever discovers improper things, ought to engage himself in their betterment. To talk at length about such circumstances, or to accuse Mission workers of ineptitude, is neither smart nor brotherly. Should my explanations not apply to you – so much the better. It will always be difficult for younger Brothers to get along with the older ones, simply because older Brothers become a little rusty, while the younger ones want to storm the heavens. Both need to keep themselves in control.

"The time will soon come when you will head south to occupy yourself in the Muslim Mission. Keep your eyes open and your heart full of love. You will have great need for the latter. Work with Muslims is the most difficult for us. The only key to their hearts is love, not arguing, preaching, and most of all, no polemicizing. Be cautious, therefore. Having now groups of Christian Batak living amidst Islamic populations might open a path for us to penetrate this fortress. We Europeans must positively stay in the background, for the Muslim does not want to hear anything from us."

In February of 1933, Alfred moved to Sidempuan, where he stayed with Brother de Kleine, a Dutchman, to be introduced to the Angkola dialect. Heinrich de Kleine became a good friend and mentor to Alfred, and in the years to come, the godfather of Alfred's daughter Ute.

In July, Alfred wrote about a forthcoming trip with Brother de Kleine to Padang, Hermann's (his future father-in-law's) efforts to find him a horse, and that he had not received a salary for three months. There was the possibility that by August he would be stationed in Sipirok.

Upon Hermann Weissenbruch's request in November of 1932 to the Mission's directorate, in which he explained that

Gertrud would do better in Sumatra with her parents, where she could relearn the Batak language, she was, against Mission policy, permitted to leave for Sumatra on May 1, arriving there on May 25, 1933. This reduced the waiting time for a bride's departure substantially and was permitted only since she would stay with her parents.

Gertrud wrote that this year was the happiest time she ever spent with her parents. She was able to refresh her knowledge of the Batak language and enjoyed talking with the people in the village. Shortly after her arrival, she joined her father on a two-day trip to one of his remotest parishes in the mountains, which she vividly recalled.

Her mother had prepared some food to take along and one of the 'boys' had saddled a couple of horses. Passing through the village, they were briefly accompanied by a gaggle of laughing and screaming children. Outside the village, a narrow path snaked up the mountain. To its left and right grew reeds, ferns, and haramo hug bushes. Gertrud expressed her delight in spotting the various small herbaceous plants, mosses, and little flowers along their trail,   companions remembered from her childhood days.

In the years to come, she was able to pass this knowledge and delight on to her yet-to-be-born daughter, Ute . They took a rest here and there, then had a wonderful vista of beautiful Lake Toba, the green rice fields surrounding it, with here and there a village poking its roofs above the tree line. And the higher they climbed, the more spectacular the vistas became. Suddenly, a deep chasm yawned ahead of them. Giant trees rose before it, their trunks and branches projecting over the gorge, while deep down a creek rushed wildly. There was no bridge. "We dismounted," she wrote, "and very carefully, step by step, descended into the gorge. The deeper we went, the pleasantly cooler it became. Already, from afar, we heard the racket of monkeys, then, ahead of us, we saw them swinging from tree branch to branch. Arrived at the bottom, we took another rest. I immersed my feet into the cool waters while the horses stilled their thirst."

On November 9, 1933 – the required wait-time of two years had not even come close – Gertrud and Alfred were married by her father in the beautiful church he had built in Balige. When Mr. Warneck, the Mission's Director, learned of the early wedding, he expressed his displeasure in no uncertain terms in a January 1934 letter. He had heard only rumors of the wedding and complained that the groom had not even found it necessary to advise him of the fact. Warneck thought Alfred to be still very young – at age 25! – and should have waited somewhat, especially when young Brothers nowadays were required to wait four years before marrying. He wrote to Hermann Weissenbruch, "I had advised the Mission branches accordingly and was therefore unpleasantly surprised by the news that this marriage had already taken place. I had thought of doing you a favor by having your daughter stay for some time in your house."

But what was done was done, and the time came for Alfred and Gertrud to leave. An old truck was brought in and loaded with their overseas trunks, crates, furniture, foodstuffs, and not forgotten – the piano Gertrud's father had purchased for them in Medan. The farewell was hard. Their destination lay approximately 300 miles (480 km) south. The couple found some not-so-comfortable seating next to the driver and off they went, for some distance accompanied by the usual crowd of screaming children. The route took them along Lake Toba, through the village of Tarutung and up into the mountains. Gertrud described how their 'marriage cart' groaned and moaned, its radiator regularly needing water to be added.

Driving along the terraced rice fields and occasional villages, and, here and there, catching a glimpse of Lake Toba, was very pleasant, with much of it remembered by Gertrud from her early childhood. For hours their drive on narrow, winding and bumpy roads went up, then down again, along precipices and waterfalls, until, finally, they spotted the ocean and the port of Sibolga. Following a short rest there, they continued towards Padang, with the road sometimes following the coast and crossing many rickety bridges. Evening came, and their driver turned on the rather poor lights of his truck, which soon completely faded, however. He stopped, got out – in the pouring rain – pulled out his pack of cigarettes, tore off a piece of its cellophane wrapper, fiddled for awhile with the truck's light cables, and voilà, light shone once more. A few kilometers farther the same happened – the fading light and its restoration – and so it went on repeatedly through the darkest of nights, while they drove along steep drop-offs on one side and towering cliffs on the other. Gertrud recounted that "one quick prayer after another escaped my soul.

"There were no places to stop, which was also advised against because of the presence of tigers. So, on we went! The driver began to sing, his way to deal with his anxiety. He accelerated on a straight-away but then, right before a curve, the lights failed again. There was a crash and we had ended up in a ditch. Fortunately, no one was injured. There we stood now, wondering what to do. We decided that the driver and his crew, who had been riding on the truck's platform, would stay with the truck, while we, the newlyweds, would walk through the night to the next village, where, after midnight, a kind soul was willing to drive us to the next larger village, Sidempuan, where we were expected by the de Kleine family. Exhausted, we were fed a snack, then fell into bed. What a way to begin one's wedded life!"

The Rutkowskys settled in Sipirok, about 100 miles (160 km) north of Sidempuan. The older de Kleine, already stationed for some time on Sumatra, became something of a mentor to the freshman Rutkowsky. The Mission had plans to have Alfred learn the Angkola language from de Kleine in order to translate the Bible into this Batak dialect.

In January of 1935, Alfred wrote a long letter to Inspector Warneck about his experiences and outlook for missionary activity among Muslims, saying, "we did not perceive the so-called depressing character of our Islamic mission, since we did not concern ourselves with its success, but simply performed cheerful seed work. We have also found many Islamic friends who have helped us in understanding our labors." Alfred continued to elaborate extensively on the missionary work among Muslims and questioned its future effect. But he also stated that he had many contacts with Islamic shaikhs, mu'alims, and others. "Because of my knowledge of Arabic, I have found a peculiar trust among Muslims. It went so far that my contacts told each other that I was actually a Muslim and became a Protestant pandita only because I was unable to overcome my parents' demands. Should missionary work among Muslims ever come, it will require a strong Batak Church. It is not up to me to answer this question."

In December of the same year Alfred fired off a strongly-worded letter to Director Warneck, expressing his concern about the Mission's 'retreat' by reducing staff, and the complacency of

141

older Brothers, the advance of Catholic Missions, the rise of Independent Protestant Churches and the sometimes wholesale switch of entire villages from the H.K.B.P. to Catholic parishes. He lamented the Mission's incorrect dealings with the rising nationalism among Bataks and Indonesians in general. Concluding, he suggested that, instead of reducing staff, more help was required to oppose these influences and to work for the eventual independence of the H.K.B.P. some fifteen years in the future.

A couple of months later, in March of 1936, Warneck replied by agreeing with the deficits Alfred listed in his letter, but objected to certain pointed expressions and the tone of Alfred's letter. He entered into a plenitude of justifications and, in closing, asked Alfred for greater humility in his critique.

In quick succession Gertrud had given birth to Christa, on October 17, 1934, in Tarutung, then Ute, on November 10, 1936, also in Tarutung, Peter on December 28, 1937, and Hans Michael, on May 8, 1939, in Balige. A stillbirth was also known, but was not recorded.

On July 21, 1938, Gertrud wrote from Tarutung to her parents, now living in Germany, that her son, Peter, had died on July 17, and that Ute was also ailing. Twice Alfred had brought little Peter with their car to a doctor in Sidempuan, but was both times assured that blood in the boy's stool was nothing serious. Well, it became worse, with Ute also showing the same symptoms, so the entire family took off to see a doctor in Tarutung, who diagnosed the two children with suffering from dysentery. They were given shots, alas, too late for Peter.

Alfred was busy supervising the construction of a mission building in Laguboti. Having been promised funds by the government in Batavia for the hiring of a nurse, he also had to build a home for her. An isolation barrack for the hospital was also most urgently required, because of the many cases of dysentery. A man who had been admitted with severe dysentery to the hospital, had died on Sunday, and on Monday Peter had showed the first symptoms. Gertrud wrote: "This illness was terribly contagious!" On September 1, Gertrud was still in Tarutung, writing that the one-and-a-half year old Ute was recovering extremely slowly. She was given a very restricted diet, which, only slowly was enriched by more complex nutrition. Alfred and Christa had been separated from Gertrud and Ute for seven weeks with more time likely to pass. Nevertheless, Gertrud felt well. On an excursion to Siantar she purchased more wool to knit pullovers for the children, all in preparation for the visit to Germany they hoped to make in the coming year – or, maybe, in 1940/41. After nine weeks, the family was reunited in Sidempuan, but not before the doctors at the Tarutung hospital had told Gertrud that they were surprised that Ute had survived her affliction.

At the end of October 1938 there were rumors and concerns among the Dutch population in the East Indies that, with political matters settled in Germany, Germany might take Sumatra from Holland.

Pregnant again, Gertrud and Alfred's hope for another boy to be born in May of next year came true, following some complications. On May 8, 1939 Hans Michael saw the light of the world. And times had changed. Letters no longer took four to six weeks to travel by ship but came now by airmail, a great improvement in communication, manifested by Gertrud's frequent mail to her parents in Germany. Most of her correspondence dealt with the children, stories of their utterings and behavior, in short, to keep the grandparents informed, who were so far away and were missing the exploits of their progeny in real time.

Gertrud told the story of her 'boy,' Ladimer, whom she was fond of. He wanted to marry. At the last moment it turned out that his fiancée's parents had deceived him by saying that the girl's age was 16 years, when she was actually five months shy of it. This discrepancy now caused the customary back and forth among the relatives. Pressure was exerted on Ladimer to marry anyway, and he agreed. Of course, the Rutkowskys could no longer keep him, although he would have loved to stay. And shortly after his departure, Gertrud had the house full of guests and no help, with more guests arriving in the coming weeks than in the prior five years. She had hoped for a getaway, but there was the need for Alfred to continue work with Raja Matoea on the translation of the New Testament. And, oh, her teeth! She was losing them left and right, and was afraid that by the time they would get to Germany, she would no longer have molars on either side. Getting to a local dentist was difficult. She expressed her gratitude for her parents' gift of 70 guilders, which she was going to put aside for their Germany trip. And, to the couple's delight, they were now out of debt as of last year. "At last, we are now able to save a bit for the future," she wrote.

Had she only known what great upheaval lurked just below the horizon! Referring to a newspaper clipping her father had sent about the moral standards of behavior among Europeans on Bali, she described how this situation was first exposed on Sumatra's east coast, after which the government checked also on Java and Bali, only to find them there as well. The same homosexual practices seemed to exist across the entire East Indies, with the situation erupting into a huge scandal. Even one of the Mission people was found involved in this scheme and was held in detention in Siantar.

Alfred sold his motorcycle and purchased a small car, an Opel. They were both glad that he had traded two wheels for four. Enjoying the independence the car was providing, they were able to take a three week vacation at Lake Toba and enjoyed swimming there very much. Gertrud hoped that her swimming exercise would assist with an easy birth. But although she was due soon, the family was still traveling quite a bit visiting friends. One day, when Alfred went with the children for a swim and returned an hour later, they were greeted with the news that a son had arrived. The birth had gone smoothly and Gertrud laughed happily at Alfred when he arrived. Thus, Michael was born in Balige. And about Ute's antics, she wrote, "one could make a movie, which, surely, would not be boring."

In Gertrud's letter in May of 1939 to her parents, she extensively described the troubles that had arisen in missionary work after the older generation had left. According to her, the younger generation was lacking in dedication, with Alfred saying, "they only want to marry and get their money." Gertrud assigned blame for this attitude to Mission Headquarters, where people, in her view, had made a business of the Mission and transferred this outlook to the people they sent out. One of these newcomers was said to have told some people, "I'll take on five Dutchmen!" and, of course, had trouble extricating himself from this statement when the Controller heard about it. Another newcomer cursed the Batak before he had even made real contact with them. How will this man ever establish a good relationship with the people? It brought to her mind how her father often had to slow down Alfred shortly after he arrived, so that, contrary to these new arrivals, he would not become too close with Bataks.

She reminisced about her engagement to Alfred eight years earlier and their pleasant hikes through the Ruhr Valley and the Bergische Land, then speculated where she, with Alfred and her family, would live when they returned to Germany two years hence! As a postscript she added that Alfred was off on another nisang hunt, a catlike, long-tailed animal which lives by eating fruit and small animals. He had shot three already this past week, because the creatures had taken all their doves and chickens. When, in the early sixties, their last-born child, Dorothea, lived with them on Sumatra, she recalled that these animals often made a racket in the attic and had an evil-smelling gland system. They trapped these critters, after which the natives ate them.

In June, Gertrud mentioned two newcomers, Graumann and Schildmann, who traveled to Singapore to marry early, where a religious and civil wedding was simultaneously performed. Supposedly, their superior did not have the courage to forbid this early wedding. One of them even claimed openly that he was a pagan.

All this was peculiar! It appears that the conditions the Mission was facing among its members, European as well as native, were a reflection of the state of the world, or the conditions it was drifting to.

It was August 29, 1939, and Gertrud was expecting her husband to return from a school meeting in Tarutung, from where he, hopefully, would bring also some political news. Gertrud was enthusiastic about Hitler's accomplishments, his pact with Russia, but Alfred worried about the entire situation and what would become of Poland. If only there would be no war! The newspapers told of various countries mobilizing and that Germany supposedly was withdrawing its merchant fleet from the oceans. There was more friction among the Mission's members, and a Dutchman, who could no longer hold back his hatred for Germans withdrew from the organization.

And various troubles persisted with the Mission, some at conferences, others with individuals, and all these required Alfred to travel quite a bit. Then there was a dire shortage of teachers, so that he even had to do some teaching. The latest news from

Barmen was that future home visits would only be permitted after having stayed ten years abroad. In the meantime, there was an increasing concern that the transfer of moneys, their salaries from Barmen, might be cut off. In a December letter, Gertrud wrote that some airmail took six weeks to arrive, and special arrangements had been made for the transfer of their salaries. Whatever other moneys had come through in recent weeks, had been shared among missionary personnel percentage-wise. Barmen had advised that the Rutkowskys had been formally discharged from missionary service, meaning that they were unemployed and only eligible for minimal unemployment payments from the Dutch colonial government. Of course, they expected that, once funds from Germany would come through again, these unemployment benefits would be revoked. Prices were going up, but the government watched firmly that no profiteering was taking place. Nevertheless, the price for milk had increased 30%. Butter came from Australia and was therefore not affected by the war.

Gertrud expressed her satisfaction that the letters coming from Germany, including those to other missionary people, were all very optimistic about the war effort, whereas the East Indies newspapers presented the opposite. "Let's just hope that the war will not take too much longer," she wrote. She felt pity for the young missionaries on Sumatra, who now had to wait for their fiancés to join them. There were some futile attempts to have these young women travel to Sumatra by way of Genoa. In future all moneys were to be administered by the H.K.B.P., including the missionaries' salaries. And in Batangtoroe, Pandita Jason introduced all kinds of new rules, such as that the congregation no longer stood up for praying, but remained seated, as adat, Batak custom, supposedly called for. Another pandita, Hercules, tried to introduce similar changes, but was checked by his superior. Alfred added to her letter, "It isn't as bad as Gertrud describes it, but these war times make people uppity. The trombones we had asked for have finally arrived, but we were charged 250 guilders in duty. So far, the parish has come up with only 60 in donations, and we will likely have to make up the difference from the parish account. At least the players already do a good job playing them. De Kleine and I were present at the service in the Balige church. Little is coming through about the war and it is mostly bad news. We have often wished for a radio to get our information directly from Germany, but it hasn't materialized. We must keep relying on newspapers."

Gertrud in 1939 with Christa, Michael, and Ute

The War Years on Sumatra

On May 10, 1940, German troops invaded Holland. As a consequence, all German nationals – planters, businessmen, and missionaries in the Dutch East Indies were taken into 'preventive detention,' the men in Bukittinggi, formerly called Fort de Kock, located north of Padang, and the women and children in Raja Brastagi. Family lore tells of Alfred being arrested on the road on May 10, traveling with his car on some business, his vehicle being confiscated.

A collection of postcards bears witness to the tenuous contact the family was able to maintain between the two internment camps. These cards date from February 1941, ceasing on January 7, 1942. Of course, all mail was censored, so that its content was always 'innocuous.' At least, it appeared that, at times, the women and children were able to step outside the camp's perimeter. Gertrud had still not learned the whereabouts of her sister Else with her children, Renate and Irmgard, who had lived on Borneo with husband Heinz Otto, a businessman. For Christmas in 1941 Alfred was able to send various toys he had made for his children. From February to December 1942, the Rutkowskys, minus Alfred, lived in Bukittinggi. In March of 1942 Japanese troops entered the Netherlands East Indies and, eventually, in December of 1942, freed the German internees, actually all Axis nationals including Austrians and Italians.

In turn, the Dutch civilians were now interned by the Japanese, which included Brother de Kleine, Ute's godfather, and these Allied internees had it much worse during their imprisonment by the Japanese than the Germans under Dutch rule. Prior to the Japanese invasion, the Dutch transferred their German male internees on three ships to British India. One of these ships, the 'Van Imhoff,' was torpedoed by a Japanese submarine with almost all prisoners lost, a total of 411, among them six missionaries. Verbal reports claimed that the exit hatches on these ships had been wired shut, so that the prisoners were unable to escape upon the ship's sinking, and the Dutch crew did not open the hatchways. While rumors had circulated about the sinking of one of the ships and the loss of life, Gertrud did not know on which ship her husband had been traveling!

'Liberated' by the Japanese, Gertrud and the children, lived as of January 1943 in the city of Padang in one of the houses previously owned by a Dutch family. Of her children, Christa, was now 8, Ute, 6, and Michael, 3 years old. On April 3, 1943, Gertrud wrote that she would try again to maintain a regular diary. A couple of other missionary families had vacated the house they all had occupied and moved to Brastagi. Now, she had her own room and desk, and hoped that this would make writing easier. Her own furniture and pictures had been arranged, and she felt more at home, with the earlier two years of cramped internment camp behind her. She wrote, "How much did I long for my own room and how grateful am I for having it again. Our life is much quieter now with fewer people around. However, I must get used to sleeping by myself; while it was nice to sleep together with the children, the peace I enjoy now is wonderful. I have allowed the children limited access to my room, and to make it special, we hold evenings a prayer service there. Afterwards, I read to them. Christa has started to read Grimm's Fables herself. I am surprised how well she can repeat previously read stories. It is well that she hasn't inherited my memory," Gertrud concluded.

"Last night I leafed through my music notes and the longing for music gripped me so strongly that I did not sleep for most of the night. If only I could rent a piano, then I could also begin teaching Christa to play. I recently read Kierkegaard and am deeply moved how this great Danish man went through life. I've also read Tholuk, a German religious writer, who, with his emotional depth, appeals more to me than the polished dialectical mind of the Dane. I am so happy to have access to my books again; I have unpacked them, put them in the sun, and will now read them to my heart's desire." That same day, Gertrud was able to play Händel's 1st Organ Concerto on a piano with Mrs. Brandt, another missionary's wife. "But, oh my fingers," she said, "they don't want to obey me any more."

In April, she bemoaned the oppressive heat at Padang, a city located at sea level, close to the equator. "The least bit of work causes streams of perspiration, and at night I fall dead beat into bed. The skin begins to itch – and we might have to endure it here for years yet." She kept reading other books, trying to reconcile them with her Christian beliefs.

On April 12, 1943, she was required to move again! "If only the Japanese would leave us in peace and let us stay put," she wrote. "Now we must give up our nice masonry house here on Hoeroen #12, to move – God knows where – to some other assigned dwelling to make room for some Japanese 'lordships.' We live life like chess figures and must put up with being moved hither and yon. Only a few days ago did I unpack our ten crates in this heat and nicely arranged our house. Now I must go through the process of packing everything again. If only we could be back home in Germany or, at least, hear what is going on there. But we are totally cut off from what is happening. This is the worst to bear!"

But there was also some light in her gray daily life. Mrs. Brandt had received a long letter from Mr. Schneewind in Japan, in which he reported also about internment camps in India. Schneewind wrote that the internees there had it fairly good, lived in a good climate, were permitted an extensive hike once a month outside the camp, and were allowed to write monthly to Europe as well as to receive mail from there. This meant, however, that their wives in the Dutch East Indies were still cut off from any contact with their husbands. That same day, April 13, more than a year after contact on Sumatra had ceased, Gertrud received a letter from her sister Else, saying that their husbands were supposedly held in an internment camp at Doeli/ Ajsur in British India. "Oh, how delighted we were getting this news. And as we've always said: 'The British are more generous than these small-minded Dutchmen!' "

"Something in Else's letter from Japan saddened me," Gertrud commented. "Else wrote, 'you may have regretted not to have traveled with us to Japan. We never understood it, but you went your own ways. This was not good!' This is not true, but it seems the people who made it from Raja (Brastagi) to Japan, do think this way, saying, that we had not wanted to. But when I recall the pains we suffered, when we weren't permitted to join this group, I could still cry. Only God knows why it happened this way. I have decided to write down in detail all the 'buts' and 'ifs' for the time when we will be able to talk about this failed 'escape' to Japan."

Djibada, a local Japanese official, gave permission to send a monthly postcard to Gertrud's parents. These cards were censored first in Sumatra, then most likely again in Japan, the country they were routed through. Schneewind reported from Japan that five German men who left the East Indies months ago had arrived in January in Germany. "What all they will be able to tell there?" Gertrud remarked in her diary.

"At noon, on the 15th of April, we were told to move the next day. Head over heels we packed, then a Japanese car and porters took our entire household to a little house on Damar street #7. There was barely enough time to air and clean the premises before the ten crates were delivered. Only after the locks were broken were we able to enter – no keys were available. It is a nice, small masonry building with two rooms for me and the children and two small rooms for the Meyers. There are many shade trees, flower beds and pots. I have planted some flowers already. Unfortunately, the house has no air passing through, but one cannot have everything! I hope that this will be the last move we have to make.

"We quietly celebrated the 'Führer's' birthday. Mr. Beck, our local German representative, gave a simple speech, and we sang 'Deutschland, Deutschland über alles,' among other songs." Referring to the books she was reading, or rather rereading, she remarked how her understanding of the content and depth of these books, after the recent years of suffering and experiences, had increased. The same was true for music. She felt enriched, but wished for a place where she could be by herself, and need not observe dreary consideration for others.

Heinrich de Kleine, a Dutchman, Ute's godfather, had been interned by the Japanese under the most miserable conditions, while his German wife with their children was 'free' under Japanese occupation, and had decided – surely after due consideration with her husband – to join the 'liberated' Germans instead of her interned husband, a wise choice. When, however, years later, the East Indies returned to Dutch control, this choice was held against her by the Hollanders.

"Tomorrow is Easter," Gertrud wrote. "It is a year now, when, just released from imprisonment at Fort de Kock at Bukittinggi, we celebrated our new-won freedom at the Hotel

Central. This is how time passed, uselessly and without sense, and I ask 'what is life's worth if one only sits around and waits, waiting for times to change and being able to return home from homelessness?' I and my fellow-missionary wives are still waiting for any message from our men and news from Germany – just a short one, be it ever so brief and impersonal, if only it can be trusted! And tomorrow is Easter, yes! I have painted Easter eggs with Christa and Ute, which, together with the egg nests the children made, will be hidden over night, to be displayed and enjoyed by the children tomorrow. They are happy and full of expectations. Hail to them that they can still enjoy themselves from the sweetness of their hearts."

Easter behind, the family joined the Tiemeyers, de Kleines, Kirschners and her house mate Thea to go to Ajer manis, a most pleasant trip, which included swimming in the ocean. A few days later, the group hired a bus to drive to the Juliana Spa, something Gertrud had suggested. They spent the day swimming and playing games with the children and, after a few words of Mr. Beck and singing the Deutschland hymn, returned home. A couple of days later, the children were school-bound once more, it being high time for Christa to have something to do. After living for three weeks with Thea, Gertrud found their differences beginning to grate. She commented about more books she read and her understanding of them, but also her rejection of the contents of some. The children's education rested like a heavy burden on her. Now, in May, the heat had become unbearable. She wrote, "One takes a bath and right afterwards, little trickles start running again. How much longer must we sit in this furnace? Ute seems to have some kind of flu. When she's illl, she looks like a flower with its leaves drooping; it is heart wrenching. Our group of 'liberated' Germans has become ever less talkative, more quiet. I am grateful to have my own room and my books to carry me through the emptiness. Today, the 8th, is Michel's fourth birthday. His friends bring presents and the little boy impatiently barely acknowledges them, but hurries to tear the wrapping from the gifts."

The following day, Gertrud described how Christa complained about her food, after which she beat the child more than necessary. Afterwards, she commented about Schrör's book 'Flucht aus dem Alltag', 'Flight from Mundane Days,' about a pastor, who, unhappy in his position and full of inner conflict, dumps his joyless existence onto his parish. Realizing the similarity, she felt ashamed before her daughter. And she read more, quite different books; it is only the Bible she is unable to open, asking, "When will I be able to obtain an inner relationship with this book?"

On May 23, she quoted from a book of Heronimus von dem Dome: "Every human being must create his life on his own. One pays dearly if one is not rooted in oneself!" But then she asked: "How many people can do this still today? Does not the restlessness, the drivenness of our time produce the exact opposite? To become rooted in oneself requires solitude, or better, the escape from daily routine. Is it that the deeper I'm rooted in myself, the deeper I'll be rooted in God? Oh, Alfred, could I only be with you to ask for your advice. As it is, I stumble along not knowing whether I walk the right way. But if I earlier thought I always needed your help, I now know I must go my own way, with you being only a railing I can hold on to occasionally.

"No money has been received from Tokyo yet, although it was transmitted over a month ago. Mr. Beck has allotted some from his fund, so that we have something on hand. It is all so unjust, when five single people living in a house must pay 50 guilders rent together, but we mothers must pay 40."

At last, the longed-for rains came. Gertrud claimed, "that these last weeks were so terribly hot that one thought the brain would dry up." But the cooling rain soon dissipated and the sun returned, producing an oppressing, humid greenhouse atmosphere. A couple of days later, Gertrud cited a book she was reading, describing an exchange of letters between two no longer young people. It was a book of love as she had never read before, describing purified love, love no longer driven by the heat of the blood, a love between mature people. The book's language was like music, a communing of souls. "But I'm still so young," she said. "The story churns up my innermost depths, the love, the longing, the homesickness – and the years of loneliness. Alfred, do you sense it? Are you aware of my loneliness? Oh, and you are just as alone, I do know!

"It is an eerie time we live in. Prices go up and up with the merchants setting prices. The poorer folk can no longer pay for these high-priced goods, resulting in impoverishment and hunger. One has difficulties fighting off the daily beggars and if one does not pay attention, theft becomes commonplace. Last night, when I was still reading by my window, I heard steps approaching. Looking up, I saw a well-dressed gentleman standing outside on the grass. I kept sitting by my light while he remained standing, smoking and looking at me. Finally, I asked: 'Apa?' 'What?' No reply. I got up and walked towards him, seeing that he was a Japanese civilian. He replied in broken Indonesian: 'Ada orang?,' 'a man?,' pointing to the house, speaking in a low voice. I repeated aloud: 'Apa?', with him looking displeased with our neighbors sitting on the emper. With my heart in my throat, I loudly asked: 'Ada orang disini?' 'Is someone there?' Another couple of brief exchanges, and I returned to my book. He understood and left, but my knees were trembling."

Gertrud described her ideas about van Gogh, saying, "he was made a dramatist of modern painting by the sun of Arles. He no longer painted just a tree, but the growth of trees, their being, and no longer did he paint blossoms, but their blossoming. He is life personified, painting its tension.

"Last night, on June 8th to the 9th, we had a strong earthquake, or was it a seaquake, like I've never experienced before. It was so strong that I considered taking the children outside our masonry building. Then, at noon today, there was an aftershock. We ran outside to look for the children, hollering, until some kind souls brought them to us. Animals were shying and people were lying on the ground. A wooden house across from us had collapsed. I do not know for how long the quake lasted, but we were lucky, as little was broken in our house. But many poor folks, who barely have anything to eat, may now no longer have even a place to live. Two days later, there were two more light quakes, with the Merapi volcano having a second crater now. Aftershocks continued through the following days. The heat of the days before has been replaced by uncommon cold – and that in Padang! I can hear the ocean waves and imagine them rolling in on us."

In June, the German General Consul, von Ramm, flew in from Medan to check on his countrymen's well-being. Through him, they learned of the battle of Stalingrad, causing Gertrud to say, "compared to this, how small is our own fate. What oppresses us is that we have no contact with our country, get no news, and must rely on the piddling Padang newspaper. The visitor promised to send some papers from Shanghai from time to time. During a pleasant evening get-together, von Ramm told us about his work and the arrival of the Assama Maru. This ship had brought the German women and children repatriates from the East Indies to Japan. They were hosted, then put up in hotels in various cities, since, by that time, Germany had invaded the Soviet Union and a return to Germany via the Trans-Siberian Railroad was no longer possible. Thus, the Germans who had thought to make it back to their homeland were stuck in Japan for the remainder of the war. No German was accepted for Japanese service; it's the same there as here – the Japanese don't trust their allies."

Gertrud grappled with the education of her children and their behavioral education. For it to work, she told herself that the ABC of education was self-control, equating it with the labors of a gardener. As an example, she mentioned her oft-repeated requests to Ute to do a certain thing – which Ute did not do. She wrote, "When I then come with the cane, she is startled, frightened, so that I often think that she's not even aware of her misbehavior. This situation with an otherwise so sensitive and easy-to-direct child is disconcerting, at times even depressing. I believe that it is not conscious misbehavior, but a non-realization of what she has done wrong. She plays her games with body and soul, which is why I feel that my reminders don't get even through to her. How am I going to solve this problem?"

And there are more books Gertrud has read and discussed with a woman-friend. Some contain sentences she felt like underlining boldly, not for one's descendants, but because they speak to the reader's heart. And yet, in an earlier comment, she complained about underlining, by saying, "one comes across sentences thickly underlined in pencil strokes. Imagine that you walk through a beautiful countryside and arrive at a spot with a warning' poster: Do not miss the beauty of this place! Such a poster not only disturbs the sight, but is literally an insult. This is what I think about bold underlining of the best statements in a book. I can accept a fine line, but not too many, and that in someone else's book . . ."

Getting back to behavioral education, she commented that Thea complained that she had difficulties with the children obeying her. Observing such situations, Gertrud found that 'orders' given in a grumpy way – and children ought not to be ordered around, but guided by friendly requests – lead to rejection and disobedience. To entertain the children, she hand-drew playing cards with flower images, another game for the children, and a reminder of home.

Then came the news that 40 letters from Germany and husbands in India had arrived in Medan. Gertrud's hope was, "Will there be also one for me? May God so provide!"

"Today, it is July the 17th, a Saturday, just like the Saturday when our little Peter died years ago," she recalled. How wonderful it would have been to have two boys, an older brother for Michael. But that might have been too much of a blessing."

In July of 1943, the Rutkowskys lost the companionship of a pleasant couple due to their required move. "Last night, we had another Japanese visitor. I leave aside what he actually wanted. He asked for a match for his cigarette. I asked him to sit down, he offering me also a smoke. I joined him as if I were a habitual smoker. The conversation was slow, using signs, English, and whatever, mostly about husband and children. He promised to send more cigarettes, then, with a courteous bow, disappeared, and I tried desperately to get the evil tobacco taste from my mouth. Will he send cigarettes? If so, I respect him. If not, well, then he was looking for something different."

As shortages grew, a few days earlier, she had waited five hours at a distribution center for light bulbs. "This is how one's time is spent: standing in line for bulbs and sugar. Oh, and when, if at all, will a letter come for me?"

With the help of a laborer, Gertrud rearranged and renewed her garden and seeded it. "If only these stupid chickens which keep destroying my hard work were not around. After my gardening, I enjoy going to a pool to relax. I can do this now twice a week. Another German family has moved into a neighborhood house, so that there are now nineteen children living in the four 'German' houses on Damar street. I'm reading more books and study English, thinking that my 'lost' time finds some use after all. Only my sewing suffers from these activities, but – so what." And the families get together for singing, but no operetta tunes!

Gertrud's Japanese 'friend' of some days ago did come back twice. He truly kept his promise to bring cigarettes and, in addition, a bag of raisins for the children. But he quickly left every time. Today, he showed up once more bringing two packages of cube sugar for the kids. "When I got ready to offer him something, he had again disappeared. In the evening he was back. I had put the children already to bed, but got them out again; then we talked as much as that was possible. Sometimes, the misunderstandings are precious. Tonight, he explained that he is the manager of the Hotel Centrum in Bukittinggi. He asked us to visit him there. He is simpatico, and I feel it is the children who draw him. He may also be homesick for his family and appears to commiserate with our own broken family life. Well, let's see for how long this friendship will last?"

On a day in July, friends decorated Gertrud's desk with many flowers surrounding a picture of Alfred's. "Amidst the daily grind, my thoughts go out to my husband's heart, wherever he may be. Nothing is known – a hole in my imagination. It is a hole I simply cannot leave be, maybe if I would receive a sign of life were it even of an old date," Gertrud wrote. "Last night we were at the consulate, where we sang folk songs for a Japanese, who, in turn, sang for us some Japanese melodies which I enjoyed very much. It turned out to be a pleasant, casual evening."

The family enjoyed a Saturday trip to the ocean at Air manis, which they hoped to repeat once the children's school vacations start. But fever struck everyone, one after another. Gertrud read more books, including Sven Hedin's 'Germany and World Peace,' which she liked. She expressed her concern about Germany's military situation in Italy, and whether Italy would remain allied with Germany, saying, "Oh God, what Germany must all endure. No other people could ever perform like this! If nations would only become rational! Ute is off on a 24 hour vacation with the de Kleines, and I wonder how the little girl will 'survive' it."

August brought some good news. A German ship sank several Allied steamers and escorted eight captured enemy ships with their cargo to Japan, where the German captain was received with honors. A woman-friend received a letter from her husband, an event everyone enjoyed and this provided some hope. The letter was dated December 1942, meaning that it took approximately eight months to be received. Then, Gertrud commented on another book she had read, written by Stefan Zweig, 'Maria Stuart.' She found it a masterly portrayal, but critiqued the writer's 'digging in dirt,' something she found typical of Jewish writers.

The German community in Padang gained some members on August 30th. All Europeans still residing in Bukittinggi had to leave. The still 'free' Dutch, that is doctors and nurses, working under the Japanese, were interned in Padang. Other moves could lie ahead, as rumors went. "If we could only stay put!" Gertrud commented. "We heard these days that, one year after the Japanese invasion, eight Dutchmen, among them a general, were captured in the jungle. Since then, the still freely operating Dutchmen, 'half and quarter' Dutchmen of mixed race, were interned." Bukittinggi had been cleared even of Indonesians, only business people and employees were permitted to stay. A construction boom was taking place there, with Bukittinggi becoming an almost entirely Japanese town. The native people must find whatever place to live.

Gertrud wrote another comment: "Presently, the children have developed a giant hunger for bread, which I make using mostly rice flower with a bit of corn and ubi flour , one pisang, and some sourdough. If I can mix in some butter, when it becomes available, the children's desire for this bread finds no limits. We don't even miss real flour any more. Funny to think how worried we were when wheat flour ran out."

It was September 10, 1943, and Italy had capitulated. "Our heart is shaking when we think of our fatherland. But the mighty is strongest alone," Gertrud wrote. "The German community's trust in its fatherland is still unshaken. And we sit here and cannot do anything. We wait and wait, and in this way one year passes after another!"

The patriotism of these expatriate Germans was unbroken. It would probably be wrong to call it nationalism. Far from home and receiving little if any information of what was happening in their believed homeland, most of them could not do otherwise!

Gertrud was practicing playing the piano at the consulate. On September 8, their chorus sang on the radio with another performance coming up. "I was asked to complement the performance with several piano pieces, for which I selected some of Schumann's work and a Bach piece. We even received 30 guilders for our performance.

"Odd things happen in this world. A few days ago Mr. Beck brought me a postcard written by my parents in Germany on October 2, 1941! It took two years to arrive. Although this was 'old news,' it was comforting to see the familiar script. Nevertheless, the 80 letters we were told were sitting in Brastagi have still not been delivered." Gertrud remarked about Mussolini having been liberated in a daring rescue by German troops and that Germany still triumphs in Italy with the help of Fascists.

Her piano trials for the forthcoming radio transmission went well, although Gertrud was unhappy having made three mistakes. But with a new and much better instrument, she envisioned her playing to improve together with finding greater inner strength. When the performance eventually took place she was delighted and proud that the two Bach minuets, the gigue, and others went very well, and that the children's singing was also much better.

Gertrud concluded her day's report mentioning that her drapes were stolen one evening while they were sitting on the verandah. Someone climbed up the back of the house and simply cut them off the rods, grabbing a table cloth and towel in addition. And there's no use getting the police involved; they aren't going to do anything anyway. During the coming two days, the Japanese have ordered a practice drill with road blocks and lights-off, and Gertrud wondered whether Padang might become once more a battle zone. "Maybe we will all be moved to Brastagi after all?" she wrote on Sept. 21, 1943.

It was her intention to practice twice a week playing the piano at the consulate. She said, "Playing music has become a necessity for me; it enables the heart to speak without revealing oneself to others. I'm playing the D-minor Fantasies of Mozart, also Bach and Beethoven pieces." Becoming more and more involved in her music, she had begun to 'sing' Bach and Beethoven pieces, and found that, by doing so, she entered deeper into the essence of music.

By mid-October news arrived from the German Foreign Service that the husbands of wives living in Padang were all well. It was poorly defined, general information. The past two days, the Dutch men, women and children who had been interned in Padang were taken to Pekanbaroe, to be interned there. They were marched in long lines to the railway station and had to carry their belongings. Some were so weakened that they had difficulties doing that. Gawkers, lining the road, yelled and screamed at them. Where they walked, the streets were littered with all kinds of items, little bags of rice, cups, kettles, and small bundles they had dropped, which these poor people were not permitted to pick up again.

Some more books she read: 'Love and Death on Bali,' by Vicki Baum, and 'Tropics Fever,' by Las von L. Szikely (of course in German). Christa's birthday went fine, with well-wishers coming and going. "Even Ohatasan, the radio announcer, who visits our group quite often, showed up that afternoon with a bouquet of orchids and a cake. The children played with him, giving him a hard time. I invited him for dinner. Ohata was very quiet during our dinner, which he is usually in the company of adults; at heart he is a child. Last night, after a long absence, our friend Tadasan showed up with a can of dried seaweed, a Japanese delicacy. It is just too bad that he does not speak Malay or English, while we do not speak Japanese. This makes conversation cumbersome, but we succeeded, little by little. He delighted in giving presents to the children and promised to play St. Nick. Next time he comes, I'll invite him to stay for dinner. Let's see whether he will accept the invitation?

"The children have a short school vacation and today went with Ohatasan to the Juliana Spa together with a few other adults. We are wondering about our likely move from Padang, maybe to Brastagi or Kabandjahe. While we dread another move, we would also be happy to get away from Padang's heat.

There's something happening which troubles our community greatly: Mrs. Kniesch is expecting, the child's father likely being an Indonesian, married to a Japanese woman. The woman is a slut, and our German community is ashamed of the situation. The children more or less know about it, and we must be prepared for them to ask, "why are we not getting a baby?"

It is November 10, 1943 – Ute's seventh birthday. "Early in the morning she crawled into bed with me, telling me that she was so happy that she could cry – and she did."

The German community decided to gather every second Thursday for an easy-going evening with everyone contributing something. Last night was the first event, to which ten Japanese guests were invited. "It took some effort the get the Japanese to relax and to mix with us," Gertrud commented. "Our guests enjoyed our singing and playing of some classical music pieces of Schubert, Schumann and Mozart; the Händel seemed a bit too long for them. The evening went very well; it is a good way to cultivate the relationship with our allies. But then, the other night, I heard heavy steps sounding in our house. I smelled the reek of alcohol and knew that another 'butterfly,' " as Gertrud called them, "was on the prowl. Thea, still living with us, appeared, and tried to get the man to leave. When it did not work, and the Japanese mariner offered her money to sleep here, we called one of our Japanese contacts who got the fellow to depart. The Japanese soldier, thinking Adjuk, our contact, was military police, trembled all over when he finally took off. We will likely have to expect more such visits, but by now, we have learned how to deal with them without becoming all shook up."

Gertrud read Leon Feuchtwanger's book 'Jud Süß' with great effort and reluctance. The author, himself a Jew, delved, like all Jewish writers, into, what she considered 'human dirt,' appalling to her. For two nights earthquakes rattled her and the children. When, after days of continuous rain the sun came out, they were delighted. More moves were required in the community, fortunately none affecting Gertrud and her children.

"My camphor box has arrived from Medan and everything is as I packed it. I'm glad to see my parents' letters as well as the letters I wrote as a fiancée. Alfred's letters are somewhere in Batavia. I will read them all again, after which I shall burn them. During the past days I read my letters from my time in Kaiserswerth, and by doing so, relived the joys and miseries of these years in the Mission home. How terrible was my lack of joy as a fiancée in this Home! Even today, I'm outraged about the petty upsets with the Alfs, and how right I was to oppose them. Looking back, I recall what all arose in my soul at this time, the urges and stirrings, the hunger for understanding, and the desire for the expression of my soul. Had

I been able to do so and not been held back at the time, and had I had the help of a guiding, understanding hand, I'm certain that I would have entered my marriage as a more mature human being and would have been spared many a bitter experience during the first years of my marriage. But instead, dirt was dumped on me, and the most impossible motivations were assigned to my need for solitude and the tempest of my soul. All the Alfs spitefulness, their envy, the malice they vented on me, have left a pile of rubbish in my soul, which, to shake off, I found only this year the strength to do so. Yes, I do feel it and I'm grateful, to, finally, try being able to be myself. The misery of the years of separation have helped me to grow and mature, to move more freely in my daily life, just as I have been able to in my music!"

[I, the author, who, of course, knew Gertrud personally and through some of her writings, and am now married to her daughter, Ute, for 50 years, have frequently wondered how Gertrud's life might have evolved, the different direction she might have taken, had the Mission and its people not impacted her as they did.]

They celebrated Thea's birthday on December 12 among ten people. Last Thursday, they had another German evening at the consulate with an Advent and Christmas motif. It was a rather large gathering and many seemingly failed to find the right mood. Quite a few of those present also had no understanding of the Christmas motif. "I played the C-minor Fantasy," Gertrud wrote, "but was so very 'off' that I was unhappy for the rest of the evening. I had very much looked forward to playing this piece, but the acoustics were so bad, maybe I was also influenced by the many candles, that I felt like playing to a wall. As much as I tried, I could not relate to my music and even less to my surroundings. I felt sorry for my beloved Fantasy. Later, when I played the first set of the Moonlight Sonata, I did better, but only because I made a mighty effort to find its proper expression. I did not enjoy my playing, but, fortunately, most of those present did not notice my lack of enthusiasm.

"What an unpleasant Christmas season this is! We are amidst packing for another move, and don't know whether it is to Brastagi or to Penang. The German Navy establishment in Shirnan and Penang had asked whether German women would be prepared to assist in their local mariners' homes. Singles and

163

mothers with up to two children are supposed to move to Shirnan, while we mothers with more children are to move to Brastagi. The German embassy in Tokyo refused to pay for the transport; the Japanese also refused, since they don't mind us staying where we are. It is Beck, our supposed organizer, who wants to move and has registered himself for Shirnan. Thus, if we remain in Padang, Beck must stay, too. This is why he tried everything to get us to move. While we large-family mothers wouldn't mind moving to Brastagi to get away from the Padang heat, we were asked to pay for the move ourselves, for which we don't have the money. The issue has divided the community, pitching singles and small families against larger ones. It all makes for a miserable Christmas season."

On December 21, 1943, several women received letters from their husbands in British India. Of course, those who did were more than happy. But the letters were over a year old! Thea learned indirectly through one of the letters that her husband was working in a hospital. Every writer emphasized his humane treatment with hikes and swimming being allowed. But there was no word from Alfred. "Will I be one day so lucky?" Gertrud asked.

They celebrated Christmas in a pleasant atmosphere. The children were happy with their presents, Ute being the most delighted and 'giving' of the three. And, lo and behold, the cost for moving to Brastagi had been resolved. "We need not pay for the move. Once Mr. Beck really wants something and his self-interest comes to the fore, he can do wonders."

More books were read, and Gertrud expressed her enjoyment of a Japanese movie, a decently-portrayed love story.

In mid-January 1944, Gertrud addressed a subject she, too, had to deal with. It was the relationships of the husband-less women, separated now for many years. She asked, "might our men know about the battle we are waging, the fight for our purity? This is the frontier: here, on one side, are the women without husbands, while there are also men without women or wives, the Japanese, who, with Asiatic bluntness think they can make demands of every woman. There's only one way to protect oneself from stumbling, which is: reserve, utter reserve! Whoever believes she can maintain a purely friendly relationship with a 'butterfly,' fools herself. It does not seem possible with these people, even if they may be the most decent and educated men.

For a while it will work, but then it will be over, and woe to the woman who loses self-control. There are women who trade compliments, touch and let themselves be touched, but even if it is only the little finger – it will not remain so, soon it will be the whole hand and then more. These women have many friends and a lively homestead, and they get to know many really nice people, but among the visitors are also many less worthy subjects. In the end, they are talked about, even by their visitors, and their reputation suffers. Often without noticing it, these women drift astray. It is a slippery slope, and whoever is no frog ought not to step onto it. My personal rule is: What would I do if my husband were sitting next to me?

"I cannot condemn a woman when she stumbles. Times are too difficult and dangers too great for every woman to properly deal with them. If I do not permit mitigating circumstance for myself, I can do it for others. It calls for case-by-case judgments. For me, there's no hesitation. I'm totally aware that I can pass before my husband and the children by maintaining total purity. But it is something impossible to do by one's own strength.

"And, still, there is no decision for the move. No one knows why. Maybe there are military reasons. It is hard to live without knowing what's going to happen," she wrote.

She read several presentations and sermons of Alfred's that had arrived in her camphor box from Medan. "If such year-old writings bring us closer together, how much more would a new letter accomplish? But I'm not one of these lucky ones, yet. These days, Alfred feels close to me. I try to retrieve old pictures and dream about the future. But then there are weeks when the distance is so great that I become frightened for myself."

One evening, Gertrud entered her bedroom wanting to turn on the light. No light – the bulb was gone! Another look to the window, and she noticed that her curtains had also disappeared – again. They had been sitting on the emper, when the thief must have approached the home from behind. The next three evenings brought visitors, a Japanese officer and, on one occasion, a doctor-friend who brought various treats and toys for the children. The officer's repeated visits became unpleasant, since he did not show any interest in photos or songs, but acted distracted. It became suspicious. Then, one evening, when it had started to rain, he claimed that he could not get home and wanted to sleep here. "After he became offensive towards Thea, we complimented him with some true Japanese smiles from the house. It is so sad to experience these repetitive disappointments. We receive them in a friendly way, offer them something, try to make conversation – in short, cultivate confederacy – but in the end one shudders."

Some time in January of 1944 Gertrud mentioned again her pleasure in having Alfred's letters and documents, which she found useful in bridging the distance to him somewhere in India. Reading the letters, she described her attempts to gain insight, to enter into the being, thinking and feeling of the beloved person, or simply to let them affect her. She wrote: "It is odd; the longer we are separated, the more I feel the need to live joyously, now, as if it were in our future life together. I want to use the time to gather and create inner values of whatever nature they may be, such as music, literature, English, theology, and more. I do it because it brings me joy and enriches me, and because I know that Alfred will appreciate it very much. It is my gift to him for our future togetherness! For the children, I must live in the present as best I can, but I, myself, live in the future, and the present is only a transition. That women, especially singles, kill time with daily dusting and perform a weekly general cleaning, simply because they have so much time on their hands, is incomprehensible to me. Oh, the wonderful time I have! Never again in our future lives will we have the time to engage ourselves to this extent in intellectual and spiritual activities. But these folks are so dissatisfied and moan and groan about having nothing to do, and complain about the senselessness of the times, and say, 'oh, were we only home in Germany and could spend our time for our country!' "

A few days later, it looked like their path to Brastagi was open; however, the promised truck would only become available three weeks hence. Gertrud read about Michelangelo's life and enjoyed the description of the artist's paintings in the Sistine Chapel, the beauty of the depicted figures, so natural, yet in their nakedness lacking all sensuality. She found that this man lived his personal Christianity, with a historian-writer calling Michelangelo a 'Christian Heathen.' Gertrud visited a friend, Lene Gunther, who had a phonograph on which she was able to listen to Beethoven's violin sonata no. 1 in B-major. She recalled how she and Alfred had tried to play this piece together in the past, yet did not quite succeed at the time. And more books she read!

Mrs. Kniesch gave birth to a son, the father being an Indonesian. Gertrud tried to prepare for the children's questions on the subject. And their questions came: "If aunt Kniesch can get a baby, why can't we get one?" And so it went. With all the questions arising, it was difficult to tell them that of some one ought not to talk about. How to make the difference in the child's mind?"

March came, and Gertrud was finally able to write from Brastagi! They had made it! The families did not travel together, since insufficient transportation was available, thus they dribbled in, a few at a time. Prior to their departure they were utterly busy packing, selling some of their belongings, shopping, and saying their good-byes. Gertrud did not develop a sense of leaving Padang until some good-byes arose: those with Nelly and Lydia brought forth some tears and even leaving Thea was not easy, who now lost her only close contact. When the time finally came to load the truck, a torrential rain delayed it to the next morning. She said, "At last, with everything tightly stowed, we still found some seating. I had to leave two of my crates of books behind since there was simply no more room. I was so tired of loading and reloading, or I would have left some other items behind instead of the books. The Kaisers will bring them on their trip."

Describing the journey, Gertrud wrote, "The trip as far as Bukittinggi went well, but when we arrived there, we were told: 'Reload onto a bigger truck!' The reason was that two giant oil drums had to go with our load! What were we to do? We sat by the road, and I sharply watched the reloading to make sure some decent seating was left for us. It was already dark when the drive continued. Then, only five kilometers after Bukittinggi, the truck came to a stop, its generator out of commission. Another vehicle drove back to bring a replacement. After that, the brakes were found defective, requiring another jaunt back to Bukittinggi for new brakes. By now, our mood had collapsed to nothing! The children were unable to sleep in the cramped quarters until I found a way for them to stretch out on a wooden plank. At five in the morning, the drive continued with the headlamps not working properly, a fearful experience.

"After a few more minor repairs, we arrived in Sidempuan, where we were able to clean up and sleep in beds. In the morning the trip continued, with the children having difficulties where to put their legs in the cramped quarters. But we made it to Sibolga, where we had lunch, and then to a one hour stopover in Tarutung. We passed by the sulfur springs, which had been fashioned into a magnificent spa facility. We crossed Tobaland and, regretfully, passed Lake Toba by night, then had supper in Balige and afterwards continued to Siantar. By the time we arrived there it was three in the morning. We stopped in front of a Chinese hotel and were offered two beds. When I went to inspect them, two people were just vacating them. I was disgusted. But it was still a five hour drive to Brastagi, impossible to endure. This meant to crawl into the pre-warmed beds. I made the necessary preparations using a few additional mattresses and, taking some precautions, all nine of us travelers fell quickly asleep. Early up in the morning, we arrived at noon in Brastagi. There, a disappointment awaited me, for I was to house with two women I was not very fond of, and not with the family I'd have wished.

"I found the buildings' rooms rather opulent, with every room furnished. With some rearrangements and others taking some of the furniture, I was able to set up my two rooms with my own furnishings, pictures, vases, and wood carvings. Life isn't more expensive than in Padang, except that one cannot get some of the native products; there is no miniak manis (sweet oil), no pisang goreng (fry bananas), and no klapper available. This required me to change my cooking, very much to Christa's regret. The library of the German community is wonderfully rich. I will not run out of reading material. For the time being, I'll concentrate on reading historical books about Mozart, Verdi and Wagner."

On April 6, 1944, Gertrud could not believe the news. The Germans' 'manager,' Mr. Beck, had been named general manager by Tokyo. Gertrud commented: "Beck, who was unable to control us timid chickens in Padang, is now supposed to rule this bunch of people here? He'll be surprised. He has my condolences, and I feel pity for the old man. Well, we'll see."

In her new abode, Gertrud removed a built-in bench and moved her desk to the window to enjoy looking outside as opposed to facing a wall. This also provided better light for the children's school work. "Christa is doing all right," Gertrud stated, "but Ute must get it yet. She is still too slow and when reading, she's like me – she cannot quickly take in the words' meanings. I have left it to the teachers whether she can move to the next higher class or repeat the second. She's actually still too young to move up."

There remained also the question of what was to happen with the German families still living in Padang. Some could still get here but others would have to stay in Padang. She slowly involved herself with some of the new people and found that many were way too sensitive and quickly took things too personal.

By mid-April Ute was in bed with headaches and vomiting. "Dr. Heinemann is going to give her a thorough checkup, since she is not looking very good," Gertrud wrote. "Ute will likely always be our problem child. And she is not eating well. The new environment, as well as the school curriculum, seem to tax her."

Late in April, Gertrud wrote that she had 'made it' past her birthday, but was pooped by evening. Then it happened that, "Mrs. Rechenbach handed me all her silver bowls, vases, table cloths, and whatever else, giving the impression that she wanted to enjoy them once more – before she dies! She's so attached to external things, her glorious past, from which she cannot separate herself. It makes her dying so difficult. The other day, she told me: 'Mrs. Rutkowsky, I'm such an externally-oriented person; you won't believe how much this is troubling me!' I would love to help her, if only I had the proper words at the right moments. What a difference it is to see the quiet, willingly dying Aunt Müller, versus this other woman, fighting her passing with all her might."

More books were read – Hermann Stehr's 'Heiligenhof,' and Lord Clive's account of Britain's conquest of India, plus Chopin's collected letters.

But soon another move became necessary; the sixth in two years! Gertrud gave up her independence, as she called it, and moved in with Lene Gunther, whom she liked very much, to Deli Ba My 13, a street name. Another family, the Kaisers, were to take over Gertrud's previous abode. "Lene and I are happy. We now have a beautiful house, a nice garden and better view."

"It is mid-June, and all nine of us have had what we call the 'five-day-fever.' Our beautiful new house turned into a hospital. But we are past our affliction, and the children eat like horses. If only we need not have to save all the time. Prices have risen to the extent that we don't see how we can continue living like we used to. And the news is that the Allies have landed in France. God help our poor Germany!"

"Christa's school report was very good, with an A in drawing, the only one in school. She found it so obvious that she did not even tell me about it. Ute is doing the second class over and is happy finding everything so easy. Michel I often do not see for the entire morning. Only when he gets hungry, will he show up dirty, like a scamp." And there are always more books to read, like 'Letters of a German Master,' by Max Reger, Mureschkowski's 'Leonardo da Vinci,' 'Madame Curie,' by Eve Curie, Richard Graf du Mulin Eckart's 'Cosima Wagner,' which she found very good, Guy de Pourtales 'Richard Wagner,' Duff Cooper's 'Talleyrand,' and many more!

In October, Gertrud wrote: "Week after week we live in fear for our beloved Germany. The worst is our lack of information of what is happening at home. How hard it is to sit here with hands tied, in safety, quiet, and abundance, knowing of the want and misery at home. Here, we must only deal with quarrels and trivialities, oh, one could cry about it! We prepare and hope to be able to get home, no matter what awaits us there – nothing else but to get home!"

Gertrud's diary ends in October 1944, although her stay in Brastagi lasted until May of 1946, one-and-a-half years longer! This period is bridged by the mail connection that was eventually established between Alfred and Gertrud, and is addressed in the subsequent chapter.

Japanese forces remained in power in much of Sumatra and Java until Japan's surrender in August of 1945. Thereafter, Gertrud and the children came into the custody of British and Dutch forces and had to move in May of 1946 from Brastagi to Medan until June 1947. During this time, until Alfred's release in November of 1946, he remained in the internment camp at Dehradun. Following is the couple's exchange of letters, made chaotic by poor mail service between India and Sumatra.

Alfred, center, Heinz on right

Alfred's Internment in India

Prior to the Japanese invasion of the Dutch East Indies, the Dutch transferred all German internees on three ships to India. The British had established a large internment facility for male Axis civilians, Germans, Austrians and Italians, gathered from throughout southeast Asia, in Dehradun, in the foothills of the Himalayas. These men 'enjoyed' a rather civil arrangement, being that they were allowed weekly hikes on an honor basis outside the camp, meaning that they promised not to attempt escape while on such outings. They had access to a swimming pool and could maintain small gardens. For some men, inclined to be more adventurous, the imposed idleness was unbearable and they attempted repeatedly to escape, but never when outside the camp on the honor system. Two such adventurers were the German mountain climber Angermaier and the Austrian Heinrich Harrer. Both escaped independently, one group dressed as an Indian work crew under the command of a German in a makeshift British officer's uniform. After their separate escapes, Angermaier and Harrer met in Tibet, and after much suffering, made it eventually to Lhasa in Tibet, where Harrer became a confidante of the young Dalai Lama. Two other Germans in manufactured British uniforms traveled all across India, making it to the Japanese lines in Burma. Alfred, not inclined towards this kind of adventure, stayed put, went on hikes, enjoyed classical music, and tended his garden. The internees had access to a library to keep educating themselves, if so desired, which is what Alfred pursued diligently.

He arrived in Dehradun, specifically in Premnagar, in early 1942. While there had been mail contact between Alfred and his relatives in Germany, as well as with his family during his internment on Sumatra, once he was transferred to India, this connection was broken for nearly a year.

The first news, transmitted via the International Red Cross in Geneva to his father Johann in Germany, was dated January 12, 1943, advising in terse terms that Alfred was in good health and asking urgently for frequent communication. A regular exchange of letters between his parents, his sister Emma, his brother Hans, the Weissenbruchs, and other relatives ensued,

172

but was often interrupted by missing messages. There was still no contact between Alfred and his family on Sumatra!

How erratic and cumbersome communication was, becomes apparent from the following letter to Alfred in Dehradun, written by Else Otto, living at Minami Tsurugun Jamanashiken, no. 3984, in Japan, dated late August of 1944. In it she referred to a letter dated October 19, 1943, received from her husband, Heinz, also interned in Dehradun, but in another camp section. Else wrote, referring to the letter of her husband, "that you, Alfred, would like to hear how Gertrud is doing. From my official information, I can tell you that she is doing fine. Unfortunately, despite my best attempts, I have been unable to establish personal communication with her. The single letter I received from her does not confirm whether she ever received any correspondence of mine. Be advised that Gertrud lives in Padang, Damar 7, together with the Berghäuser, Michel and Meyer families. I will copy Gertrud's letter I mentioned above." Following is a summary of this letter:

"How happy I am to be able to write to you. We had always looked forward to receiving our consul's delegation from Tokyo, and I am glad to send you this letter using this opportunity. We are doing fine, and our situation has improved due to the connection with the representatives of our government. The past years were not always easy, but the more interesting and educational for it. We experience a piece of history you would have difficulty to comprehend. How very much the upheaval progresses here! We would have loved to also get to Japan, but our path was blocked at the last moment. We were rather upset by it and, had it worked, we would have been spared much. But it wasn't to be!" Gertrud closed her letter with explanations and stories about the children.

On August 9th, 1945, in a brief message, Alfred tried unsuccessfully to establish direct contact between himself and Gertrud in Brastagi via the Red Cross in Geneva. A second attempt on October 17 through the same organization brought no results either. A third try on November 20 via the Japanese Red Cross was, at last, successful. Apparently, a telegram of Gertrud's to her parents in Germany made it, and with contact between Dehradun in India and Germany established, Alfred was able to send the following telegram in English to his wife:

"Dearest! The parents have received your telegram. We are much delighted about your news. All of us are well. With my thoughts I'm always with you and the children. God bless you. My love to you and the kids. Yours . . ."

Alfred received Gertrud's first letter, dated December 9th, a long one, not just a telegram, by way of the Red Cross in Geneva. Abbreviated in translation, she wrote:

"My dear Alfred!

We have been told that the Red Cross will now forward our letters to our relatives. Supposedly, letters from India have arrived in Padang, meaning that we may soon receive also word from you, God willing. I'm waiting eagerly for some sign of life from you, although I received some indirect news that you are alive, even a picture, through local friends. The children are doing well in school. We have been spared from serious illnesses, and we've lived in relative quiet and did not suffer any shortages. Until July of this year we received financial support from our government which, while too little, helped us get along. What fell short, we had to supplement by selling linens and clothing. Since we no longer receive support, we make do by selling various items and are sewing for Europeans and Indonesians, as well as by giving piano lessons. However, we will not be able to maintain ourselves for very long by this means. It is hoped that some kind of organization will soon look after us. We are not being bothered by the political upheavals, but are uncertain as to how things will develop. If there's street unrest we stay home and stay neutral in our behavior. It's not easy for us, and we would sooner than later travel to Germany or to you in India, from where we could return together to Germany. We hope that the manager of our affairs will soon come up with a solution. The children's Christmas expectations have withered, but a letter from you would make the best Christmas present. I give piano lessons to Chinese and am grateful for being able to practice. I received a letter from de Kleine from Medan. He is doing fine, but has suffered indescribably during his Japanese internment. He has turned snow-white.

With love and fidelity, always, yours, Traut."

The above lengthy communication was followed by several brief back and forth missives through December, then a longer letter of Gertrud's, dated December 31, got through, in which she wrote:

"My dear Alfred. How great was our joy when two letters of yours arrived eight days ago. They were a real Christmas present." Gertrud cut a photo showing Alfred and another internee in two, to give the other half as a Christmas present to a woman-friend, whose husband was shown on it. Gertrud expressed her strong longing to be together with her husband, and told about her bad times, when, because of the years of no contact, her feeling of togetherness with him had drifted. "But it was a wonder what these two 'shreds of paper' produced, the few words they bore, telling me that somewhere in this big, bad world a heart is beating for me. May God provide that we can now write to each other regularly! Do you have any plans for the future, if such are possible? I only wish to be together with you again and return home to Germany. The children need schooling and medical care." Gertrud had also learned of her father's peaceful death. Describing the children's activities, she also mentioned her playing of music. "Now, have a blessed New Year. In love, yours, Traut."

In wire exchanges through January 1946, Alfred suggested to Gertrud to sell some of his belongings to support herself. Furthermore, he recommended establishing some local contacts in preparation for her return to Germany, saying that his hands were tied, living behind barbed wire. But more than a year was to pass before the family was reunited again.

With the receipt of letters erratic, some apparently being lost, Gertrud and Alfred began to number their letters. This system continued for more than a year, with Alfred writing 51 letters from Premnagar, the last dated October 21, 1946, when, shortly afterwards, he was released to return to Germany. His first letter to his wife from Germany was no longer numbered and was dated January 12, 1947. Gertrud's letters from Sumatra remained numbered, the last one being no. 49, dated June 4, 1947, from Medan, prior to her and the children's return to Germany. Thus, from May 10, 1940 to July 11, 1947 the family had been separated for more than seven years!

Following is an excerpt of the letter exchange of the family, (frequently disregarding letter numbers and dates):

On January 20, 1946, in letter #3, Gertrud wrote to Alfred about a dream she had of being in some German mountain area. "When my loneliness seemed to overcome me, I walked to the piano to play Mozart's beginning motive of the C-minor Fantasia and played away all my want, my loneliness, struggling with the music like I do with my fate. When the final bars faded," she said, "me, sitting still and listening after them, there came this noise from the door. I heard your voice, "Traudele," and there you stood in the room and had listened to me playing, had understood me. Do you know this Fantasia? I play it more and more, and the more I do, the more I love it. And my longing drives me to play Beethoven, his Appassionata and violin sonatas. I hear you playing alongside me, like in old times, in more happy hours."

Gertrud continued the above letter on February 3, writing, "God only knows what our future will look like. Should there be a way for us to get together, I am certain to take it, wherever that will take me. For the good of the children and ourselves this separation must end, and I shall fight whatever force that will attempt to separate me from you and the children again. It may be well to include these, my thoughts, in your plans about our future. Whether this future will provide a way back to missionary work is questionable, and if so, then only under entirely different conditions. Even Heinrich de Kleine is skeptical, although he's making his own plans, hoping to rebuild. He, too, has not been able to get together with his family, which is still living in Padang."

"It has been a tough week," she told Alfred. "I had 'kitchen duty'; our babu was sick for a couple of days. Afterwards, I sewed like mad, cutting up table cloths and bath robes to make children's dresses for sale. I handed the whole shebang to an inang, who is going to sell it for me. And today is my cleaning and shopping day. But I'm going to quit work now to chat with you, although I had been looking forward doing this for the past week." Not finishing her letter, she continued the following day by saying that "I received a letter from you with your picture. What joy! Now I have already three of your pictures, but it is sad that I have not been able to send you one of us yet. I'm so glad that you receive mail now, and I'll make sure by numbering the letters. I also received your letter telling of father's death, and mother's letter to Else, which I am to forward to her. But since I do not have her address in Japan, Heinz must provide it to me."

Only a couple of weeks later, Gertrud followed up with another letter.

"I had a full day, my dear. I gave five piano lessons, three at home and two at another home to a nice, educated Chinese woman and her eight year old son. Both are eager students. Another student, little Gerhard Noll, however, appears not to have much musical sense which makes it hard for me. I hope he learns as much from me as I do from him. My best student is the 17 year old Avée Lallemand. We play Mozart and Beethoven, and the one hour lesson usually turns into two hours. I enjoy teaching; but when the children do not do their duty I must control myself and not lose patience, which rarely happens, though. But your daughter Christa causes me worry. She could do much better, in school as well as playing piano. She could be the best in school, were she not so hurried and disorderly. Especially for her, I would be glad if we would soon be able to find ordered conditions. My house-mate Lene Gunther and her children and I try working together, but have our different ways of doing things, which we cannot and must not give up. But how I long to be just family again? How wonderful it would be to take a holiday from the 'I', just the five of us on a small spot on this Earth, where no one knows and bothers us, a shared week of quiet joy, with forest, meadow, creek and flowers. Will that ever become possible again? I wonder whether you will receive these lines of mine? With love and fidelity, your Traut."

Ute had written a letter to her father, telling him that they had a nice Christmas, and that they set up the nativity crib he had made. "I have four chickens; one is called Krählieschen, the other's name is Goldhähnchen, because it is golden-yellow. The other two have not been named yet, because they aren't laying eggs yet. We must help mother with the chicken coop and clean the garden, the rooms, and set the table. I have planted katjang and onions in our garden. We hope that we can soon join you."

Alfred wrote from Premnagar: "Love of my Heart! Life has renewed itself since we can correspond with each other. I received four Red Cross forms and two real letters from you with the children's inserts. How promising! Your messages are passed through the 'wings' of our camp, because they are so moving to everyone. Reading Christa's and Ute's letters, I realize how much they have grown and how I will need to adjust to my big daughters when we get together again. How is Christa's piano playing, and is Ute playing the violin? If she could only use mine here, which is in good order after it suffered a bit these past years. How come I don't hear anything from my son? I'm impressed by Ute's chicken story. I cannot compete with it, but I could with my gardening. A large gathering of missions and churches will take place in Geneva, which will also address our work. Always, your Alfred."

Another evening, lying in bed, Gertrud enjoyed 'chatting' a bit longer with her distant husband. "We share a bedroom. Ute and Michel sleep in one bed, while Christa and I have separate beds. There's insufficient room for four beds. The two are used to sleeping in one bed; it also means that I save on bed sheets, which have dwindled. Christa has grown very tall, but she still need's her little 'nose nappy' for the night. She has become an avid reader to the extent that she has neglected her school work, bringing home grades at the low end of the scale, when earlier she had been at the top. I had to forbid her to read for two weeks and also visits with her friends, a tough measure! This is Christa – she can when she wants to! Listening to native children, ours hear a lot of lewd talk and terms. It is a time when all moral rules and customs seem to have been tossed aside, and it is difficult to keep the children on a straight path. But I talk straight to them, not beating around the bush."

Only a couple of days later, but miles away, Alfred wrote to Gertrud: "My dear Traut! Last week, we had a wonderful chamber music afternoon, performed by musicians from Wing1: Beethoven's Appassionata, the 1st Cello Sonata of Richard Strauss, and others. Heinz and Gunther were able to join us. I have not been playing any music since Ramgarh. Schmidt is using my violin to play in the symphony orchestra. To play myself, I would have had to join Wing 3 and play with the Italians and their music. I hope very much that the girls are studying English. I heard that our mission in Africa has been turned over to the Americans. Heinz and I received a couple of nice photos of the parents. I would love to send you mine, but am afraid that they might get lost. Let's rather wait. I did not receive any mail from you last week, and there's still no connection with Germany. Did you get any help meanwhile, and did you hear from Albright in America? Have de Kleine write me. Greetings to you all, and with longing for you, your Alfred."

178

Within days, Gertrud wrote to her husband that Friedchen de Kleine had succeeded in getting together with her husband, Heinrich, good friend of Alfred's. Heinrich de Kleine was Dutch, while his wife was German, and their children spoke only German, troublesome in a camp of Dutch who rejected Germans. And the moral conditions in this camp had to be terrible – a total of 49 extramarital children were expected to be born soon! "When will order return once more to this world?"

The above paragraph was somewhat puzzling. Why were the de Kleines in a camp? The Indonesians had declared their independence on August 17, 1945, with the still present Japanese surrendering in Batavia on August 22, 1945. Their homeland surrendered on September 2, 1945, following the dropping of atomic bombs on Hiroshima on August 6 and on Nagasaki on August 9, 1945. Prior to their surrender, the Japanese supplied the Indonesian nationalists with weapons to fight the anticipated return of their colonial masters. Dutch troops landed in Aceh, on Sumatra's north coast, on August 23, 1945, but fought Indonesian nationalists until July of 1947. So, when Gertrud wrote on February 20, 1946 that the de Kleines were in a camp, it could only have been a camp maintained by Indonesians, who had interned their former Dutch masters, with Dutch troops not having been able to liberate them yet, almost six months after their initial landing?

In another crossing of letters Alfred wrote: "Traudele, my Dear! How very much did I enjoy your letter of January 20th. I was able to walk hand-in-hand with you and partake in your life and suffering. But I do not worry about our future, which I've put into God's hands. Wherever we shall arrive, there will be God's world, and more work than we can handle. The main thing for us is to get together again, so that everything can become all right once more." Alfred then quoted a poem of Josef Weinheber, promising more poems, but only, in jest, if Gertrud would diligently write to him. "We are now permitted two visits every month. If you like, come, and we shall make sure you'll like it here with me." The letter was quickly followed, by: "Traudele, my Dear! Since we can write regularly, I'm numbering my letters. Every numbered letter you confirm will tell me that you have received word from me. Our camp commander has tried to get you wives here to us, but I'm doubtful of success. Your thoughts

179

expressed in your letter of January 20 ring in my heart, and are a solid confirmation that our separation has not disrupted our innermost unity." This was followed by a poem of Ruth Schumann. "Please tell me more about the children's lives in your next letter."

Gertrud wrote that she had to give a home address in Germany for their eventual return. She specified Wiesbaden-Biebrich, where her mother, Martha Weissenbruch, had been able to hold onto the apartment at Dotzheimer Straße 52, which she had occupied with her husband, now deceased. On an earlier trip to Sipirok Gertrud had sorted Alfred's books according to their value, that is, putting all Arabic and linguistic volumes into one crate, while donating the rest to the German community or selling them as waste paper. Whether the saved books would ever make it back to Germany was questionable; maybe Heinrich de Kleine would be able to help. Thanks to the faithful supervision of their former church members, Philemon and Samaria, theirs were the only crates that had not been pilfered.

At the beginning of March, Alfred wrote: "Traudele, my Dear! Yesterday, I received two Red Cross forms from you, dated February 13, and on Monday your long letter of February 14. Thank you very much! The news from home is very dark, and my impression is that the suffering of our people has not reached its apex yet. We can only pray and wait." Alfred then entered into a discourse of how to deal with the children, Christa especially, responding to Gertrud's earlier letter. In closing, Alfred expressed his delight with a symphonic concert performed the previous day in camp.

Within days, Gertrud let Alfred know that, "we had our picture taken this week, so that we can send you one. Michael is busily chopping wood in the yard to make some money. He is so good-natured, won't hurt a fly, yet is a real boy. He's good in arithmetic and reading, but writing causes him still some trouble. Christa is the stimulating element in her class, if only she weren't so flighty. Alfred, you don't believe how I look forward to receive the money from New York. If we really will get that much, I'll give up our thrifty way of life, stop sewing and knitting, and dedicate myself fully to the children. And, yes, our dear Bataks! Not a single one has checked about our well-being, although they easily could. But the simple people have been tossed hither and yon, don't know what to do, and are too afraid. With the reoccupation of Sumatra by the Allies, the German expatriates are under British administration in Medan. The Germans' poor administrator was recently discharged by the British and replaced by an elected board of five people, four women and a man, who are to look after our interests."

In another mail overlap, Alfred expressed his regret by saying: "Beloved Traut! This is your sixth birthday that I cannot celebrate together with you. Melancholic thoughts pass through my mind when I think what these years have taken from us. But they did not take our togetherness, grounded in God's eternity." Alfred then quoted a poem of Goethe's, but, unable to send her much, included a picture of his with a promise to make up for much once they would be together again.

"My dear little Ute," Alfred wrote in a long letter on March 15, 1946, telling her how much he liked the story about her chickens and their egg-laying, then – lovingly – described in great detail the multitude of birds he encountered in his camp, and their antics and food preferences. He commented on Ute's report that they had set up the nativity scene he had made when he was still in a camp on Sumatra, and added that he made himself a large-figure set which was painted by an Italian friend in camp. Then he described that he was permitted to go for walks outside the camp twice a week, at which times he collected berries to make jam. "You would not believe the kinds of jams I have made already, among which are mango, papaya, and orange marmalade. Beyond that, we have even produced Limburger cheese. We can bake bread, the dark bread we like, and we get white bread, of which I wish I could send some to Germany! We have eight papaya trees in our garden and recently had a good harvest, but, unlike Sumatra, where these trees bear fruit all year, here they ripen only in March. Bananas grow all year, but they are not as good as those in Sumatra. We can grow all kinds of European vegetables which are good for us. In winter, we must wear warm clothing, especially at night, when the temperature can drop to freezing. There are 550 internees in our camp. We have a common kitchen and do all work alternately, only the main cooks remain the same. We even have cake made from good wheat flour, which are sure better than yours made from rice flour." Alfred concluded his letter, advising that he had still not received any mail from Oma, Martha Weissenbruch, and Opa, his father, in Lütgendortmund, which is why he was unable to report anything about their well-being.

According to the Red Cross, the mail embargo with Germany would be rescinded on April 1, 1946.

Two days later, Alfred wrote to Gertrud, bemoaning the terrible state of the world, but quoted from a simple woman's letter: "Love your fate, for it is God's walk with your soul." He continued by saying, "we cannot make any plans, but must remain open to the future. Let us consider our present life as if it were our normal one. If we permit our wishes to gain power over us, they will paralyze us. What you told me about Christa keeps occupying me. Some of my vices seem to find resurrection in her. She has my sensitivity with all its pros and cons." He continued with advice on how to deal with his daughter. Glad to hear that the de Kleines were able to get together, he asked for Heinrich de Kleine to write to him, to obtain his address. He was able to assemble sufficient cold-weather clothing for his eventual return to Germany. "And while this year's poor harvest has led to some shortages, we are still doing fine. What helps is that we have good specialists in camp who produce top products from what is available to us. The weather here does us good, except the summers. A few times I have suffered from dysentery, once severely, but I made it." He described how much he enjoyed the piano pieces of 'Pictures at an Exhibition' by Mussorgsky, the violin concertos of Brahms and Dvorak, and Beethoven's Eight's Symphony. He even saw a color movie featuring Chopin and his music. And more was to come, Brahms' second piano concerto, and a violin sonata evening with works of Biber, Vivaldi and Beethoven.

A week later, another letter followed to his beloved Traut. "Since February 8, we are permitted to write letters twice a week. I've numbered my letters, and if you confirm their numbers, I will know that you have received them. I performed a church service today, but my belly gave me trouble. With God's help I made it through. It is a very small circle that attends service. Most Protestants participate only on the major religious days. Camp life is not conducive to promoting interest, and the general situation adds to this lack of interest."

At the end of March Gertrud wrote in letter #7 that she had an opportunity to have this letter taken from Brastagi to the Red Cross in Medan, thinking this distance was the most difficult to bridge for their correspondence. She had not received any

182

mail from Alfred since February 4! "Our Wiedersehn seems to have moved farther away; if only we could rely on regular mail service. And while the news from home is devastating, we are drawn to our home country with every fiber of our being. We would rather suffer want and hunger with our loved-ones at home than be uprooted like we are here, without rights, strangers among strangers and exposed to the mercy of these strangers. If only we would receive the money promised us, which, supposedly, is held up in Singapore." At last, Gertrud received word with a Red Cross note of Else's whereabouts, who had apparently not yet learned of their father's death. "Did you, Alfred, receive our photos with the last Red Cross note? And might you soon be permitted to also write letters, not just these brief Red Cross forms? I would love to learn how you put our years of separation to use, who you were able to become friends with, what you have read, learned, and whatever. Please let me know! Except for some boils and itching rashes because of nutritional deficiencies, we are doing fine. What we miss is you, and the longer it takes, the more we do! And how are your intestinal troubles, Alfred?"

Crossing in the mails was Alfred's March letter, in which he told that he had been admitted to the hospital for intestinal troubles, but the bacteriological findings were okay, and his belly had settled down again. Unfortunately, while hospitalized, he missed the photo-taking event. "It is interesting to observe the effects of the war in our different camp wings. In the German camps new forces have materialized and people work with renewed effort. Not a single piece of ground lies fallow any more, even the area between the barbed wire fences is being cultivated. Never in our years of internment did we have such plentiful and good vegetables as now, and we expect our supply to increase in future. Money has become more dear, some rations have shrunk, but our food has rather improved. It is God's blessing for which we are grateful. If our current intense engagement affects our people at home as a whole, we can look forward with hope ! I have learned much in these hard times, which I would never want to miss for the remainder of my life. I think of you and the children!"

On April 1 Gertrud wrote, "that I, having written such a gloomy letter, leaves me no peace. I hope you weren't negatively affected by it? Again – we have no right to despair! And through these past days, I had to think of Sister Lau, who told us: 'We should not imagine that God would always lead us well and happily through all dangers. Just the opposite, God will lead us through more and more depths to prepare us for His Coming. This is why we should not despair, but hold on to Him ever more.' Sister Lau lives what she speaks and that in a simple, modest way. I have no close contact with her, only through school."

Letters crossed again in April, when Alfred wrote how good he felt receiving his family's photo from Sumatra. It was better than an entire letter, and he could not stop looking at it. "You, Gertrud, have changed little," he wrote. "You remain as I remember you. How wonderful it will be to have you back in real life!" Alfred expressed concern about some alarming information by a Mrs. Kirchner about the German community's provisioning on Sumatra, an earthquake, and the defection of entire parishes to Islam. "What is true about this? Go ahead and sell even the last of my clothing if it helps you. I have no need for any of it. There's still no mail connection with Germany. Is my mail getting through to you? You haven't confirmed any of it."

Two days later, Alfred confirmed once more – just to be safe – on a Red Cross form, the receipt of their photo, saying that Gertrud had changed little, but that the children had certainly grown. "I have written 18 times since February 8th, twice-a-week, with everything numbered, and once-a-month via airmail. A first letter of Heinrich de Kleine arrived, which lets me hope that you will soon receive the promised moneys. It would be best if you came here, if possible! . I'm delighted to receive regular mail from you now."

The next day, April 8th, the Red Cross form was followed by a 'real' letter in which Alfred again confirmed receipt of his family's photo and how much it meant to him. Standing on his table, it was like good medicine, catching his looks again and again. He wrote that he was doing fine, except that a pastor colleague got dysentery and that he had to replace him in giving services. As he frequently did, he quoted a verse, this time of the poet Christian Morgenstern:

"Oh, give me joy, but not enmeshed
with what I feel inferior in me,
but give such joys to me as gifts,
as spirit sends to spirit, soul to soul.

184

Oh, no more of these stale joys' pain,
that from strange sufferings were only bought.
Make heart my present to decide on YOU,
then mine will truly be delighted, too."

"The above is not 'great literature' that I'm sending you from my treasure chest. This one, and others, are just randomly surfacing pieces which reflect some of my own experiences and images. You may find yourself in them, too, gaining some small pleasure. It's just that I don't have anything to send you. When you asked what I've done in all these years of internment, I can tell you that, aside from the work camp-life requires, I have tried to work on subjects that will deepen me and support me in my occupation. This is a gleam of light in my internment for which I am grateful. The time spent here has not been in vain for my inner, my spiritual being. I've always had access to the necessary literature; unfortunately, Arabic books, despite much effort, have been unavailable. To my regret, I'm no longer playing the violin. Our close quarters make practicing difficult, forcing me to spare my comrades' nerves. At first, while I was in Ramgarh, it was still possible; then I even played in the orchestra. But know my heart thinks differently."

Two days later, in another letter from Premnagar, Alfred advised Gertrud that he had just received information that the Indonesian Red Cross would permit only letters from his camp that were written in English, French or Malay. "This let's me think that every single one of the twenty letters I wrote to you since February 8th will not have made it. Of these, I mostly regret the loss of my birthday letter to you, Gertrud, with which I enclosed a little pencil drawing of myself. And you will have missed every bit of news I wrote of these long years of separation. In case of financial difficulties, sell all my clothing items still in your possession. Our friend in New York, Mr. Albright, is very willing to help you, according to letters I received from him, but he has difficulties getting in touch with you. I suggest, therefore, that you try to establish contact with him via the Red Cross in Medan, with our friend Heinrich de Kleine, or someone else trustworthy. Bregenstrodt, on his own, has likewise written letters to D. D. Reitzer in America, asking him to help you, and I hope he will succeed. It will simply take time. Our comrade Michel received a letter from him, saying that his ministry is in want of pastors and he asked us to come to the U.S.A. If we cannot return to Sumatra, or should political troubles in Germany prevent us from staying there, this might be the right way. Let me know what you think. It is strange that I received every single one of your letters, all written in German, through the past five months. It means you can continue as you did; some of my comrades have received fewer letters, some only one or two. Your photo has made me very happy! How much the children have grown, and I fear they will soon be out of my control. You, too, have changed for the better, looking healthier. Heinz (Otto) sends his regards. No letters have arrived from Germany."

On a Red Cross form, dated April 12, #22, Alfred reconfirmed that, henceforth, only letters written in English were allowed and that he wrote yesterday his first letter in English to her. "Which of the letters I wrote since February 8th did you receive?"

Gertrud's letter #8, addressed the difficult question for German nationals of whether to stay in Brastagi or transfer to a camp in Medan. "It is a question of our security which very much depends on how the Indonesian political situation develops. We are still free here, even if we are being bothered at times. Our living quarters are good, the climate is pleasant, we have fresh fruit and vegetables, meat and milk, while in Medan it will be mostly preserves. In Medan, living conditions would be tight, with life playing out in a single room. Then there's the heat and lack of water and – not to forget – we won't be received with open arms. All in all, everything speaks against moving as long as our safety up here is guaranteed. One thing is certain: once the Japanese military departs, which may happen in six weeks or six months, our stay is no longer assured, and we cannot live by the Indonesians' mercy. I suggested, therefore, that those of us who are undecided about moving to Medan at this time, stay put, provided they can transfer to Medan prior to the Japanese departure. I have decided to move to Medan because of mine and Christa's teeth needing repair, and the children's teacher's decision to move to Medan, which would necessitate that I teach them myself. I'm also afraid that once some of us transfer to camp, which would mean abandoning our neutrality for an Indonesian-hostile position, those that remain will increasingly experience mistrust and harassment. Merchants would ask for ever higher prices and no babu would be willing to stay in a household. Thus, to maintain schooling would become more difficult than it is already, meaning more work and neglect of the children's education. There would be less work in the camp in Medan, resulting in more time available for the children. So, these are my reasons. Yesterday, I was very unhappy and in doubt of what to do; today I'm at rest and have decided to go. May God grant that I'm right! The request to move seems to come from de Kleine who is concerned about us still being up here and would like to see us all come together in Medan.

A note added by Ute, to her "Dear Vati," described how they could now rise later in the morning, having school vacations. "When done sleeping, we can stay in bed and romp. At six o'clock Michel gets his cat, Schnurri, and climbs with her in Mutti's bed. Michel lies down on one side, I on the other. A bit later Christa also comes to join us, trying to find a spot. When she doesn't, she pushes one of us out. Many kisses!"

Christa added that Germans from Padang might join them soon, which would bring some of her friends. "I received your birthday letter and look forward to seeing you again soon when we – maybe – return to Germany in November. We recently received three letters from you, two for all of us and one for me. A thousand kisses!"

In April, Alfred advised Gertrud that the local censor's office required that she write only one-sided letters. "In future, I will be allowed to write only on 'prisoner of war' paper, which will result in shorter letters. For three weeks now, I have not received any mail from you. This past week I sent my first letter, now permitted, to mother in Biebrich; I hope it will make it. I've learned that Mrs. Tiemeyer was robbed, making your own position likely worse. I strongly advise you to leave at the next opportunity! With love, your Alfred!"

A month later, Gertrud told Alfred of the song 'Shine on us, dear sun . . .,' a piano sonata, and what she could not put into words would arrive by this melody. "Do you remember it still? It is our song, but it's a long time since we sang it together. If you can, take your violin now and play the tunes, knowing that my heart is full of that which vibrates in every one of its voices. Once it was our song. Might you still know? Oh, what a happy time it was! Then, when we sang it, the dear sun was shining on us – but we were not aware of it! Will it yet shine on us again? Oh, just a little beam into some corner – how happy we would be!

"I cannot report anything pleasant otherwise. Our entire section is forced to move without being assigned accommodation at our new location. We – seven mothers with their children and four singles – must move in with other German families. You can imagine what this means. It means we must be strong and not become bitter. Our dear God simply grew all kinds of rabble on his Earth, among which are also such that reek of nastiness and disgracefulness. And plenty of them live here! Yesterday, we received a month's supply of stale rice, salt and even a bit of money. But don't worry – we keep our heads above water, happily sell our belongings, and once our bags are empty, we'll simply sell them, too. Pardon me if I spoke from my heart, I did not intend to. Don't become concerned!"

"My dear Traut," Alfred wrote in May, "today I received your letter #8, the one with the children's notes. Finally, after four weeks of a dry spell, we had a refreshing rain. It is so very sad that you receive only my simple Red Cross forms, but that my longer letters do not reach you! Yet I continue to write – a small door must open eventually. This Monday, I received a letter from my sister Emma that all is well at home, even with my father. Only Hans is missing in the East. If possible, try to get our marriage certificate and yours and the children's birth certificates. We will need these documents. Were you able to save some of my other papers? See that you can leave Sumatra, wherever God will lead you, be it Australia or the United States. Reitzer, our Brother in America, is trying to get some of our Mission people a vacation in the States, and he's trying to enlist some of us as pastors to join him."

A week later, Alfred referred to a letter received by one of his pastoral colleagues referring to the Mission's situation, in which a return to Sumatra was deemed impossible. This appeared to be the position of the 'powers' in Barmen. Alfred then referred to other ongoing efforts to retrieve Gertrud as quickly as possible. "It would be a relief knowing you can get away, to wherever that may be. Stay in touch with me wherever you go – I will succeed in finding you! It is still unclear when we will be discharged to Germany, but I would like to hear your opinion for our future, your remaining strength, and that of our children. It isn't that I'm making plans – God will show us the proper way – but I'd like to hear what you think of what might not be possible for us. Might you be able to move in with mother, although she had to sublet part of her apartment?"

On May 24, Alfred reported that he learned from the Red Cross in Simla that the Brastagi families had moved to Medan, and that this might mean that they were closer to their transport home. He then referred once more to questions in his earlier letters about their future. The 7,000 pastors who had moved from the East to the West in Germany will likely fill all requirements there. "The path left to us remains therefore to be seen. Please write tons to me, describing your limits, so that I can gain a clear insight."

Gertrud now communicated from Medan, Linschotenlaan 27, on May 26, letter #27, that she regretted that Alfred had to wait for three weeks until she was able to write again, due to the move to Medan. They had found kindly refuge with the Salvation Army. "The de Kleines live here, too, and we must thank the organization's woman-manager that we can stay here. We live a right romantic-adventurous life in the various rooms, get plenty of good food, drink a lot and sweat even worse. The children love it and I enjoy not having to cook and to take care of things. Heinrich de Kleine has grown a full beard and looks like a reverend priest. I'm just surprised that Friedchen (his wife) hasn't discouraged him yet. He's looking out for your books, and I think it will work. We are supposed to be shipped out soon, whether to Germany or another country is unknown. We hope it will be home!"

Ute added her impressions on how they got from Brastagi to Medan, writing that "a truck came at eight o'clock, and after it was loaded with our belongings, we climbed on top of them. Then we took off with a stop at the post office, where we waited for other trucks and people to arrive. Since mother was afraid that Michel and Christa might fall off the vehicle, they were allowed to ride in the cab with the driver. Upon our arrival in Medan at the Salvation Army quarters, we were greeted by the de Kleines. I wish you the best for your birthday and hope that we can soon see each other."

Christa commented that she had met many Dutch children at the Salvation Army with whom she played often. The families had to pick up their food, some of it hot, some cold, at different houses in the compound. She expressed her hope that they could soon travel to Germany.

In May, Gertrud wrote, "the heat is awful. I'm longing to be back in cool Brastagi. But it is only the climate I long for, nothing else. I feel that our move to Medan brought us a bit closer to our eventual return to Germany. But life here is primitive. There is no table, no chair, and six families are squeezed together in a large hall. The setting is impersonal and noisy, and not conducive for a longer stay." The letter ended with the usual question of when and where they might be able to travel to leave their present conditions behind. However, Gertrud was grateful for the friendly reception they had received and that she and her German compatriots could be among themselves and were not exposed to the shenanigans of the natives.

In June, Gertrud followed up her earlier descriptions with another letter, in which she expressed her difficulties writing in the chaotic conditions of their residence. "De Kleine has conducted the first service to the delight of everyone. He held even two Sunday Batak services. All in all, he looks confidently on the Batak Church's future. I hope he is correct. We judge it from what the families experienced in Brastagi and have scant trust in Indonesia's independence. The native people are like children who are given power but do not now know what do to in their wantonness, especially what to do with the few Europeans that are left. They quarrel among themselves and envy even the least bit of their neighbor's possessions. We are glad to have found sanctuary here, even though we are not allowed to leave the facilities – not that we want to! I have not received any mail from you since March, only a form letter with a group photo. Did you get our pictures? The first letters from Germany have arrived, but none for me yet. It is good to know that this path seems to be open now."

Five days on, in letter #15, Gertrud exulted, writing, "fifteen letters, real letters, in one go! Can you imagine my joy? Thirteen letters from you and two from mother, mailed in April. I can't believe it yet and am totally beyond myself! Where might they have been sitting? Did you receive my letters from last week? We had difficulties with the Indonesian Red Cross in Brastagi; here in Medan, our mail goes directly to the International Red Cross. But let me take care of your letters for which I'm more than happy. I shall reply to every one as soon as possible. Who knows how long I may have to draw on them? Thank you for your picture! Now, I have you before me again, can look at you and talk to you. It is you, the way you were, and yet different. I look at you and sense the difficulties of the times, the heaviness of the years which have carved their creases. You look so serious, and there is an expression which I do not know, is it sadness or just tiredness? But none of that comes through in your writing. It must be just tiredness. De Kleine has mailed you a ten-page typewritten letter. He is our 'camp father,' and we are grateful that our affairs are handled by a man we can trust. How difficult it was for us to have, for years, 'representatives' one could only despise from the bottom of one's soul. I'm happy about the verses from your little 'Treasure Chest.' They are like iron for blood. Tell me more from your Chest! Your letters breathe so much inner peace – peace of the soul, ripened through need. They make me happy! Through these years, my greatest problem has been to get off the treadmill of duties and work. My longing for solitude or contemplative dialog remained unfulfilled. And hereabouts it is totally hopeless. But God knows about this need, thus I am quiet, and hope it, too, will bear fruit.

"I am sorry that Heinz (Otto) complained about me. Is it that I don't mention him? I wasn't aware that you see each other so often, but am glad to know now. My regards to him, and I shall try to do better. I'm glad about mother's letters, which breathe of peace, so that I have no worries for her. The batch of letters I received include the nos. 4, 5, 7, 9, 10, 11, 12, 15, 16, 19, 20 and 21, plus an unnumbered one, dated April 22. My recent letters to you were rather dry. Forgive me! I was missing the lubricant of your letters."

In his mail of June 7, #29, Alfred complained, "writing is no fun when there's no response, and especially if I do not know whether any of my letters make it to you, thus I can only write and hope. There is some general correspondence making it through to us, but nothing of any consequence."

Three days later Alfred reported some good news. "Albright has notified me that he wired $ 4,000 as 'first aid,' and that he hopes to be able to repatriate you soon. On Saturday, I received your letter #11; #9 and 10 are still missing." And, once more, not having received confirmation of his earlier requests, Alfred repeated his request to secure their marriage and birth

191

certificates, asking Gertrud of what she thought about their future. He expressed his opinion that it would take some time yet before he would be repatriated.

Another letter crossed in the mails, Gertrud's of June 11, her reply to his letters #4 and 5. In celebration of a friend's birthday, one of the women played records of the Brandenburg Concertos and a violin sonata of Mozart's. "Here and there we can play a record, but this is the extent of my musical refreshment, which cannot compete with your past wonderful musical evenings. I almost envy you for the Appassionata, which I've never heard performed. It is beautiful. Earlier, I tried almost daily to play it, but with little success. However, it was enough for me to be able to follow it, and I hope we can play it together at some future time. It is amazing how one grows into all kinds of things over time, and I learned that, what I call 'hunger cures' worked wonders for my perceptive faculties. There were times when I longed so much for music that I picked some Bach tunes and enjoyed singing the voices one by one.

"Christa's piano playing has become a thing of the past. I tried lessons on Ute, but she is such a tender little flower who needs time to grow into things, and I must take care not to tire her. Tears come easily to her, but sometimes I wonder whether reluctance is not hiding behind them, and it is not always easy to find out whether these tears are a pretense. Sister Lenchen told me the other day that she thinks that Ute, based on her disposition, will later be better at mental work than Christa, since she is more steady and thorough. Ute is more like a quiet mountain lake of clear depth, while Christa is a bubbling brook, happy and bright, but erratic and superficial. Unfortunately, life here in camp is unsuited to dedicate oneself more intimately to the children. Michel seems to have overcome his earlier difficulties. I administered some quinine, after which he eats better, mostly milk rice with cinnamon-sugar. But when, just now, I ask him to take a bath because he is so dirty, he objects against this 'inundation.' Since I am not so averse to water, he must have inherited it from you. Yes, the sins of fathers!

"I love your greetings from your Treasure Chest, Josef Weinheben's poem and that of Ruth Schaumann. And you are allowed visitors? Oh, how much we would love to come! And you can leave camp for hikes, while we cannot take a step outside and must make ourselves invisible, because we are Muffen, as the Dutch call us. My greetings to Heinz; I sent Else a letter today and included one from mother. And, wonder of wonders, we just received word that we will get some money."

Gertrud's note of June 16 described their Sunday sing-along at the Salvation Army, in which she participated for the first time. "It is an international gathering with English soldiers being regulars. At first, Salvation Army melodies are sung and other spiritual tunes, but everyone can make suggestions, even for solos; everything is very informal. There's no feeling of hate or us being outcasts, just a community in God. How good that feels! When one sees these fresh cadets with their harmless joy, one's heart could bleed. How many of their likes, these human flowers of this wide world, the war has taken!"

In June, Alfred wrote that he received a long letter of mother's from June 14th. "She confirmed receipt of your letter of January 1st, Gertrud, about which she cried. She says to let you know that there are 36,000 parties looking for rooms in Wiesbaden, which is why she had to sublet a room. This is why she may not be able to provide shelter for us when we come home. Whether we find some other place remains to be seen. You may need to change plans and get in touch with the Mission. It would be best if I got home before you and might thus be able to look for and provide a modest, warm nest."

"My dear Alfred," Gertrud wrote on June 22, "it has taken me longer than I wanted to get in touch again with you. Not knowing when and how school for the children will begin again, I have started, as best as I can, to teach the children myself. Do you know that we women with our children are expected in Kaiserswerth for recovery? It's a nice thought and it is good to know there will be a place initially for us. Yet, I'm not drawn there! Ten years of me in a foster home, six years in camp, or at least some confinement, are enough, and I'm not looking forward to extending it. Just now, de Kleine has told us that the English administration intends to repatriate all Germans and that this would include you. We may yet see us this year. How wonderful that would be!

"De Kleine held a very nice service, its theme being 'Prayer is the Breath of the Soul.' I am so grateful for his services, and, oh, how much I look forward to being home, the spiritual life, to forests and meadows, and the thousand little things that make our home country so dear. Tears come to my eyes when I think of it. What is our future going to look like?"

In June Alfred wrote that he had received four letters from Gertrud plus another from Christa. "Imagine how happy I am after these long weeks of want. But I'm still missing your letters #7, 9 and 10. I do not know where your path will take you, but keep your eyes open. Wherever we go a future will open for us, except that our old tracks may be closed. Remain open for whatever comes, openings which are not averse to our calling. Remember, 'The entire world is my parochial home.' We are still young and flexible enough to adjust to whatever comes."

"Although your birthday is still a bit away," Gertrud wrote on June 29, "I am writing now, because, who knows, how long this letter will take. We are enclosing a photo of us as your birthday present. Did you hear something about our journey home? Forces seem to be hard at work for it. Recently, a woman from the Singapore Red Cross was here and spoke of the possibility that you might join us on our ship in Bombay or somewhere, since we women and children would not fill the ship. It sounds too nice to be true! And what the future is to bring, we will see. America? If necessary. But I'd prefer to go home!"

A few days later, Gertrud wrote again, reporting that Alfred's letters #18 and 22 arrived. "You seem to write so very often, but where are all your letters? You asked about the earthquake in 1944? It was a terrible one, caused by the eruption of the Talang volcano near Padang, thought to be extinct. The ocean was very much agitated, but the tremblor caused no loss of life." Continuing a couple of days later, she added, "a big letter arrived yesterday with your photos. I'm so happy!" Gertrud then commented upon the appearance of Alfred's, of Heinz, and the other men she was familiar with, finding them all looking in good health. "Christa is in bed since a few days ago with malaria tertiana. It is awfully hot at present. We received some money from de Kleine, an advance of the promised $ 4,000."

On the 8th, Alfred wrote, replying to Gertrud's letter #17, how much her longing to be Home touched him. "But one thing I'm sure of, which is that we five will become a 'Home' more than ever before. We have now mail connection with Germany, and I must see that I fulfill my obligations of writing home."

Twelve days after it was posted, Alfred received Gertrud's birthday letter "with your beautiful picture," he said.

On July 19th 1946, Gertrud informed her husband that she had received a letter from her mother, which elaborated on the misery their relatives and friends had experienced in Germany, the deaths, the illnesses, the bombings, imprisonment by the Gestapo, and the destruction of homes. She wrote that mail from Germany was now arriving on a regular basis, except that the postal service from India to Sumatra was still wanting.

"Alfred, three of your letters made it, the #25, 26 and 27," Gertrud wrote. "But it is amazing that mail from Germany gets here faster than mail from you. Except for some documentation of minor importance, I have not been able to gather anything of consequence. Whatever I had, I sent to the Swiss consulate in Batavia prior to our intention to travel to Japan, but then, despite repeated requests, never heard anything from them any more. What concerns me most is the future of our children, and I ask myself to what extent this question ought to be influenced by Mission life. Under normal conditions, it would have resolved itself automatically. They would have been sent to Germany at age ten for schooling and occupational training, with intermittent vacation visits by us parents to Germany. But what now, when the situation has shifted so much, after we have been separated for six years? You have a son who does not know you at all; a nine-year old daughter who has only a vague image of you, and an older daughter who urgently requires your influence. Once home, our children will need to go to school. We would need to leave them alone, should the question of our renewed departure arise. Would we need to part once again from our children? Does Christ's command to do missionary work cancel every obligation to the family? Where is the border between obeying God and the duty to one's children, also requested by God?

"This question occupies me even at night, so that I wake up and think about it until I start crying. If I imagine the three, each in need of love in their own way, and when I then imagine them living in a Mission home, where everyone is treated alike, then think of warmhearted Michel, alone among strangers, my entire being fights against this, and my heart says: 'God cannot demand this of us!' I would prefer to stay in Germany, but America or any other country would be all right. Should you ask me as your wife and life's partner, I can tell you that I could live even less away from you than from the children. Thus, me and the children staying in Germany, with you going to who knows

195

where, alone, is out of the question. But should you ask me as a missionary's wife, then know that I do not possess the inner strength and joy to answer this question. It would be a path of obedience to which I do not have the strength – and if I had to travel it now – I would spiritually collapse.

"Heinrich de Kleine is sending his family home to Holland; they will take the next ship. He will stay, being the only male member of our Mission. Depending on how the situation develops, he will have her come back or go home himself. As to our work: with some exceptions, it's a sad fact that our Protestant coworkers, pastors and non-German missionaries leave their work without any scruples and return home, while on the Catholic side, whoever can, stays put to jump into the abandoned parishes. As to our repatriation, we have learned that the Dutch will not evacuate anyone after August. Your books are taken care of. Supposedly, the Dutch intend to take over our work, but do not have the personnel to do so. There's also the question of what the Batak Church has to say. Since yesterday, I've been assigned two small rooms, enabling me 'to close the door.' "

On July 29th, in letter #39, Alfred wrote, "I completed an application for my return to the Dutch East Indies. However, I registered also for my repatriation to Germany, considering the questionable situation on Sumatra and the uncertain position of the Batak Church, this with regard to the absence of any information from Barmen." Alfred maintained his contact with Mr. Reitzer in America, who had promised a decent salary and the support of parishes he wanted to establish in English and German language. Should those joining wish to enter the missionary field four to five years hence, they would be free to do so. At least, they would not suffer from hunger now. "But a decision for or against will likely be made only once we are in Germany," he concluded.

Gertrud's #22 mentioned that she and the children were able to take a bus trip through town, a wonderful change for the children, especially since it concluded with some ice cream for the kids and coffee and cake for Gertrud. Alfred's letters #29 and 30 arrived, as well as #8 to Christa. Continuing, Gertrud wrote: "This week the Germans that remained in Brastagi have also moved here, but three of them, a man and two women, have disappeared without a trace. They were either kidnapped by

Indonesians or have joined the 'Opposition' on their own accord. However, the event has complicated our situation here in Medan. The result is that we are once more under house arrest, when, for a week, we had been allowed to move freely in the section of town surrounding our camp. We can only wish that some kind of decision about our fate is forthcoming; it's just that we aren't folks who are liked. But don't be concerned for us; we are well provided for. Give my regards to Heinz. Does he get regular mail from Else?" Two days later, Gertrud was able to add that de Kleine did not rest until he had regained the camp residents freedom to move, at least within the camp grounds.

Only a day later, August 3, Gertrud remarked again about de Kleine's efforts to organize their supplies and tend to the needs of the German residents. Christa, as well as Gertrud, were learning English, with Christa listening to English soldiers for proper pronunciation. Gertrud wrote that she hesitated speaking English, but said, "once we are in America, I will surely 'swim.' I wrote to mother, checking with her about the possibility of moving in with her."

"Today, I have sad information for you, Alfred," Gertrud told him on the 10th. "Heinrich de Kleine and I tried everything to get your two book cases, but I learned yesterday that they were left behind when Mrs. Meyer's moved from Brastagi to our camp. She and Mrs. Tiemeyer were badly robbed the night before the move, and when the truck finally arrived late afternoon, it supposedly was nearly full, and the drivers refused to load the heavy cases. The only thing the two women wanted was to get away, so one of them ran to a Batak Christian, asking him to safeguard the two crates. Had she only contacted the English administration right away, with which the Germans in Brastagi have such a good relationship, Major Davis would surely have taken care of it."

A month later, Gertrud wrote that Alfred's letter #32 arrived. "You mention a letter of mother's. Could it be her response to your letter, or was she writing independently of it? In her letter she says that we cannot live with her. I had expected that, since she never responded to my respective question; it must have been difficult for her to tell me 'no.' And she cannot simply terminate her renters! This means that only the Mission facility at Kaiserswerth is open to us, which, aside from its similarity to 'camp life,' which I am sorely tired of, also has some advantages. In light of the hard times in Germany, it is better to live in the country than the city. The Heimatfreude Haus has a large garden, which has been further enlarged and planted for us returnees. There's no problem with school for the children and it isn't far to Düsseldorf. The only bitter note is that mother would be so far away, which I cannot accept. I wish to take over the household duties for mother and to ease her twilight years as much as possible. Might mother be willing to move once more? Or could we possibly find housing nearby? Am I then to register for acceptance at the Mission in Barmen?

"De Kleine is now at the conference in Batavia and will address the question of the whereabouts of the $ 4,000 the I.M.R. sent for us, of which we haven't seen a red cent yet. As of today, we have received only some money from the funds Reitzer sent directly to our group. It is peculiar that only de Kleine remained of our Mission society, he, who was never fully accepted by his colleagues, who was neglected, and who was not forgiven for his German wife to join us Germans and, therefore, escaped the horrors of Japanese internment. He is now the only man who remained at his post and tries to save what is left. All other (Dutch Mission members) have quit work and returned home. The Lutheran Mission is totally orphaned, but how different it is with the Catholic Mission. Medan swarms with nuns and priests, who conquer one city block after another, where they, among other things, establish hospitals. None of them leaves, except when they become totally incapacitated. Thus, the way for them is free, and they will, it is expected, conquer all of Sumatra in a couple of years. It will be interesting how the H.K.B.P. will react to the question of European missionaries. According to de Kleine's opinion the independence of the Batak Church proved itself. Whether they will ever accept missionaries in superior positions again is questionable – under their control, yes. The latter is what de Kleine expects to happen. Should it ever come to it, it would mean a most difficult path of self-denial. We experienced ourselves what it means to be under the control of Indonesians! Dutch Brothers are unlikely to be found for this work."

Alfred expressed his gratitude that his family celebrated his birthday, thinking of him. "I invited my missionary colleagues from my 'Wing' for a pleasant coffee get-together; Jordan was able to join us from Wing VII. I did receive your letters #21 and 22, from which I learned your concerns and thoughts. Since they are also mine, I have contacted Reitzer in America, because Sumatra will be closed to us for some time to come. The situation at home seems to develop into a mighty occidental crisis going well beyond Germany. Reitzer's offer would give us peace and work, yet leave the way open to future developments. It would be risky and call for our total engagement. Brush up on your English, therefore, and also that of the children. We must remain flexible in this world of today!"

The next day, another letter of Gertrud's arrived to which he responded: "It is good to receive regular mail from you now. On Saturday I got your letter #23 describing our three children. I long for such notes! You cannot imagine how difficult it is to gain an image of them; the six years of separation have taken their toll. Their letters show me that their orthography is wanting, but with some help, they should be able to catch up. Tomorrow, Vollmer and I will go for a walk outside the camp to enjoy beautiful Nature. These walks make our internment tolerable. We are presently getting ready for repatriation. My books are packed, only my clothing must yet be tended to."

Several letters were exchanged between Alfred and the children on the 20th and 21st; then, on the 23rd, Alfred wrote to his "dear Traudele" that he received her #24 and 25th, plus one from his sister Emma and sister-in-law Erika in Germany. "Hans, Alfred's oldest brother, Erika's husband, is likely a P.O.W. in Russia. The bombing war has cost 6,341 lives in Dortmund, and everything lies in ruins." Alfred then described at length the fates and doings of various relatives and friends, ending with that they must trust in God concerning their future.

Gertrud told Alfred on August 27 that Friedchen, Heinrich de Kleine's wife, had left for Holland and that he had returned from Batavia. "Since Friedchen's ship departure was delayed, the two were able to enjoy half a day of togetherness. Having been in Batavia for two weeks, he reported that about 30 men participated in the conference. The German members of the Basel Mission will travel this week from Java on a Dutch ship via Holland, Belgium and France to Switzerland. It has been said that the German borders are still closed, making our return impossible. Could that be correct? De Kleine has made an attempt to make our return via Switzerland possible. But who knows? De Kleine battled the Dutch authorities as best he could but was told that the Rhenish Mission will no longer be allowed to operate in Indonesia. Only a few Brothers may be permitted to come back. The question as to which country is to take over the Batak Church, whether Holland or America, has been left open. De Kleine suggested a minimum number of ten Brothers for Sumatra, six for Nias, and two for Mentawei. In the course of the conference, the translation of the Bible into the Angkola dialect was raised, de Kleine being asked to do it. He, however, pointed out that you, Alfred, had begun the project and would surely be prepared to finish it. He sees it as a good way to get you back into work here, especially since you weren't a Nazi party member."

[It appears, however, that the translation project for an Angkola Bible was never completed.]

A day later Gertrud added that de Kleine was asked to work at a theological seminar in Batavia. "It's a hard decision for him; he cannot avoid it. This will be hard on us, since we will lose our advisor and protector, but he may be able to do more in Batavia for our repatriation than he can here."

Alfred responded on August 30 to Gertrud's letter #25: "You write that you want to have mother with you to relieve her loneliness and the burden of old age. This is also my wish, but there are obstacles. You won't be able to get to Wiesbaden. We will first need to find a place wherever possible. In Wiesbaden relatives will look after her, but what could you do for her when you arrive there? If we would go to America, we could take her along; there would be no problem with housing, even though we would start there with nothing. My concern is: 1. To remain true to my calling. 2. To find within it sufficient support for you. 3. Not to lose myself in dreams about the distant future, but to work for solutions of the present's pressing problems. Clear goals force us to be hard on ourselves, so that we do not, against our better judgment, enter into some chaotic situation. The thought about mother will not diminish in me; once we are together, we will take her in, provided she wants to. But there's nothing new about my repatriation; I just wish I could be home before you to prepare a 'nest' for you."

September had come, when Gertrud was writing: "I had hoped so very much for a letter to once more 'resonate' with you. Mine and the children's letters seem to get to you, but where are yours? For how long will they keep you penned up, and when, oh when, will the path home open for us? It is almost irrational to push and long so much for home, when mother writes 'I hope you will not arrive during the winter.' But, whatever is true of the story – it looks that our people will finally get the $ 4,000. De Kleine has been appointed official representative of the Rhenish Mission Society. Here are some details from the conference: There are plans for educational facilities on Macassar for Indonesian preachers and teachers, with the required means ready in Holland. America is providing more than 80 million dollars to get work going again. Every church damaged during the war is said to be repaired, and every Christian is to get clothing material. Every Mission station is to receive an account, a typewriter with paper, and a car, which would mean ten for Sumatra! I don't recall what all de Kleine told us, but I became dizzy. There is to be a motor boat for Mentawei, down to the last fish hook. It sounds truly American! With what simple means did we conduct our mission and not to its detriment. It is odd how differently people look at missionary work! When going to Batavia de Kleine will travel via Padang and visit our people there. He will once more check after your books. I let him have some of your books I'd kept for his studies, hoping this is okay with you. My greetings to Heinz. Mother received Else's first Red Cross letter."

In #29, Gertrud told of several letters that arrived, yet none for her. "For some time now we go also to the English services and feel good there, except for some minor details that appear strange to us. Every Sunday evening there's singing at the Salvation Army with everyone welcome. There is a regular group of English soldiers and chaplains, a few Dutchmen, at times a Batak, and some of our people. At first, the Salvation Army and English songs felt good, but in the long run became boring. At times, we feel like belting out some of our old, vigorous church songs, like 'I know what I believe.' How elevating this would sound coming from these young men's throats.

"Last week came another request for registration of Mission members, here and in Padang. It was said that we would shortly be repatriated to Hamburg, together with our husbands in Dehradun. But too much has been promised already!"

"Oh, Alfred, six of your letters arrived today, September 10! What fortune! One each for Michel and Christa, and four for me. My heart longs so very much for you and your love. I have the letters lying before me and the photos you included. I look at you and commune with you. I was so restless these past days that I could have screamed at times. In two hours lying awake this past night, I held a dialog with you, after which I found my equilibrium again. Your response was this blessing of letters. You scared me. Why are you afraid that our way home could be a long one? Do you have plans? De Kleine suggested that it might be smart to complete the application for an eventual return to Sumatra now, better to find work presently than later, especially for you with your translation work. De Kleine returned yesterday from Padang. He also visited the Swiss consulate in Batavia, where they keep lots of cartons with German documents, but no one can get to them, not even the Consul General. They must wait for some kind of permit."

On September 12, Alfred received a letter from Gertrud's mother, who was looking optimistically to the future, "just as de Kleine does," Alfred reported, "and your letter #26, which I received today, describing how de Kleine sees our problematic situation. It will likely take years before orderly missionary work becomes possible again. Whether the Dutch plans will materialize is questionable and will depend on the British. I keep all my avenues open, but I very much like my work and feel obligated to it. Nevertheless, I do not want to be a father who is not known by his children. America would still be our best bet, from where we could observe developments at home and the Mission. It is questionable whether you will be able to get to Switzerland. Who is to pay for it? The last Italians are leaving our camp for home."

"I want to write you a few lines, yet, Alfred," Gertrud wrote on September 15, "although I'm tired enough to go to bed. But tomorrow is Heinrich de Kleine's birthday, and I'll need to make ready for a pleasant evening. Heinrich does not want any celebration, which is why we leave him alone for the day and will get together only in the evening. Did you get his letter? I'm glad he communicated his thoughts to you. It would be well to make an effort now for your way back here. Now, it would be easier with the respective administrators knowing us, when later we would have to deal with new people, not knowing us, across a great distance. For me and the children, being born here, it is easy; the law allows us to remain. At present all doors are shut for us due to the political situation and who knows how long it will yet take, maybe a year or two. A vacation at home would

202

certainly be welcome in between! Do you still have the translation you made, or was it taken from you? It must be a year since your coworker in Siantar inquired about it. There was again a robbery at our premises, something that has become very common. Two of us must stand guard duty at night, alternating every two hours, but these crooks are so shrewd that they still dupe us. We assume that some bois, boys of the Salvation Army, are in cahoots with the robbers. Christa wants to write you a letter in English, and I'm looking forward to see what she will produce."

On September 18, Christa wrote a lively, fantasy-rich letter to her father, saying, "today, it is the kakilima, the concrete footpath, leading from one of our buildings to another, who's telling this story: ' In early morning, some children come, tip tap, with baskets to fetch bread. Then comes, klipp klapp, someone in wooden shoes walking on me. It is an adult with a bucket, mop and a cloth. Often, there are more people, who wipe and scrub while they pour water on me. Oh, how good that feels! Afterwards, all the others walk over me, children and adults, to bathe, and right away I'm dirty again. Now, the bread fetchers are returning, walking noisily over me. Every one of the children and adults gets some bread, after which they walk over me, making a racket. It's truly terrible! This is how it goes all day. Only at lunch time do I have a bit of quiet. But then they come once more to rinse dishes, and again I get wet. Then the children go to school. At lunch time they go to pick up food and milk, at which time many drops splash onto me. Then, there's midday rest. Oh, it's a rest in the truest sense of the word. Only here and there something drips on me, but only softly. In the afternoon everyone is at work, and it gets quiet. But then they go for dinner, after which they clean dishes, then step in front of the house to walk back and forth. Following this, the children take their baths and go to bed. At nighttime, guards walk over me with a stick and a bell, watching for thieves. Suddenly, the bell rings, and everyone jumps from their beds, since they know a thief has come and is hiding somewhere. Usually, everything remains quiet. But the next morning everything begins anew.' Well, dear father, how do you like my story? 'Don't I have to bear much?' "

"My beloved," Alfred wrote in September, "at last our situation appears to be clearing up. The Dutch General Consul in

Bombay asked for our ship-passage. If all works out, we may 'swim' within one to three months. We were given already some details of the transport, which makes it look more real. If only you could join us! De Kleine's letter arrived. We were pleased about what he reported from the conference. If the Protestant and Reformed Church would take over our work, it would at least mean some continuity of our labors. Whatever you cannot bring along, sell or entrust to good people. We will head for hard times at home, a poor, hungry and shivering world, but we don't want to be a burden to others."

In another September letter, Alfred elaborated to his beloved wife about what to plan for their repatriation to Germany and what to expect there, that is what he had learned from home. The situation was supposedly worse than after W.W.I, with five million German prisoners of war still being held in Russia.

Gertrud reported to Alfred about various Confirmations performed, and that Ute was bedridden with malaria. Two days later, her father sent Ute a letter from Premnagar, wishing her the best for her forthcoming birthday on the 10th of November.

"My Alfred, so dear to my heart," Gertrud wrote on September 29. "The children are playing in their room and de Kleine is away this morning. I took the opportunity and retreated to my room where I enjoy my solitude with you. I received a letter of mother's, who was in Miehlen for a week, where she was able to have some good meals. Unfortunately, it turned out that she did not receive any of my letters written between January and July. She expressed her hope that she might be able to get the guest room of the landlords, who live downstairs – in case we make it home. In afzienbaren teyd, in a reasonable time, the Mission Consulate told us, we will be brought together. How nice that would be! How I long for home, when we will be able to roam the fields and woods. All three children look at nature's beauty with open eyes, for plants and animals, all in their own way. I see little Ute, and how she would want to embrace everything to her motherly heart, her eyes shining from an inner joy. Christa, how she talks at length about whatever she sees and hears, looking at the larger things without overlooking the little ones. How she determines the genus, collects flowers, grass, and herbs, never getting enough. Then there's Michel, collecting beetles, climbing and somersaulting, and flying his kite. He has long since lost his shyness with Heinrich de Kleine. Ute is the most affectionate with Heinrich. She can sit next to him and is delighted when he addresses her. From whom might she have inherited this thoughtfulness? My greetings to Heinz. Did he get any letters from Else?"

"In all probability we will be shipped home by the middle of November," Alfred wrote on October 3. You likely, too. I look forward to seeing you again, wherever that may be. Just remember that it will be winter, which the children are unfamiliar with. The Sisters and missionary wives from China were transported to Ludwigsburg and, following many checkups, were then released. We are allowed only little in the way of luggage and will try to have some shipped as freight."

"What magnificent joy, Alfred! Seven letters from you at one time," Gertrud wrote on October 6, 1946. "I've read them, all of them, again and again, these past two days," telling him that she loved most of his thoughts expressed in his letter #41, of Aug. 6 (of which, unfortunately, no copy exists). "From it, your love and deepest affection speak to me from every line, like dew to a thirsty soul. That these years of separation did not reduce our love for each other, but even increased it, makes me feel so very happy and enriched.

"De Kleine has put out feelers to the H.K.B.P.s Ephorus, who is ready to talk with him. They are aware that they must make provisions, so that the Brothers of 'the other faculty' will not preempt their own efforts. The Catholics are lying in wait to rush upon their prey, and they do have the upper hand. De Kleine hopes that Bos will come soon come from Holland to share responsibilities with him, which are more than he can really take care of. He hopes to push his departure to Batavia as much as possible into the future. I often feel pity for him and don't think that taking care of 30 women, among which are a number of blockheads, is much pleasure. Write to him and also ask the others to do so. You won't believe the problems he has had in caring for us! At some future time he may be able to tell you about it. We are grateful for every day he will be here yet."

Alfred, still writing from Premnagar on October 10, 1946, reported that he received Gertrud's letter #32 and Christa's letter, of which he thought that "every good spirit in Medan must have been drafted into service for its composition. I doubt that it brings anything to respond to it, since I expect us to be repatriated by next month. It seems that 'normal' mail takes six weeks to get to you. I learned that one of my colleague's request for return to the Indonesian Church has been declined, something de Kleine will find interesting. I wrote to him already that I think our return there to be rather difficult, from what I've heard from Holland, Barmen, and you. Much must happen until some bridges can be rebuilt. In the meantime, I'm looking forward to seeing you at home, as hard as living there may be. And there will always be work for us."

Gertrud wrote to Alfred on October 12 in #35, of their excitement at the Salvation Army after they had been told that they were to leave for Germany in November – and that with the Dehradun internees. The Germans still in Padang are to come shortly. All kinds of forms had to be completed; then it was said that a ship would arrive on November 15 which, stopping at Calcutta, was to pick up the men for a common trip home. "We were all unable to sleep. Imagine – we will see each other in six to eight weeks! We all talk about seeing each other again in all kinds of variations. Some of us women have claimed already a smoke stack behind which they want to welcome their beloved husband. Mrs. Müller even said that she'd need two stacks next to each other, and even those would not be enough, should her 'better half' have acquired a like circumference. But enough jesting – one must imagine the feelings of joy, the past suffering and need. The children's joy is precious to observe. 'Mother, is father like uncle Heinrich?' Michel asks at times. He has become so comfortable with de Kleine that he finds it magnificent to sit on Heinrich's lap to hear and to tell stories. Heinrich and Major Davis are the prototypes of fathers for the children. The moment Davis shows up in our yard, the little ones come shooting from every door and window, trying to catch hold of a piece of his uniform. He's like the Pied Piper of Hamelin. Unfortunately, he will leave on the 24th of this month. We are so very grateful to him. He is an unassuming but very fine human being. He intends to visit you, but will he still catch you? How many more letters will I write yet, and which will be the last?"

"My dear Traudele," Alfred wrote once more from Premnagar on October 21. "I'm glad you agree to my plans. Once your departure is certain, there is no use writing to you any more, and I will do so through de Kleine. I was touched and delighted by what you've written about him." And still there was uncertainty about the time of departure on both sides.

Gertrud notified Alfred on October 22 that her ship would leave Batavia by mid-November, after picking up the Germans there. It was expected to arrive in Padang around the 20th. By month's end, they expected to arrive in Calcutta to pick up the men.

"Farewell parties and other obligations pile up during these weeks," Gertrud wrote on October 27, "that it gets to be almost too much. Last week we bid Major Davis, our children's friend, goodbye. A few days from now the chief of this house, Brigadier Meyer, who is returning to Holland, will be given his farewell. Then, on Saturday, there will be a church concert, in which my little chorus will take part. And not to forget, we must still prepare for our own journey home. Reports from home are shattering, with starvation apparently everywhere. And that we can expect to arrive in the middle of winter won't let me rest either."

A month later, Gertrud wrote to Germany in letter #41, "My dear Alfred! 'Welcome home!' Who will be the first to shout this 'Welcome' to you? So it turned out that you hurried off before us. Who would have thought that? We take it as a sign that we will soon follow. We still don't have a certain date. On the 20th, the Padang people were brought to Onrust, where they are to board, joining the Java-Germans. We hope it will not be our fate to be taken there. My thoughts search for you somewhere on the ocean, wherever you may be. Could it be too late to send a letter to Port Said? Anyway, I'll give it a try. We just learned that 1,100 men are on board the 'Sloterdayk.' Since you registered for the first transport, you may very well be on board this ship. Who knows now where we will meet? In any case, I have registered us for staying at Kaiserswerth. It would be marvelous if you could obtain warm clothing for the children. Much of their clothing has become too small and is difficult to replace. I will make do myself, and by the time we arrive, it won't be too long for spring to come. December 1 has come and we are still here. This is as far as I made it on Sunday. We had rather restless days and nights and experienced a little of what our loved-ones at home suffered these years. Since yesterday noon the guns on both sides here, the Dutch and the Resistance, have fallen silent again. Peace for us!

207

"Might you be home by Christmas?" Gertrud wrote. "It feels odd not knowing where to seek you in my mind, whether in Premnagar, in Calcutta, in Bombay, on the ocean, or already in Germany? I received a letter from mother telling me that she may have to vacate her apartment for occupation troops, and that I would need to find shelter with the Conradis to share there a room with Lisbeth. I find this terrible, with aunt Ria's house already more than full. I wish you a blessed Christmas and despite the problems, a joyful return home.

"My dear Alfred! When this letter, which I wrote on December 8, gets into your hands, you will have long since arrived home. Where will you be and what all will you have found? My heart is restless since the bridge between Premnagar and Medan was broken and the one to Germany hasn't been established yet. But your response is unlikely to reach us still in Medan. There's still talk that we shall leave by mid-December, but we don't believe anything anymore, only after we've boarded a ship."

A week later Gertrud sent a letter for Alfred to the Barmen Mission House, saying: "We learned from Holland of Alfred's ship's arrival in Kiel, where the men are to be processed, then to be sent on to their final destinations. What a feeling it must have been to be free again after seven years of internment! Our departure has now been pushed back by two months, supposedly because the Germans at Serangan have difficulties leaving. However, it is not known whether they don't really want to stay. Christa hasn't digested yet that you are already in Germany. She still prays evenings for us to travel together to Germany, that the peoples of the world have enough to eat, and all soldiers and fathers may return to their loved-ones.

"Christmas lies behind us, my dear Alfred," Gertrud wrote on December 29, 1946. It was somewhat difficult to prepare for the holiday, but in the end we found something for the children. At Holy Night, I had terribly much to do with cooking dinner for imprisoned Bataks, Japanese and Europeans. This enabled de Kleine to bring a little Christmas joy to these people. He delivered each little parcel personally to the prisoners with many touching scenes taking place. De Kleine is tireless in his kindness to bring some light into darkness, especially when dealing with Bataks. It almost looks as if he wants to make up for the years when this wasn't possible for him.

"I received a moving letter from mother, describing how, for an entire week, she collected beechnuts. She could get about 13 pounds into a bottle. I picture her tirelessly bending down in the forest to gather these many pounds. I could cry over it! She will be able to stay in her apartment, and the rooms she had rented to Prof. Hopf and his wife will become free on November 1. She hopes to be able to keep them available for either Else or us. Should Else move in with mother, since her family's house was destroyed, then this is okay with me. Barmen will have a nook for us. I learned that you arrived already on the 3rd of December in Germany, and I'm now eagerly awaiting your letters."

Wiesbaden-Biebrich, January 12, 1947, it was when Alfred sent his first letter to Gertrud, still stuck in Medan. It was a long one! In it, Alfred wrote, "coming from Kaiserswerth, I landed with all my luggage at mother's place. It may take weeks for me to get permission to move in with her. My first attempts at making some purchases have failed. You don't believe how poor Germany has become! It is cold here, which is why I'm presently trying to get some firewood. By March it should be better, and we are glad you will miss the cold. When I returned home yesterday from the city, I found two letters from you, those from November 24 and December 8. It is good that I arrived before you; this way I can spare you many unnecessary tasks. In my talk with Heinz, we agreed that he and Else will move to Kaiserswerth, while we stay with mother. Last night I read to mother from some of your letters I had received in Dehradun. In this way she learned more of your situation than from my many words. The two of us have made ourselves a comfortable and harmonious life, only you are missing for it to be perfect. Sitting together, mother and I make plans for when all of us will be together."

He elaborated on his various visits with relatives and their well-being. Among them, Hans, who returned sick and debilitated from imprisonment in Russia, but good care pepped him up and he will resume work in his profession. Friedchen and Heinrich (not de Kleines) were lucky enough to have their cozy home spared through the bombings and succeeded in reestablishing their business. Alfred's sister Emma suffered most in the chaos of war, but remained her old self. Except for her, none of the relatives lost their houses in the bombing, sparing them the worst.

"We learned through Friedchen de Kleine that you have arrived in Germany," Gertrud wrote on January 7, 1947 to W.-Biebrich. Upon her arrival, Friedchen was shocked by what she found in Germany. "We are doing fine here in Medan and are now outside the danger zone of military activity, except that the resistance movement cut off Medan's water supply as a New Year's present. Not that this troubles us, since we have a well and pump in the central yard, only that the water must now be boiled. I'm now waiting for your first letter from home."

Five days later, Gertrud wrote in her #45: "There's still no mail from you. As long as this is not the case, there cannot be any contact of the mind. My heart searches for you but doesn't know where. How may you be faring in our ruined home country, where thousands may daily die of starvation or freeze to death. What we read in the newspapers is devastating. I received a letter from mother, dating from October 18. Might she have found some firewood by now? Was mother able to hold her apartment for us? And has Else come home or is she still in Japan? The children are able to go to school again. Letters we received from Onrust have calmed us; the situation there appears to have turned for the better, especially their food supply. Only the isolation and lack of activities makes waiting hard. All the Germans from Surabaya, or those calling themselves that, have already arrived and those from Semarang are expected shortly. Things seem to be moving.

"Heinrich de Kleine sends his greetings. He is extremely busy and looks into every dive for Batak Christians. And he's so happy for every new contact he can make. The Mission Consul has put him on the evacuation list, although he did not ask for it and has no intention for leaving. It appears the 'higher powers' want to get rid of him, possibly because he is so active."

In January 1947, Martha wrote from W.-Biebrich, apologizing for not writing earlier because she and Alfred expected Gertrud and the children to be already on the way home. She assured the children that their beds were made and that hot water bottles to warm them were ready, because it was so cold in Germany. Heinz visited for a day and informed them that Else, when she arrives with their two daughters, could live in Kaiserswerth. He hoped to find work with his former employer in that region. "I was so happy when my renters suddenly decided to move to Nuremberg, which freed the rooms for you. It will be

210

tight with you five, but thousands are living even tighter these days. I will be glad to have you here; it was lonely since father passed away."

Shortly thereafter, Alfred wrote of his distrust of the information that Gertrud was to arrive by mid-February. "I will therefore continue writing letters to you, even if they no longer reach you. After our Sunday service, we retreated to mother's room and made ourselves comfortable. Our firewood will last only for half a day and one room. I ventured into the woods yesterday in search of firewood and enjoyed working in the clear winter air of the Taunus mountains. [Imagine that whatever firewood he was able to collect on his outings had to be transported home for several miles – by bicycle!] You may recall our hikes in the Taunus at the time of our engagement. Fortunately, the house mother lives in was not bombed, except that some window panes still need replacement. I use my plentiful free time to gather firewood, it being the basis of our mutual life. Before I came, its lack made life difficult for mother, who, at times, had to find refuge with strangers in order not to be cold."

"There's still no letter of yours, my beloved Alfred," Gertrud wrote on the very same day he was penning his letter to her. She expressed her concern for sufficient clothing, should they arrive during the winter, and mentioned that some of the children's clothing had been outgrown already twice in the course of their wait. "In some cases I have made one from two pieces, but once those are too small, it will mean the end."

"And still no mail on January 28," Gertrud moaned. "It seems just about every one of my recent letters began with my expression of this regret. Did you receive some of mine? I received two postcards from Else who mentioned their lack of heating material and woolen clothing in Japan. She has not heard anything about their repatriation, only that 1,200 people are waiting."

Still, no mail had arrived for Gertrud in Medan. On February 2, she wrote that another woman received her husband's fourth letter via Holland. "Why don't you also write using this route? Others, too, have written. Why not you? Where are you?"

211

Martha wrote on February 9th, that they would try sending their letters via Friedchen de Kleine in Holland. "Did you receive word from Alfred that we are comfortable here and are only waiting for your arrival. Thank you very much for your parcel! I just hope that you did not spare this from your own food. So far, we have had enough to eat, even if it isn't as plentiful as in earlier times. You pitied me for my beechnut collecting. But that's not necessary. Indeed, it was cumbersome, but also nice in the woods. I went there daily with Mrs. Dr. Hopf and enjoyed our wonderful German forest. We each sat on an old sofa pillow, then slid on the ground around the beech trees. Next year, God willing, we will all go, including myself. On a sunny, mild day, Alfred was able to get another load of wood from the forest."

Alfred wrote from W.-Biebrich that he just returned from a conference in Kaiserswerth, and that he made some contacts to facilitate access to his future area of work in the French-occupied zone, the synods Nastätten, Usingen, Selters, Wied, etc. "This is why I can only now respond to your three letters of December 15 and 29, as well as January 1, 1947. Opening your parcel was troubling, when we found all the good things you took from yourself to send us. It would have been better had you eaten them yourself. We manage here, although fat, sugar, potatoes and vegetables are hard to come by. By the time you arrive, it will soon turn summer. Today, I paid Bishop Kortheuer a visit and with his blessing will soon be able to travel to the various parishes neglected by the Rheinische Missionsgesellschaft."

Gertrud's postcard, dated February 16, said, "rumors of our repatriation are increasing. But there's still no word from you! You men may now have gathered in Kaiserswerth, and I'm wondering what all you will produce there. Bring a bit of life into the Society; it seems to have become rather ponderous. Our Mission group is still waiting to receive the first letter from Barmen, a sorry experience when one expects seeing the place again."

Again, Gertrud expressed her disappointment on February 23 for not receiving any mail from her husband, thinking that he had not written in the belief that they had left Sumatra. The wait without any news from home was terrible. "But how hard it must be for the people in Onrust, who, separated from the world, live in barracks without furnishings, even beds, and are poorly supplied. How much longer will it take?"

A week later, Gertrud wrote to her 'dear Alfred' that she was taking care of one of the sick women, one of many, who were at the end of their rope, health-wise, induced in large part by the uncertainty of waiting. "A few letters of husbands have arrived, but none from you. What do you say about your oldest's drawing? She is becoming quite good. A couple of times, I have been able to go to the movies with de Kleine which was a nice change in our monotonous life. Otherwise, I spend my time reading books, magazines and newspapers. If I had a piano, I would love to play. Occupying myself with music, be it playing an instrument or with my little chorus, has helped me to maintain my equilibrium. It is therefore too bad that our singing has largely gone to sleep.

"A few days ago, I experienced great joy. A Batak soldier had addressed de Kleine on the street and, in the course of the conversations, asked, 'Ai dison do si Christa?' A pleasant, fresh face, he visited us the following evening, all spruced up in a Dutch uniform. It was Togar, the youngest son of Manga Raja Hoeria, who is no longer alive. He became a soldier in May of 1940 and was interned on Borneo by the Japanese. He's now here for additional training. For four years he did not hear anything from his relatives, and even now must pay extreme caution trying to contact his people. Should the 'Extremists,' "as Gertrud called the Independence Fighters, "learn that he is with the Dutch military, they would make his relatives suffer for it. These are the problems many are exposed to and the majority of the population would be happy if the Dutch would put an end to this situation. Togar was a reminder of old times; I very much enjoyed his visit. He sat with us for a long time and promised to come again. De Kleine is always so very happy for the trust these fellows extend him, making him feel as if seven years have not passed for nothing. He does whatever he can for these people, and may yet become well-known across Medan for his activities. Enough now. Should you be at home, greet everybody. Always, your Traut."

"We are so sad to learn from your postcard that you aren't getting any mail from us and that your repatriation drags on," Alfred wrote on March 2. "We did write regularly, but somehow our mail seems to get hung up somewhere. I did send a letter by way of Friedchen de Kleine in Holland, and hope you will receive it. We are preparing more and more for your arrival. A bed has been set up for you in the living room, while I sleep on the couch. The children will sleep next door in lent beds, eventually we hope to get our own. I have so far been unsuccessful in finding blankets and clothing for the children. Mother will retain her little room. The kitchen is terribly cramped, but it will have to do. I have not been able to find any clothing for myself and was lucky to obtain enough in India. For the end of March I was promised a pot, a bucket, and a dish. We will need to improvise until things get better. I finally received my residency permit and am now a proper resident of Wiesbaden."

In a March letter – waiting now for three months – Gertrud once more expressed her disappointment at not receiving mail from her husband and the continuing delay of her repatriation. Continuing it a few days later, she wondered whether to put her earlier outpouring into the mails, but then decided, "read it and make of it what you want. But I'm not going to continue writing in this way. At Onrust, the women have received mail from their husbands, Mrs. Meyer five times. I wonder whether you know already the area of your future activity, Alfred? I hope it will not be in a city but in beautiful countryside. I will need the woods, fields and meadows to recover in body and soul. My longing is so great, I could cry."

Martha wrote on March 9, expressing her regret that no mail had reached Gertrud, to learn about the kind of nest she will land in with her three chicks. "Many people on our street sympathize with your situation and keep asking about you."

Alfred added to her letter, writing, "there's still plenty of snow and it is cold. Yesterday, I walked in the Taunus for hours through heavy snow imagining how it would be when we can do this together. On the way home I found some cattails and picked them, imagining they had been given to me as a welcome bouquet for you. That evening I was engrossed in 'welcoming joy.' Mother had put an old photo of yours on the table, which I hadn't seen for years. It appeared to me as if it had been taken only yesterday. It is well that I'm beginning to work properly, preventing my feelings from overcoming me. I can imagine how you must feel, seeing home before your eyes, yet having to wait and wait. Winter, the cold, keeps us at a distance, reminding us too much of that which has been. We must think more of that which is to come – spring. This past week we ran out of wood, but new firewood arrived meanwhile. We make plenty of plans – light, airy structures. If they collapse, it won't hurt. We simple build new ones, you know, like children in a sandbox. I watch the birds in the woods, who, despite the cold, fly happily about, and must make do with what they find.

"No mail from you this week. I feel as if a telegram could come at any moment, telling that you are on your way. Don't worry about mother at her age. The past years have been hard; she had to walk and work a lot, which has steeled her. She is in better health than she was on Sumatra. My thoughts long for you. Your Alfred."

Another long letter of Alfred's in March to his beloved Traut, told that he would send it via Friedchen de Kleine in Holland. Yesterday, he learned from Friedchen that Gertrud's departure was again pushed back by several months. "Maybe you know already that I have found shelter with mother and that you and the children will do so, too. It will be cramped, but you aren't spoiled and being close together will keep us warm. I have found work here in the Rhineland and Hesse which also determined my place of residence. We have only two rooms, maybe we can rent another nearby in the future. As long as you aren't here, nothing of the kind will be possible, since all housing is controlled with everyone receiving only limited space. There's nothing available for purchase, not even a nail to hang a picture to a wall. And not a thought can be expended on clothing and blankets; household utensils are unavailable. There are no spices except salt, the only one freely available. Cinnamon is a word in the dictionary. Other foodstuffs are dear, especially fat and sugar. And whatever rations have been assigned us are just on paper; only a part becomes available."

"My dear Alfred," Gertrud rejoiced on March 16, "finally, I received mail from you, three letters at one time, one of yours from January from Kaiserswerth, another which came via Holland, and one from mother. They revived me! You would not believe how far my soul ventured through the world, not finding rest. Now I can imagine you sitting in mother's kitchen, cutting wood, how you travel about to return cold to the bone. And it will be wonderful to be able to live with mother once we are there.

"I cannot quite imagine your work. A traveling pastor? Theological 'gofer'? As far as I can recall, church life in the Taunus area was rather lethargic and there was not a trace of interest in the Mission. Did this change? Do you enjoy your work? Although your work is different, I wish for you the same joy and dedication I see here in Heinrich de Kleine." Gertrud then elaborated at great length about the H.K.B.P., the Batak Church.

The very same day Gertrud, still in Medan, wrote to her husband in W.-Biebrich, he penned a letter to her, saying that in the past week a postcard and her letter of February 23, arrived. "It was music to my ears, together with the amsels singing now, promising an end to winter. But whatever I hear, your return will drag on for some time. Let us remain tough to survive this final test." Alfred then entered into a lengthy discourse on how to make it through the dire times, once his family would arrive in devastated Germany. He then voiced a personal request, that is, to bring some of the delicious Sumatra cinnamon he so sorely missed. A family relative visiting requested that he perform some services at nearby villages. With another visitor Alfred discussed a possible employment for Heinz Otto, hopefully before his wife Else arrived from Japan. A ship from there was thought to be on its way. There were few trains moving in Germany, all of which were full to the hilt, and travel on fast trains was possible only with a special permit. A similar situation existed with buses and street cars. Travel in Germany was difficult these days and was often restricted to the use of his bicycle. "Please keep notes of whatever is happening to the Batak Church to provide me with reliable information when you return," his letter ended.

Alfred wrote again at the end of March of his travels and visits with various friends. He reported that he was able to make some provisions for Else's return, expected to arrive this month, her husband presently staying with them in W.-Biebrich. "This afternoon Heinz and I were out on a botanical excursion in search of wild vegetables and healing herbs, of which plenty are growing in the Wiesbaden area. Nature is alive once more, the trees are in full bloom, and a number of plants have become available. We brought some Scharbockskraut home, which made for an excellent salad for our evening meal. I will be off on another trip through the Taunus in preparation for my future work there. It will mean also a trip into the fresh greenery of the new year, where I will find the wonders of nature again. It is too bad that you will be unable to experience spring. And, I'm happy to say, that, by now, I feel at home here; it's only the oppressive crowding I still must get used to.

"Your extensive report on the H.K.B.P. Church pleased me very much, as you can imagine. Aside from personal matters, we are lacking information on the real life of the Church, whatever progress or backward steps have happened is what people want to know on my travels. One good thing – with the warmer weather we can now live in the entire apartment and are no longer so cramped. Unfortunately, the supply of foodstuffs has become worse. We can only hope for betterment with God being in command. Always, your Alfred."

One day after Alfred's letter, a long letter of Christa's went out to her father in Germany.

"Beloved Traut," Alfred wrote again in March, "I'm thinking of your birthday – so close. Spring shows signs everywhere with blooms and sprouts. A ship from Japan is to arrive on April 1 in Bremerhaven; maybe Else will be on it. It is well that you don't arrive together since there would neither be enough space nor beds, nor sheets. And nothing is available for purchase. Last night there was a break-in at our house, but only an ax was stolen; there was nothing else to take. The owner of the house has a dog, which, today, however, doesn't mean much. This is already the fourth break-in at this house since the end of the war on May 8, 1945. It is that the 'big' guys steal big, while the little ones steal small. They are eager students and learn more every day. God's rules are scorned, and ethical standards apply only to others. Claims with the police are useless.

"Through Easter I will be away for some services in Oberkriftel as a substitute for uncle Wilhelm. We have planned some other short trips, visits with relatives. I miss hearing more from the children. Tell them about our home in Germany, and, I promise, when they are here, I will try to pay off all my debts. Please collect literature about the Batak lands, for instance the Batak adat and also Batak sayings. It's just too bad that all my documents were lost. I can't just rely on my memory for these things."

In a brief note on March 30, Gertrud mentioned how much she missed being able to play and hear music, and wondered whether she would be able to join some kind of chorus once in W.-Biebrich. That same day Alfred wrote about his visit to a Lutheran church where various Bach pieces, including some chorus works were performed. "On Good Friday the Johannes

Passion by J. v. Burck will be performed, to which I will go. We have definitely not fallen short on spiritual assets and enjoyments. Volmer and Tiemeyer have invited me to visit them in the Ravensburg Land, intending to improve our supply of foodstuffs a little. Thereafter, my travels to the Westerwald and Rhine areas will begin, because of which you won't find me that much at home. It is a widespread area with travel made difficult because of the poor means of travel and having to cross occupation zones. My services will cover the synods Wied, Selters, Nastätten, Nassau and Usingen. Barmen has been in contact with Holland and America concerning your repatriation; it isn't as if nothing is being tried here. I am deeply sorry that you have still no mail from me. I have written regularly and hope to have found the proper routing now."

"The day before yesterday, my dear Traut," Alfred wrote, "your letter dated March 16 arrived with the happy note that you, finally, received some mail from us, apparently by my new routing. Heinz will visit us tomorrow, and we hope for Else's arrival. 250 women and 350 children are supposed to have arrived in Bremerhaven. Hopefully, we will not be disappointed! Thank you for Ute's photo. The child looks awfully thin, and it will take some calories to get her proper human form back. Tiemeyer and Vollmer expect to have some carrots, potatoes and peas, they were able to garner for me. Even the smallest quantity of vegetables must be fetched from far away. Eat whatever you can before you get here so that you do not arrive half starved. Bring whatever you have in the way of bed sheets; I'm unable to obtain any. My entry here in Nassau is difficult. The parishes are not very alive, a hinterland of the Baseler Mission. It is uncertain what I can accomplish there for the Rheinische Mission. Spring has come full force, yesterday with a mighty storm. Shortly, everything will be in full bloom."

Martha told her daughter on April 20, how much she enjoyed Alfred's presence, and that she thought her son-in-law matured in the seven years of internment, and that Gertrud should look forward to meeting him again. "Heinz is staying with us, and while his family did not arrive with the first ship, we hope that Else, Renate and Irmgard will arrive with the next boat in about ten days, which left Japan the middle of March."

"My dear Alfred," Gertrud wrote, still in Medan, on April 20. "I received four letters from home, all written in March. You won't believe how good this feels. I'm shocked about all the problems you describe, even having to borrow beds. I have eight woolen blankets, which I will try to bring. And I have three good cooking pots, a dish, and some silverware. I just hope these items will not get lost on the way. I was sorry to learn that Else and her children did not make it on the first ship. The money for it was provided by the Swiss government. I'm happy to learn that mother is doing so well. We received another circular letter from Vedder in Africa, something he does regularly. In this way we learn a little of what's going on in Barmen. Bos, a good-natured fellow, arrived last week. He is a man, whom Heinrich, the rational one, can trust unconditionally. The two complement each other. Both traveled this past week to the outermost front, even some distance into the opposite camp, where they met 40-50 Batak soldiers from just about everywhere. They talked with them, heard them out, and finally left, having been told that the men would check with Colonel Sarumpait in Siantar whether Bos and de Kleine would be allowed to conduct Sunday service at the border. Should that become possible, it would constitute a mighty break in Batak land." Gertrud continued reporting more on Bos's ventures and successes in the course of his mission. Christa added her lengthy report on events at school.

On May 5, Alfred reported to Gertrud that his ability to write was becoming more difficult due to his travels. "I received a Good Friday greeting from you and Ute, but mail from you was meager these past weeks. It was better in India. I wonder whether I shouldn't wish myself back there, where I had more free time. Just now, your letter from April 20th arrived. How glad I am! But I think the worst time is yet to come here. Our food supply has deteriorated to 1000 grams of bread per week and 50 grams of fat. Since being in Germany, we never got any fresh potatoes and only once half a pound of vegetables.

"Tomorrow, I will head out to the Neuwied synod, which I'm looking forward to. There's plenty of work in Germany, but not enough to eat. Twice now, I have been offered work; once by bishop Kortheuer with the Nassau Church, another to enter the Nassau Gemeinschaftsverband. I declined both offers since my path with the Mission is still open. In one of your letters you asked whether mother still has her sewing machine. She does, but no yarn; that you'd have to bring. Something like this is unavailable in Germany."

It was the 11th of May in Medan, from where Gertrud wrote: "It is now a full seven years that we have been separated. And what now? I still don't see an end for it. Nothing is happening! It truly seems to be a problem with the British occupation authority which does not permit entry into Germany. However, the Germans from Suriname have supposedly arrived in Holland, but aren't allowed to enter Germany. Should that be the case, it is better we wait here, than to be stuck in Holland. This morning, Bos held a nice service in German. I was surprised how good his German still is, totally without accent. He feels very much at home in our circle, just like a family father. De Kleine is traveling and may stop in Padang to check for books and documents of German owners and property of the Rhenish Mission."

"Yesterday, on May 17, we received a telegram from Friedchen de Kleine that you will depart on June 5," Martha wrote, while Alfred was traveling. "Let's hope it is true. This may very well be the last letter you will receive, though we will send another, just in case. And how much I am looking forward to have you all here with me! I still have some clothing of father's, even some woolen material, and have already knitted a pair of children's stockings, except for the heels, since I'm not sure of what length the socks must be. Alfred helps me a lot. You ought to see him doing dishes, carrying firewood, and cleaning the kitchen. We worked hard the other day, getting eight hundredweight of heavy firewood from the coal merchant. Alfred will begin sawing it tomorrow and split it. For the time being, his occupation is thus quite different from what it was on Sumatra. But he looks fine and is doing well. Greetings from your Oma."

"We came a step closer to home," Gertrud wrote on May 18, 1947. "De Kleine sent a telegram that our departure is scheduled for some time between the 5th and 10th of June – but likely later. We had the date confirmed locally, but it is as yet unknown whether we can board in Belawan or must travel via Batavia. Is Else already with you? How very nice that would be! We will experience some restless weeks until our boarding. It's just too bad that we have so little money to purchase a few things. Just about everything can be had, if one has money. I will try to bring whatever possible, like coffee, tea, tobacco, etc., but it will be limited by our luggage restrictions. We will see the local administration tomorrow and try to obtain new papers, such as marriage certificates and birth certificates for the children. The originals are supposedly held in Batavia; maybe we will get them some time later."

Ute added to the letter by writing, "I barely ever play with dolls anymore, but climb trees every day. I find good fruit up there. I stay up there until Mutti calls me. Then we go to the spring to fetch water. Nearby flows a river, where mother lets us bathe at times. There is a place where the river is very deep. Michel is afraid of the deep. Yesterday, the river was especially deep, which is why we were unable to bathe; where it was earlier only 8 inches (20 cm) deep, it now went up to my hips. I hope we will soon be with you."

On May 18, 1947, Martha sent one more letter, telling her grandchildren to watch what they are going to see on their long trip home, so that they could tell about it. "Look at the port cities and watch out for flying fish. Father will pick you up at the railway station in Wiesbaden, and I will be very happy to greet you. You will marvel about how nice it is in Germany, where everything is fresh and green, birds are singing and flowers are blooming. But hold Sumatra dear in your hearts, because it, too, is your home. There will be a big school for you where you can make many friends."

"You two dear old ones!" Gertrud began her final letter from Medan on June 4, 1947, "Sunday is almost gone and I must hurry if this letter is to leave in time. I received Alfred's letters of March 12 and before that, one dated April 4. We are living in great suspense with the rumors of our departure increasing daily. But nothing's been said yet officially. Will it still be this month? De Kleine is off to Batavia again to another conference but will try to be back as soon as possible in case we are leaving. There are plenty of things to prepare for, among which is Bos's and de Kleine's move to new quarters, at which we are helping. The church and pastor's house have been freshly whitewashed, inside and out, and look pretty again. But de Kleine will miss his 'family' once we are gone. Bos finds good acceptance everywhere, especially with the Bataks. He just isn't as well known as Heinrich de Kleine and must gain the trust of the people yet. But with his excellent Batak and his comfy, folksy ways, he is quickly accepted by them. De Kleine returned today from a prison visit, where a newcomer hugged him, crying bitterly – a boy from Sidempuan, where he once went to school with de

Kleine. He suffers terribly from homesickness. It was a Wiedersehen with the boy, now a political prisoner! And there is more. De Kleine experiences many pleasant things, but has had to swallow many a bitter pill, too. Just to let you know: The Lutheran Church is to take over the areas of Sumatra and Nias; the bishop would prefer to get only those people who are familiar with the land and the people and speak the language. Thus, you may not believe it, but 'my two men' want to keep me here until you come! I received a telegram from Friedchen de Kleine that she wasn't allowed to stay in Germany with her folks, but had to return to Holland. Heinrich is distraught; while, at first, he wanted her to stay in Holland, he would now prefer her to remain in Germany. Now they must change everything again. The children might be better off in Holland, although they will always feel like strangers there and feel more at home in Germany. Yes, it is a problem to belong externally here and internally there! May God take care of you. I hope we will soon see each other. Your Gertrud."

And at last it came true, Gertrud and her children boarded a ship in June of 1947. The ship arrived in Rotterdam from where the returnees were transported in railroad freight cars to Neuengamme camp near Hamburg, where they arrived on July 7, 1947. Four days later, on July 11, they were released from the camp.

Reunited in Germany 1947
Ute, Michael, Dorothea, and Christa

Returned to Germany

Ute's recollection is that her father picked up the family at Neuengamme camp for the railroad trip to Wiesbaden. Another of Ute's recollections is that she was ready to return to Sumatra, after seeing the destruction that had been wrought on Germany's cities. They took a bus from the railroad station to the house on Dotzheimer street no. 52 in Wiesbaden-Biebrich, where the family spent the next nine years.

The house had three floors. The ground floor was occupied by the owners of the property, the Rossels. The second floor, consisting of three rooms and a small kitchen, became the Rutkowskys' domicile. One room was assigned to Oma Weissenbruch, the living room served also as bedroom for the parents, and also held a desk for Alfred's work. The third room, with some partitioning by a wardrobe, became the bedroom for Christa, Ute and Michael. With little heating material available, Ute recalls how cold their bedroom became in winter.

While the family settled in and the children were registered at school, Alfred pursued his task of visiting various parishes for religious services and presentations, and whenever possible, the acquisition of foodstuffs and heating material. With the crowded public transportation system unreliable, a bicycle was the prime mode of transportation of man and goods over short and not so short distances.

The Rossels' property included a large garden with numerous fruit trees. At times, when in season, some fallen fruit became available to the Rutkowskys. A small garden plot helped them grow some vegetables. Several nurseries in the vicinity, in the postwar years dedicated to growing vegetables, also provided 'reject' vegetables and lettuce; the better quality produce was diverted into official channels.

Ute recalls that money was scarce, just as foodstuffs were, and the family had to make do with a minimum for several years. The purchase of a pair of shoes, for instance, provided they were available for one of the family members, was a major outlay and had to be planned carefully.

Between March 15 and April 12, 1948, Alfred and Gertrud visited the Tropen-Genesungsheim in Tübingen. The diagnosis for Alfred was:

"Multiple exposure to amebic dysentery prior to his internment in 1940. No exposure to malaria. During his internment at Dehradun, he experienced several bouts of bacterial dysentery. Otherwise, he had not been ill. Between 1935-37, Gertrud was afflicted by some light sprue which was cured through proper diet. During the same period she also suffered from some amebic dysentery. She never had malaria either. During her time of internment she was never seriously ill, only suffered from headaches, dizziness, and weakness. Except for the latter condition, Gertrud was healthy, with no indication of any tropical disease." None of the children was tested at the institute.

Of the three children, Ute was in the most fragile health, afflicted by hook worms, for which she was treated. Through efforts of the Barmer Mission, she was able to spend three summer months on the farm of a Swiss family in 1948. This greatly appreciated, beneficial stay was repeated the following year, when Christa and Michael also benefited from such a respite.

On November 21, 1948, Gertrud gave birth to a daughter, whom the couple called Dorothea , nicknamed Dörthe. To accommodate this fourth child, a room on the third floor of the house was made available for the family, which became Christa's, the oldest, now 14 years of age.

Alfred became more and more engaged in his work, which now included conferences at the Mission in Barmen, taking him away from home for weeks. In a letter he wrote on February 19, 1950 to his "Beloved Traut," he 'confessed' to his long absences, leaving her alone for long stretches at a time. The territory he covered had also been increased, but at least some travel by car became possible, even if only as a passenger. Eventually, in 1952, Alfred obtained the use of a business vehicle, a Volkswagen Beetle. Ute was by now attending Middle School in Biebrich, where she had made friends, among them Gerda Michels, a cousin of the author. The Michels' household in Amöneburg, a suburb of Wiesbaden, provided a gathering place for an age cohort consisting of Gerda, her one year older sister, Liesel, and her two-year-older brother Fritz, Ute, and myself. In 1952 Ute and I were both 15 years of age and may have met there for the first time. In the years to come, boyfriends of Gerda and Liesel joined the group for occasional outings, dances and sing-alongs at the Michels.

Spring of 1953 brought Michael's performance troubles at school to a head. In early 1954 Christa was also falling behind in school. But by Fall Gertrud had acquired a piano to play her beloved music. Her playing and the children's noisiness, together with the pickiness of the landlords downstairs, made for an unpleasant relationship. An attempt in early 1954 to obtain a larger apartment came to naught.

In April of 1954 Alfred, with twenty-five others, attended a 14-day long conference in Büsum on the North Sea coast; most participants were from the Barmen and Basel Missions. The conference rooms, as well as their accommodations, were extremely limited in space. Alfred found the subject matters presented at the conference somewhat shallow, but said also, "maybe I am a bit too demanding." He remarked about the well-supplied dinner table, an indication that living standards had improved. He inquired about Michel's left foot, which had become afflicted with bone tuberculosis and was in a cast. Responding in a letter, Gertrud wrote that Alfred's youngest daughter, Dörthe, now five years old, had picked the first nettles of the season, making for some inexpensive vegetable in their diet.

At the end of May 1954 Alfred was tending the household for awhile, while Gertrud was away for a vacation in Runkel by the Lahn River. A vacation for Oma Weissenbruch was also in the works. To lessen Gertrud's work load a washing machine was under consideration for purchase. Christa was working at a PX, a store for American military personnel, and as a baby sitter. In his June 1 letter, Alfred told Gertrud that Christa had received her first wages, 100 deutschmarks, most of which he was going to put into a savings account for her. And, she had a boyfriend!

Michel had been hospitalized in Herborn for his leg ailment, where Alfred visited him at the end of October 1954. Following her graduation from Middle school, preparations were made in January 1955 for Ute to go to Königstein after Easter to the Dr. Amelung Clinic, for her training as a dietitian's assistant, where she stayed until March 1956. A month later, Ute got a surprise when she answered a knock at the door, finding Michel standing before her. He had been released from treatment in Herborn and simply taken a train to get home. But it would take another year for his full recovery. Having missed months of school, the question was now in what grade to put him.

In a letter to her traveling husband, there is a telling remark of Gertrud's: "It would be time for you to show up again!" – an expression of her feeling of 'abandonment.' Ute recalled that, when her father, called Vati, showed up at home, it was usually for just a few days. Then, clothing had to be washed and all sorts of business, like running a household, had to be discussed. Often, these brief visits ended on a sour note. Not that Alfred enjoyed his constant traveling for services and slide presentations, spending just about every night in a different bed! He was now often traveling with his VW Beetle and, it being winter, he frequently got stuck on the road when entering remoter, higher elevation areas, and where then poor footgear got him wet and cold feet.

Times were achanging when, in a letter dated June 3, 1955, Heinrich de Kleine, now Mission Director in Barmen, wrote that Brother Verwiebe, who was to go to Siantar on Sumatra to teach Old Testament at the theological seminary, was found too ill by his doctor to travel. De Kleine asked Alfred whether he would be prepared to take this teaching post, and to conduct refresher courses for panditas. A visitor's visa, good for three months, would readily be available and could be renewed locally. De Kleine had discussed it with the Mission's directorship and suggested that this experience, temporary, of course, would also benefit Alfred's activities in Germany upon his return. "But are you willing to accept this temporary separation from your dear wife and children? No one can help you there; you must decide yourself and discuss it with your wife. I, personally, would be glad if you would find the joy to say "yes" to this call. I know that your name has been mentioned several times in Sumatra. This trust, expressed by our Batak Brothers is a great gift. I hope that this request will not complicate your plans for a new home."

Four days later, Alfred responded to "Dear Heinrich," saying: "Your letter brought no great joy to me! Your request to go to Sumatra constitutes a somewhat questionable adventure which I would not advise others to take. Added to this is that I am now 15 years away from this kind of work. You also expect me to perform a task that, with its own problematic, would not tolerate any bungling. Let me tell you also that my ideas for the coming years go in a very different direction. I asked myself very quietly, whether I could not claim an irritated pancreas, which would easily relieve me from this awkward situation. But that won't work; my glands are working well, and this task has a good 'taste.' What remains then is the imposition this adventure represents. Well, I figured you didn't ask me to go to Sumatra for this project because you considered me particularly clever, but because you did not have anyone else to ask. I also received a letter from Fritz Tiemeyer, reporting on students at the University who, after five years in attendance, had no knowledge whatsoever of the Old Testament. In short, 'much has been neglected with these people.' It gave me the impression that there's lots amiss.

"I have subsequently discussed your proposal with some knowledgeable friends, who boosted my courage to say "yes" to this mission and thus I dare to dive headfirst into the waters. I'm saying this unconditionally, but add that the entire project remains a risk and can only be executed with the very best support. I ask you to pursue the project and to implement the requirements for my departure. Tiemeyer wrote further that I would need to be available for a new course beginning at the university on Sumatra in September, which calls for an August departure. This is a very short time in which to settle much. It would be best if I paid you a visit in Barmen to discuss the situation in greater detail.

"My wife asked that the question of our housing would need to be resolved prior to my departure. Please let me also know what kind of theological literature is available in Siantar, especially of the Old Testament, for me to know what needs to be brought along. I do not know much about the Old Testament and would need to familiarize myself more deeply with the subject. To what extent is Barmen prepared to assist in this matter? Tiemeyer wrote that I am to present an exegesis of Genesis, Jesus, and Paul and, in addition Old Testament theology. How much time would be left for other subjects is difficult to see at this time."

Not quite three months later, a telegram, dated September 20, 1955, advised Alfred that his departure by ship from Rotterdam was scheduled for September 29. Two days later, a letter addressed insurance questions and the availability of photographic film, mentioning also that his cabin assignment was as yet unknown. De Kleine wrote, "I can therefore not tell you how many meters distance lie between your cabin and the ship's propeller. Anyway, it may be best if you don't know this in advance. But a man like you is able to work under just about any condition."

When the time came, Gertrud and the children, together with Heinrich de Kleine, accompanied Alfred to Rotterdam to bid him farewell.

Off again to Indonesia

At the end of February 1956 the Rheinische Mission received a letter, written by Mrs. Rossel, complaining about the unacceptable 'behavior' of the Rutkowsky family, asking for assistance in finding them a new home. While the relationship between the Weissenbruchs and the Rossels had apparently been amicable, the children's activities, etc., brought the problematic situation to a head. A polite, formal response from the Mission promised to help making an apartment exchange with some other party possible. Housing was still rationed, and nothing came of these attempts.

At this point in time the children's ages were as follows:

Christa was 22, Ute 19, Michael 17, and Dorothea 7 years old.

Following her one year training in Königstein, Ute left there at the beginning of April 1956 to attend the Dietitian School in Bad Hersfeld, where she stayed until March of 1958.

In a letter to Friedchen de Kleine, dated September 18, 1956, Gertrud poured her heart out, telling of her conflicting emotions, being torn between being a good wife to her husband versus being a good mother to her children. She wrote: "For weeks and months now, I've been grappling with the problem of separation from the children. So far, I have been unable to arrive at a positive result. I can only say that it is a bitter path, having to choose between husband and children. I am aware that my husband is prepared to remain abroad, but on the condition that I will join him and that my mother and the children are properly taken care of. In no way must the children pay the bill. Now that the Barmen Mission has made it official, I certainly hope that the question of his staying in Sumatra will soon be decided. Not only has it been stressful for me, but also for my husband. He, too, is unsure what to do and has not come to a conclusion." She quoted Alfred as saying: " 'My work here requires that I stay for some time. My responsibility to you tells me that I am a fool, should I give in to this thought. If I visualize the consequences of this decision for the family, I am at a loss of what to do!"

"Alfred and I are faced with an enormous decision, and I think that we, ourselves, are unable to arrive at one. Where is the border between the responsibility to the family and that of work? Friedchen, you won't believe how much I would enjoy to go abroad, not from curiosity or interest, no, but because I see the promise of an inner gain. But if I think of my mother and the children, I do not have as yet the courage to say 'yes.' It is an inopportune time for the children, even if we would remain a family only for at most two, maybe four years, before the two girls enter some profession. And thanks to Mrs. Rossel and our tight quarters we did not have an undisturbed family life anyway. Both are of marriageable age. Ute has a firm relationship, which we, as parents, can only support. Christa, too, has been in a relationship for some time, but neither she nor we are clear what will come of it. I therefore ask myself whether, at this critical time, it is responsible to deprive them of the backing of the parental home and to leave them on their own?

"Michel requires most the firm hand of a father or male, and I have expressed my refusal to my husband to continue being solely responsible for his education. I cannot be a substitute for a father! Were we to leave, I would try to find him a home-away-from-home with another family. He is the one who would suffer most from the separation. Since Christa would stay in the neighborhood, and Ute could spend her vacations with my sister Else, the siblings would at least, at times, be together and would not be scattered to the four winds.

"My mother would have to find accommodation at the retirement facilities at Kaiserswerth or Barmen. We are also faced with the enormous cost of this move, like rent for a room for Christa, Michel's accommodation, Oma's move, and the dissolution of the household, the storage of our furniture, which it would be foolish to sell only to have to purchase it again a few years later. How am I to deal with all this on my own? I shudder at the thought!

"And against all my concerns stands Alfred's work, with all its needs, which my husband is happy to fill. Weigh this all and then decide! Can you? I can not! If someone would tell me: 'There's no other choice; you must join him abroad!' Yes, then I would see it as God's directive and with a bleeding heart would go with joyful obedience, knowing that He would provide and that a separation might even become a blessing for the children. This is why I said that we, ourselves, cannot make this decision. It must be made by the Mission in Barmen, which must then also assume the responsibility.

"Well, Friedchen, now I've relieved my soul! And tell your husband he ought not keep me much longer on tenterhooks!"

Three months passed, when, in January 1957, Gertrud wrote a letter to Heinrich de Kleine, in which she referred to a telegram of his which, she said, was a poor substitute for the letters she was missing from her husband. She then asked, "Have you heard more from Sumatra by now? And what do you think of the telegram I received this morning, saying: 'Don't change anything. I come back. Alfred.' I'm still terribly beat from the shock, my mother even more so, who, simply isn't up to taking these back and forth decisions. I'm not sure whether I should cry or be glad. I have the feeling to have landed between two millstones, or like something which, without sense and reason is being pushed from one corner into another.

"After your visit in December, my mind was set for Sumatra, and I had pushed all the negatives of this venture into the background. I had also looked forward to the move like a child does to Christmas. Now, the call is for switching back once more, after which the mind turns off completely. If I only knew the reason for this reversal. Is it yours or my pistol pointing at his chest or that of the Simbolan? Please write a few lines, responding to my letter."

De Kleine quickly wrote back on January 12, saying, "I have as yet not received a reply from Alfred to my letter I sent to him on December 18, 1956, of which I enclose my copy, which I ask you to return. I am of the opinion that my letter was written in such a way that it did not require him to return home. Following my conversation with you, I made arrangements for your departure. Only the building of a house in Siantar was to be arranged, for which our directorship can decide only after receiving your husband's statement of being prepared to stay. Since I have not heard from him, I'm unable to give any advice. We simply must wait until we have definite news from Alfred. If he said, 'I come back,' one can conclude that he has decided on it. So, what am I to say? Remain patient! From our side, your husband's stay, as well as your departure, have been okayed. Provided your husband tells us that he is prepared to remain in Siantar, it is all right with us. However, if he does not have the pleasure to do so, we must face his return."

Quickly, Gertrud responded, wondering whether de Kleine's letter and one of hers, could have caused Alfred to send his telegram, saying: "I come back." Gertrud commented: "I am still in shock about Alfred's letter of January 8; the entire letter is a puzzle to me! You may have received more information by now. I must assume that we are dealing with substantial misunderstandings by my husband; how could he, otherwise, become so excited about obvious things? I hope that he will not take any rash steps. It is hard for me to think that the troubling events of the past months have been for naught. When earlier he talked about the responsibility for his work, for which he was prepared to sacrifice the peace of his family; now, because of a few paltry pennies, he's prepared to dump the entire responsibility from one day to the next. I do not understand Alfred! For months, I begged him for his very personal opinion to all these questions, but in vain. Now, that you and I have put a gun to his head, he acts as if bitten by a tarantula. Excuse me, please, but I must air my heart's grievances, or I may yet end up in a psychiatric clinic. May God provide that everything will fall into place."

Two weeks later, in another letter to de Kleine, Gertrud expressed her gratitude to him for his 'gentle' letter to her husband, which must not have been easy. She said, "my letter wasn't as gentle! I'm now looking forward to his reaction. I have the feeling as if we poked into a wasps' nest. You were probably able to make sense of his accusations, while I had no idea what was going on, and Alfred's tone simply flattened me. As far as I can see, its cause is a major financial upset. After your generosity towards Alfred, the locals seemingly are crossing him, now that he is on location. This all leaves me in a void, and I am uncertain as to which outcome I should look forward to. But let's wait; for the time being, I will not prepare for anything."

Things settled down again. The household in W.-Biebrich was dissolved and in preparation for her departure, Gertrud moved with Michel and Dörthe to Wuppertal. Oma Weissenbruch entered the Mission retirement home, Haus Heimatfreude, in Kaiserswerth, where she met many of her former missionary friends and acquaintances. In July of 1957 there was talk of Gertrud leaving in September and, of course, taking their youngest, Dorothea, along to Sumatra. "If not in September, then it will be in October," she said. "Should I make the September ship when the Batak girls are returning, who would travel 3rd class, I could hardly travel 2nd class."

Gertrud was troubled leaving Michel on his own. In her mind the 'girls' were 'taken care of,' but not Michel. He had always been the most sensitive of the siblings and had had to deal with his leg troubles for close to a year while he was away from the family. In one of Gertrud's July letters she expressed her concern that Michel would be the one who, in the end, would pay for their venture. Still, she worried about the children, who, now, were 22, 20, and 18 years old, and would be left without a home, a place to return to when needed. Once she had left, it was thought Michel could find a home with Friedchen de Kleine and would be taken care of physically, but not mentally. Gertrud found the Barmen environment wanting, focused too much on spiritual matters and being stratified. Michel recalled with sorrow the family's togetherness in Wiesbaden and the stimulation he experienced from the 'older' children, Kurt, Christa's friend, and Fritz, Ute's friend. In a letter to Alfred, Gertrud, wrote, "It could have all been very nice – but, now, it is probably gone forever!"

By mid-August Gertrud's visa for Indonesia had not yet arrived, which prevented her from catching the September ship. Should she make the October departure, she would not have to travel 3rd class, but could do so 2nd class. A month later, she had made up her mind that Michel ought to live in Wiesbaden, and she was in the process of finding a 'foster' home for him with pastor Herold and his wife. Eventually, the Herolds accepted and Michel lived with them for approximately two years in an environment without warmth.

Alfred wrote in September about the troubles the Missionaries were having in getting their belongings through Indonesian customs. He mentioned the efforts of a colleague who, using wax, soot, petroleum, and other means to make new equipment look old and used. When the time came for Gertrud's departure, a Camembert cheese was put into a petroleum-powered refrigerator to declare it as used. Once through customs, it was packed, but the removal of the cheese forgotten. The fridge must have smelled atrociously when it was opened upon its arrival in Sumatra. One of Alfred's colleagues wanted a harmonium, and she was asked to obtain a good used one through Heinrich de Kleine, then to bring it along. And not to

234

forget some razor blades for Alfred, for they were very expensive in Sumatra. But there was still no news about her visa!

A project Alfred was involved in, together with Mrs. Klaiss, was the design and layout of the H.K.B.P. university to be built in Siantar. "Unfortunately," he wrote, "we lack the funds, requiring us to do it the cheap and time-consuming way. Still, I hope that it will eventually turn into a nice complex. The property is large and beautiful like few in Siantar." However, his foremost engagement was the teaching of Comparative Religion and History of Religion at Nommensen University in Pematang Siantar.

Alfred had entered Indonesia on a visitor's visa and now had difficulties getting a permanent visa. The Indonesian authorities were only prepared to extend his visitor's visa and Gertrud, having applied for a permanent visa, seemed to have difficulties obtaining it because of this discrepancy. He was, however, hopeful to have her and Dörthe arrive in Sumatra before Christmas. His advice to his wife was to immerse herself in learning Bahasa Indonesia and to practice English. He wrote on October 9, 1957 that there had been a rebellion by some 'irresponsible elements,' leading to a shoot-out, but which had been brought under control by the government. "Fortunately, we were spared any problems at the University, and curfew is now at eight o'clock in the evening."

A couple of weeks later, Alfred wrote Gertrud, "What you will enjoy most is the garden with its pond. We have built a dam, so that we will never run out of water. Just today, we have completed building a new trellis for the botik bolanda . I hope it will bloom by the time you arrive. We may still be able to eat some of the fruit from the old bolanda whose trellis collapsed recently. Part of my activity is still with the layout of the university grounds. Some student stipends have been applied to work, and several students are now engaged in digging holes for trees and bushes. We receive the vegetable refuse from the town's pasar , with which we fill the holes and thus get the best possible compost. If we keep at it, we will eventually have a good stand of fruit trees and will also grow plenty of vegetables, so that our people will get good vitamin-rich nutrition. I have set up a small garden patch in front of our house to grow things for our personal use."

Good news came with a letter on November 10, in which Alfred told Gertrud that his visa has been renewed for three years instead of the three month visitor's visa. Simultaneously, Gertrud had been issued a visa, but its duration was as yet unknown; an eventual extension should not pose a problem. He wrote, "Coming from Holland, the good ship 'Willem Ruys' will arrive in Sumatra on December 20, which lets me hope that I will finally have you here by that time." A long list of all kinds of items to bring followed, things hard to get in Indonesia, and all had to be made looking 'used' to save duties. The central government was still under threat by 'unsavory elements,' as Alfred put it, and the military was recently needed to put down a rebellion intent on usurping the government.

On December 4, 1957, Gertrud and Dörthe boarded the 'Willem Ruys' in Rotterdam. The ship was almost empty until it reached its stopover in Southampton. This was due to an anti-Dutch campaign by the Indonesian government, causing 63 passengers to disembark the ship before it left Rotterdam. In Southampton Englishmen came on board, but even more Indians and Chinese. Gertrud thought that about three-quarters of the passengers were 'coloreds.' "And every day one sees too many of the black frocks of our colleagues from the 'other faculty,' who read a mass three to four times a day. But there are no representatives from the Protestant side!"

Gertrud enjoyed the ever improving warmth and the weather, spending her time mostly on deck, while Dörthe, only eight years old, helped with baby sitting and was seen carrying babies of every kind of skin tone around. Their dinners were rather sumptuous, with 'boys' behind each passenger to react instantly to every whim of a diner. The ship's welcome dinner included 13 courses! They passed Gibraltar, Crete, and arrived in Port Said, where 13 more Dutch passengers disembarked to return home because of the political situation in Indonesia. It was said that the Indonesians were planning to repatriate 50,000 Dutchmen!

In the meantime it turned out that the 'Willem Ruys' would not enter the port of Belawan on Sumatra, but land in Singapore, raising the problem for Gertrud and Dorothea of how to get to Pematang Siantar on Sumatra. But Gertrud expected the shipping company to pay for the expense of their stay in Singapore and the transfer to Sumatra. While they were still at sea, Friedchen de Kleine died of cancer. Ute wrote a kind letter of condolences to her Uncle Heinrich, her godfather, Friedchen's husband. As things turned out, the two travelers arrived on December 23, 1957 by airplane in Medan, where Alfred picked them up, to take them to Siantar.

During the first days, many visits had to be paid to Batak families who wanted to see Gertrud again after the many years that had elapsed, and also to see her young daughter, Dörthe. The little girl was flabbergasted by the many people, sitting on woven mats on the floor and speaking in a, to her, incomprehensible language. Repeatedly, Alfred took them in his car to other families, until, finally, they returned home, where Dörthe was taken by a brown-skinned woman for a walk in the garden. She was Lasinah, their cook for many years.

Gertrud became quickly involved in getting their home into ship-shape. A menagerie of ducks, turkeys, and chickens populated the backyard, not to mention a couple of cats, all a delight for their young daughter. To protect some of the fowl from being butchered, Dörthe put the key to the coop overnight under her pillow. Wildlife – nisangs – paid regular visits to their small backyard pond, partly covered by a vault of yellow bamboo. These critters were always intent on eating the chicks, threatening even the mother ducks. It became Dörthe's duty to cage the animals for the night. Once, when she forgot to protect the fowl overnight, one of the nisangs, to her dismay, caused a slaughter. At another time, Dorothea, sitting on the roof, observed some workmen below talking in hushed tones, their gestures looking suspicious to the girl. Her parents shrugged off her report, but when the family returned home that evening, they saw a figure peering through a window into the house. Shouting "pentjuri, pentjuri, thieves, thieves," they drove the suspicious man away.

On a drive to a valley near Parapat the family visited a chief who was still a pagan. Alfred wanted to obtain from him a book on adat, the Batak's customs. While Alfred talked with the chief, the women, sitting separate from the gathered men, offered betel to Gertrud, who declined accepting this horrible stuff. The women kept talking, giggling and laughing, obviously about some subject that delighted them. After the Rutkowskys left, when Alfred had traded the adat book for a Batak bible,

Gertrud explained to Dörthe why the women had had so much fun. They had asked for Dörthe's age and determined that she was well-suited to become the wife of the chief's son!

On a visit to the town of Balige, Alfred and Gertrud wanted to meet Alfred's former 'right hand,' Situa Jacob, the oldest son of the former sorcerer-priest Laban, whom Martha Weissenbruch mentioned in her diary. Jacob was a member of the Marga clan that dominated Balige. Alfred had previously been inducted into the Marga Siregar clan. Subsequently, Gertrud was made an honorary member of the Marga clan. The married Rutkowskys had to become members of different clans, since Batak adat required that clan members must marry outside their own.

The major reason for the visit to Balige was to attend the wedding of a granddaughter of Situa Jacob. Dörthe recalled the ceremonial setting: "On the yard in front of the old Batak house with its sweeping roof, the guests sat on woven mats. It was a vast gathering; likely the entire village population had been invited. A buffalo and several pigs had been butchered. In the midst of a large fire lay the buffalo's head. Huge, yard-size pans had ben placed on the fire's periphery in which cut-up meat was cooked in the typical black sauce. The blackness was due to the meat being cooked in the animal's blood. Buffalo meat was shared out to the guests in their order of importance, the closest relatives, following rank and age, receiving the largest pieces. The Rutkowskys received their share, but in smaller pieces. As a going-away present Dörthe was given a beautiful rooster. Food animals were generally given away live because, if butchered, they were liable to spoil quickly. Once at home, the creature kept running off, and when Dörthe came home one day, asking for her beloved rooster, she was told to look for him in the freezer chest.

In a 1959 letter Gertrud described an outing to Balige and from there to the village of Sianipar. "Walking past the village, we came across a huge Batak house beautifully decorated with wood carvings. Just when we arrived, a large coffin, carved from a tree trunk, was carried by 30 laboring men with lots of noise to the yard in front of the building. The coffin was elaborately carved and decorated with brass, in short, it was a showpiece. It held the body of the supposedly wealthiest man of Balige, as we subsequently learned from speeches. What was not said was that he had also been the most miserly man in town. As it turned out, the funeral ceremonies were already in their fourth day and were accompanied by gondang music, dances and feasting, all according to Batak adat, including death wailing. A buffalo had been butchered and was now waiting to be shared out to the family members and guests according to their rank. Then the sons of the deceased walked up to the coffin, each supported by two men, since they, supposedly, were weakened by grief, to begin their death wail. We noticed, however, that their performance did not seem quite true. We were later told that these young men had refused to take part in this ceremony, being modern Indonesians who no longer had a relationship with the custom. But Batak adat   had proved stronger!

All the while the widow sat near the coffin, swaddled in black clothing, which, because of the heat, had been lifted somewhat to fan cooling air at her. Complete removal would have been a violation of custom. Speech after speech, all based on adat, was given, interrupted by singing and praying. Although there were plenty of Christian panditas and teachers present, not one spoke. At last, a wizened little man was called forward, a former teacher, who said something like: "Dear people, don't act as you do! Don't be so hard on yourselves. Remember, we are Christians, no longer pagans, and as Christians we can rejoice, even in sorrow." "After two hours we left, very much touched by the experience, wondering what grandfather Weissenbruch would have said to this mixture of adat, paganism and Christianity.

"Especially in the Toba region there is a call among the older population for a return to the customs of their fathers. However, since adat cannot be fully separated from paganism, it leads to this mishmash we had just observed. The son-in-law of the deceased, the University's president, had disallowed the andungen, the death wailing, but had 'run into granite' with his mother-in-law. He must have felt very unhappy during the ceremony. Fortunately, such big funeral events are rare these days due to their cost few can afford."

In addition to his university lectures and organizational tasks at the university, Alfred also conducted religious services which, as Gertrud reported, were so well attended that people even sat outside the church, listening to loudspeakers. He also arranged to have more than a hundred coconut palms and a number of oil palms planted on the University grounds, all this with only two helpers when he actually needed six. The Rutkowskys' own garden was suffering from the current dry spell and they had to chip in with watering.

The political situation in Indonesia, and Sumatra especially, was tenuous. It was aggravated by the Indonesian government's effort to relocate people from overpopulated Java to the less populated Sumatra. Some areas, like Toba, were off limits. Warfare, so far, had remained 'civilized,' without much shedding of blood. Tribe stood against tribe and newcomers against residents. In order to make their always short monetary allowances last, Alfred had to travel occasionally to Singapore to exchange money at a better rate than the official Indonesian one.

A partial solar eclipse took place, which Dörthe observed through a soot-covered piece of glass. The light had paled and their washer woman wanted to prevent the Rutkowskys from going outside into the sakit, the 'sick' sun. Tomorrow was hari raja, the beginning of the most important Muslim celebration. Hari raja was the local term for ramadan, the four weeks of fasting for Muslims between sunup and sundown. Hardly ever was so much food consumed than at the time of ramadan, that is – after sundown. However, during this period the people were all somewhat whacky and of little use. Gertrud said, "We are glad when these weeks are past and normal life begins again. Our three household helpers are Muslims. For hari raja they receive new badju, new clothing, money for cake and sweets, and two days off, during which we must take care of ourselves. Fortunately, we have been invited for ristafel by the Ottos (not relatives), owners of a hotel in Siantar. However, the hotel had become a billeting place with plenty of tents set up on its grounds."

Gertrud asked her sister Else in Germany to send her from time to time some issues of 'Der Spiegel,' the German newsmagazine, so that they would not be totally ignorant of what was going on in the world. All the while the local fighting was increasing. While she wrote, she heard artillery duels going on in the distance. "But," she wrote, "We are sitting here on a quiet island and hope it will remain so! However, in the wider area surrounding Siantar and in Tapanuli heavy fighting continues. The road to Tarutung is partly destroyed, and the same is true of the town of Sibolga. The 17th of August 1958 is Indonesia's independence day from Dutch colonial rule, and we are glad when this date is past so that, maybe, some quiet will return. The ongoing fighting is between Communist and government forces.

"Our vacation idyll at Lake Toba has become inaccessible. A missionary family visiting from Nias, who tried vacationing there, was glad to get back to their peaceful island. A woman-friend is staying with us. She left her home after a grenade exploded next to her house. However, when she arrived with us, she was greeted by a fire-fight nearby, causing everyone to take cover. Two hours later, all was quiet again with Dörthe sleeping through the entire ruckus. We are glad to live in houses built of stone, which provide some protection. And none of us has ever lived in fear in the course of these upsets. We have also been able to continue our regular work."

Whenever a trip was planned, inquiries were made prior to departure to ascertain that the route to be traveled was safe. Nevertheless, on a vacation trip by the Rutkowskys to Parapat a fire-fight had taken place on the road the night before with the bodies of the fallen still lying by the roadside. Seeing this, the family was concerned of being stopped at gunpoint by government troops or worse, rebels. Dörthe was allowed to stay with the Fritz family who lived at the very tip of the Si Piak promontory. One night, another fire-fight took place. When bullets whizzed over their house, the Fritzs took shelter in caves down by the lake where in old times pirates had hidden. Only then did they remember that Dörthe was still asleep in the house and had to be rescued. And the worse the situation became, the more break-ins took place, including in the homes of Europeans.

In a November letter, Gertrud wrote, "Our Silver anniversary has arrived, and we planned to drive to Brastagi for a little vacationing and exploring. The trip would have required that we drive via Medan, since the direct route via Saribudolok has become too unsafe, with the risk of being robbed. We had looked forward to it, when – I broke my leg in the garden, slipping on some muddy ground. Now, I'm sitting with a braced leg on the verandah!" And to make matters worse – Alfred, for awhile the owner of a beat-up Volkswagen Beetle – slammed into a tree when he tried to avoid colliding with a truck on the way home from Medan. Fortunately, he was not hurt.

Gertrud wrote: "The churches are always full, and the service is usually accompanied by a chorus. On special occasions it can happen that we have to endure up to 15 chorus presentations, and we are searching for means to curb the Bataks' exaggerated enthusiasm for singing by directing it into proper channels. In the past twenty years they have lost the guidance in the development of their taste. They were also short of suitable music material, forcing them to help themselves. At times, it can be hair-raising to hear what is presented. There are programs consisting of three beats of Händel's, several of Bach's, Strauss, Silcher and others, all joined into a beautiful, long potpourri, with some spiritual music included. If a nightingale's voice were added, the presentation would then be just right for a Batak's heart. I've always claimed that Bataks are omnivores when it comes to music. Fortunately, there are also choruses which sing truly beautifully and are grateful when we supply them with suitable sheet music. We do not recall these excesses from earlier times and hope to redress this problem, especially with Pastor Deppermann, who gives trombone lessons in Simalungen.

"Well, it isn't that we only sing! Our main task is the University which, with its 130 students and pandita trainees, is still in the process of being established. The University's faculty of eleven instructors has become quite international with Batak, Indian, American, Swedish, Norwegian, and German professors teaching; while most of the students are Bataks, some are Mentawaiers and Niassers. The latter must first be taught Indonesian, since this common language has not yet penetrated to these small-island people. The language of instruction is mainly Indonesian, but also includes Batak.

"Alfred has plenty to do, teaching History of Religion, homiletics, and dogmatics. In addition, he takes care of the administrative business of the Rhenish Mission Society. The day could be twice as long and all too often he works until late into the night. Much of the time, our house is like Grand Central Station, a continuous coming and going, and an open ear and heart must be available for all comers. This activity tends to interrupt the two to three hours of daily school lessons I must hold, since our attempts to establish a German school have, so far, come to naught."

The years to follow, from 1959 and 1966, until the Rutkowskys final return to Germany, became ever more chaotic. Mail arrived irregularly, sometimes taking weeks, or did not arrive at all. Dorothea's education took much of Gertrud's time, while she tried, with proper educational material in short supply, to keep her daughter ready for entry to a German Gymnasium.

After 1960 the working environment deteriorated substantially and the intra-Church relationship worsened. The situation became catastrophic. Shipments arriving from Germany or Holland through the port of Belawan at Medan were often pilfered, requiring Alfred to travel to the town to get shipments through customs. Following the collapse of the Indonesian currency, the rupiah, the port became clogged with shipments, since few people or companies were able to pay the duties anymore. This caused ships to lie in port, or even outside, and, with no possibility for unloading, turned to Singapore to discharge their cargo there. This led to foreign goods being no longer available or only at high cost. Basic foodstuffs, like rice and sugar, were often in short supply or only available at greatly inflated prices.

Alfred, being also the financial repository of the Rhenish Mission Society since the late '50s, also paid the salaries of its staff members. Because of the rampant inflation, he frequently traveled to Singapore, there to exchange money with Chinese traders at a more favorable rate, returning with a suitcase full of currency – a rather dangerous enterprise!

In 1959 a business trip took Alfred to Germany for discussions with the directorship of the Rhenish Mission Society. He took the opportunity to take his children, Christa, Ute and Michael, whom he had not seen for five years, on a trip to Holland. He also visited various relatives and the parents of colleagues to inform them about the lives of their children presently working on Sumatra. In so doing, Alfred helped to maintain the informal Mission information network.

And despite the political unrest, the family was able to spend a couple of vacations on uninhabited islands off the eastern coast of Sumatra, in the Strait of Malacca, to which friends had invited them. Gertrud wrote enthusiastically about the marine life she was able to observe there. Other excursions took them to Nias Island and to one of the Mentawai Islands off Sumatra's west coast, and, eventually, also to Bali, right after the eruption of the Gunung Agung volcano, when much of the area was still ash-covered.

Dorothea recalled her good relationship with the university students, males and females alike, who were funny and joked with her. Something was always going on there. However, she found the future Bible women boring. But when she wandered among the university's boarding schools with her dachshund, her parents were not too enamored by this. Upon her departure to Germany the students held a farewell devotional for her.

Dorothea was now 11 years old and needed to return to Germany for her further education. The problem was to find a place for her to stay. Thus, on April 10, 1960, the little girl, in the company of a Swedish couple, the Alms, flew with Garuda Airlines from Medan to Bangkok, and after a three-day delay there, with S.A.S. to Düsseldorf in Germany where she was picked up by her foster mother-to-be, the Mission Sister Gertrud Sassmann and the Mission's chauffeur, Trenkel.

In the spring of 1962 Gertrud and Alfred were able to 'vacation' in Germany. A week after their arrival, Martha Weissenbruch passed away. Like her husband hanging on to see his wife make it past W.W.II, she may have done so to see her daughter, granddaughter, and son-in-law once more. Alfred and Gertrud also met their 'new' son-in-law, Herbert Windolf, Ute's husband, and their grandson, Dirk, just three months old, for the first time, and stayed at the Windolfs' home in Watzhahn in the Taunus mountains. In early 1961 Ute had divorced her former husband, Fritz Michels, Herbert's cousin, after a marriage of only half a year!

Alfred's and Gertrud's main concern was the serious condition Michel had developed, which required psychotherapeutic treatment. At one point, during Gertrud's subsequent visit in 1964 to Germany, the question arose whether to take the young man with her to Sumatra, so that he would no longer be alone. After lengthy discussions with doctors, Michel was permitted to continue with his studies, and Gertrud returned to Sumatra alone.

Indonesia's political situation did not improve; unrest continued, and, eventually, a neighbor's house was even incinerated. Then, in 1966, just prior to their return to Germany, President Sukarno was removed from office by General Suharto. Communists and those suspected of cooperation were murdered. Victims were often killed on bridges from where their bodies were tossed into the rivers. There were also lots of Europeans they wanted to eliminate. A plan to kill the members of the University staff was revealed and prevented. These events, together with the concern for Michel's health led to their eventual return to Germany in 1966.

Gertrud & Alfred back in Germany

Final Return to Germany

In 1966, Alfred now at age 58 and Gertrud at 55, returned to Germany for good, where Alfred took his leave from the Mission. He subsequently joined the Rhenish-Westfalian Church as a pastor in Hagen-Boele. Upon his retirement from the Church in 1976, the couple moved to Helmenzen, a small village in the Westerwald area, where Alfred substituted for colleagues at religious services, weddings and funerals.

In 1980, a family reunion took place in Jackson Hole, Wyoming. In addition to Alfred and Gertrud, there were Christa and Ernst Schubert, Ute and Herbert Windolf with their son Dirk, daughter Karen, and niece Sabine Sponer who had been living for a year with the Windolf family in Schaumburg, Illinois.

Another reunion was arranged in 1983, also in Jackson Hole. It was attended by the parents, Dorothea Rutkowsky with her companion, Günter Klingebeil, Michael and Hannelore Rutkowsky with their son Bernhard, and Christa and Ernst Schubert, with Christa's daughter Deborah Wuliger, Herbert and Ute, as well as Dirk. At this occasion, Alfred and Gertrud's 50th wedding anniversary was celebrated.

And once again, family members gathered, this time in Murnau, Bavaria, in 1987, attended by Alfred and Gertrud, Dorothea and Günter, Herbert & Ute, and Michel with his wife Hannelore and their son Bernhard.

In 2000, with the couple now almost 91 and 88 years old respectively, their household in Helmenzen was dissolved, and the two moved to the Seniorenheim am Kurpark in Bad Marienberg. Just shy of 94 years old, Alfred died there on June 24, 2002. The obituary of the Evangelical Philipp-Nicolai Church Affiliation read:

"Alfred Rutkowsky worked for more than thirty years for the Mission in Indonesia. From 1956 until his retirement on October 1, 1976, he was pastor with the Evangelical Church Congregation in Hagen-Boele. Most dear to him was children's service and pastoral care of older people. The Rutkowsky family always maintained an open pastoral home in Boele. Even today, many parish members have fond memories of their former pastor.

Gertrud lingered on, passing away on the 16th of May 2004, at the age of 93, missed by a day by her visiting daughter Ute.

In conclusion, it may be warranted to pay tribute to a man who played a significant role in the Rutkowskys' life – Heinrich de Kleine, native of Holland. Like some other Dutchmen, he worked for the German Rhenish Mission Society. He was married to a German woman, Friedchen de Kleine. Ute seems to recall that at least one of their children, if not both, were adopted.

Heinrich, stationed in Sumatra prior to Alfred's arrival, became a mentor to the freshman-missionary. The contact between the two families never faded through the following decades. Upon Ute's birth, he became her godfather. The Rutkowsky children called him 'Uncle de Kleine,' as was customary for Mission children with adult members, and addressed him with the colloquial German "Du", also practiced by Alfred. Gertrud always seems to have addressed him as "Mr. de Kleine!"

Upon the outbreak of W.W.II, Heinrich, being a Dutch citizen, living in a Dutch colony remained, of course, free, and, apparently also his German wife and children. Following the Japanese invasion of Indonesia, Heinrich de Kleine was interned under the 'customary' horrible conditions the Japanese practiced. Most likely Heinrich and Friedchen agreed for her and their children to opt staying with the German nationals, who were "free" under Japanese occupation. This apparent decision of Friedchen to join German nationals was later held against her by some Dutch nationals, once Dutch forces reoccupied Indonesia.

During the chaotic postwar years, Heinrich de Kleine became an anchor and helper for the semi-free German nationals, especially Gertrud and the children, and for Ute and Michel a substitute father figure. He was also always ready to help his Christian Batak people wherever and whenever he could.

Eventually, he returned to Europe, where he became the Director of the Rhenish Mission Society in Barmen, from 1958 to 1966, until his retirement. His wife Friedchen had died in 1957 of cancer. Remarried, he passed away on Sept. 6, 1970 and was buried in Mennighüffen in Westfalia, Germany.

The Rutkowsky Children

In this chapter I, the author, take the liberty to introduce the Rutkowsky children the way I came to know them. If my memory serves me right, it may seem peculiar that I did not get to know Alfred and Gertrud personally until their visit to Germany in 1962, when I was already married to their daughter Ute, and our son, Dirk, had been born. But that's the way it was.

More on Ute's life may be found in my own Memoirs, which I wrote in late 2005.

Gertrud has described some of the three older children's childhood characteristics, with some more expressed in Christa's and Ute's letters to their father during his internment in India. The below account begins therefore, or rather continues, when the three older ones had become teenagers and Dörthe, the youngest, was a tomboy.

I was about 18 years old when I took dancing lessons in Wiesbaden, and it so happened that Christa, two years older than I, born the 17th of October 1934, was in the same class. It was the first time I met her, but subsequent meetings were infrequent at best. My wife, Ute, kept in touch with her while Christa lived in Wiesbaden. My first taste of broccoli was supplied by her, coming from the PX she had access to, as well as the paper diapers for our flight to Canada in early 1964. A personal meeting did not materialize again until she emigrated to the United States with her daughter Deborah in February of 1963, when she stayed en route at our home in Watzhahn for a couple of nights.

Christa had entered art school. Her relationship with two boyfriends had not continued, when, at an art fair, she met Robert Wuliger, an American. The two entered into a relationship, married, and on February 3, 1961 Deborah was born. Christa quit art school. Barely two years later the marriage had run into some problems, and Bob Wuliger sent Christa with her daughter and $ 25 on February 3, 1963 to the United States to work as housekeeper for a wealthy doctor friend of Bob's. The separation was meant as a cooling-off period but became permanent and eventually ended in divorce. Subsequently, a custody battle ensued for daughter Debbie.

Soon after her arrival, Christa met her sister-in-law, Lois Wuliger, who helper her to obtain a job at the sprawling ranch home of the Bullock family in Tarzana, CA. Mr. Bullock was a film and TV writer, whose visitors included Elvis Presley and Don Knotts. Mrs. Bullock helped Christa enter an art program and, when she wanted to move, helped her find the first of many small houses she and Debbie lived in the years to come. Eventually, Christa entered the Art Center School of Design in L.A. Some time in the late 70s, Christa acquired an MA in Art from Long Beach State University. She was able to find work as a freelance graphic designer. While she lived in Hollywood she met Seth Minas and the two married, supposedly to help him stay in the country, since Christa was in possession of a Green Card by this time. Debbie never cared for Seth.

Beginning in 1964, my business trips through the United States took me from time to time to Los Angeles. I never missed the opportunity to visit Christa and Debbie. Sometimes, depending on where Christa lived, I stayed for a weekend with her. Never did I fail to bring a couple of bottles of wine along, unknowingly contributing to her alcoholism. Christa introduced me to some California-style living. By the late `60s, if not earlier, she had become quite hip, if not a bona fide hippie. Subsequent to the Watergate Affair and Nixon's resignation in 1974, Christa felt the need to become a citizen of the U.S. and applied for it. It turned out that her ex-husband, Bob Wuliger, sore from the custody battle, had maligned her with the FBI, and Christa battled to disprove and overcome the accusations.

She met Ernst Schubert and they married in 1972, and eventually moved into a small house in Long Beach. At some time Ernst lost his job and the couple tried their hands – unsuccessfully – at starting a small computer company. Living off Christa's meager earnings, derived from her doggedly pursued job opportunities, and Ernst's savings, they had difficulties making ends meet. About 1986, Christa joined AA, Alcoholics Anonymous, and became a dedicated, livelong member. Ernst, not conscientious about taking his hypertension medication, suffered a stroke, and became wheelchair-bound. Christa took care of her husband until his death in June of 1993.

Christa rekindled or established many friendships after her husband's death. Her main companionship after Debbie had moved out were her dogs. Having been a kind of 'protester' for much of her life, she became involved in canvassing for Ralph Nader. Christa died on August 17, 2003 from complications of chronic lymphocytic leukemia. Following her mother's wishes, Debbie committed Christa's ashes at a dog beach to the Pacific Ocean.

Hans Michael Rutkowsky, (called Michel), first marriage
to Hannelore Busch, son Bernhard Rutkowsky,
second marriage to Wilja Bank

I recall meeting Michel occasionally at the house of pastor Herold, his 'home' when his parents had journeyed once more to Sumatra. It was usually in the evening, when we discussed philosophical subjects. With him, too, my contact was tenuous, at times nonexistent. Michel, born on May 8, 1939, was two-and-a-half years my junior.

At fifteen years of age Michel contracted bone tuberculosis in his left leg and was for half a year hospitalized in Herborn. In 1961, at age 21, Michel completed his Abitur, not without some difficulties.

In a letter to his mother, the 18-year old Michael succinctly analyzed his sister Ute's relationship with Fritz Michels, and obliquely predicted that this relationship would fail. He suggested that he would have a careful talk with Ute, when next meeting her. Unfortunately, this talk never took place. Had it been the case, later experiences of hers might have turned out differently!

At first, Michel studied anthropology at the university in Mainz. In 1964 Michel went to Berlin where he continued his studies of anthropology until 1967. When his parents returned in 1966 from Indonesia, they induced him to give up his Berlin residence and to move in with them in Hagen, where various problems ensued. The earlier loss of a home, the loss of the security of a family, when his parents went to Sumatra again, first, his father in 1955, then his mother in 1957, put the sensitive 18-year old youngster on a road which resulted in his admittance to several mental institutions between 1968-1971.

He called this time his 'psychiatric traineeship,' which eventually led him to sculpture. His explorations caused him to join the Art Academy in Düsseldorf under the well-known artist, Beuys, his instructor for 5-6 years until 1980. Since sculpture did not support him, Michel worked, among other ventures, at the setup of art shows and as driver for this equipment. According to Michel's own statement, he has never quite found comfort and integration in modern society, the 'automobile and media landscape,' in his words.

Michel married Hannelore Busch in 1978, following which the couple lived in Düsseldorf. Their son, Bernhard, was born in 1979.

After his divorce from Hannelore in 1985, Michel met Wilja Bank, whom he married in 1999. The couple lived a number of years in Cologne. Wilja brought a property in the tiny village of Verr in the Bergische Land region into the marriage, whereupon they built a small house. The relatively large property enabled Michel to erect several sculptures of his design on it. Weekend strollers with their children stop to admire his creations. Thus, finally he found there in the countryside, but also working with his Mac computer, a modicum of peace and integration into, but at a distance, from modern society.

Dorothea (called Dörthe) Rutkowsky, married to Günter Klingebeil

In my early twenties, the 12 year younger Dörthe, born on November 21, 1948, used to join our older group when she happened to be visiting in Wiesbaden. Dörthe was a tomboy at the time, and the blue marks I received roughhousing with her, were not indistinct. She had left Sumatra in April of 1960, then stayed at the Mission Home under the supervision of her caretaker, Gertrud Sassmann. She was schooled in at the second class of the Elberfeld Gymnasium, but was unprepared for the demands placed upon her. Only half a year later, due to her poor grades, she was sent to the Theodor-Fliedner boarding school in Kaiserswerth, where she was placed in a lower class. She remained at this facility until receiving her Abitur in 1968.

In 1966 her parents had returned from Sumatra and her father had assumed a position as pastor in the city of Hagen. After her Abitur, Dörthe attended classes in sociology and philosophy at the University in Bochum. She became politically engaged and eventually attended a Vietnam Congress in Berlin in 1967. Dörthe was appalled by the lies and deceit of contemporary society. Lacking the knowledge, the wherewithal, of how to study properly, she despaired of her performance and quit university. This led to a major family upset, since her father had hoped that at least one of his children would finish with a university degree.

In order not to be a financial burden to her father, Dörthe decided to study to become an occupational therapist, the minimum she thought she would be able to accomplish. She now attended a psychiatric hospital in Düsseldorf for a year, but her actual training took place in Berlin, where she had moved to. Her years of living in the boarding school had not been conducive to the development of social skills, of how to reach out to others. Thus, living by herself in Berlin, she grew lonely.

She was able to join a working group, later to become the Institute for Psychotherapy, Group Therapy and Group Dynamics, under the leadership of Josef Rattner. She entered therapy, became better able to deal with life, and upon completion of her occupational therapy training in 1974, began studying pedagogics with an emphasis on art. While waiting for her examination, she studied psychology. She then passed two examinations in pedagogics in 1980 and 1982, resulting in her diploma. Already by 1980, she had worked at two elementary schools. In 1990 she gained her diploma in psychology during a sabbatical. Parallel to these engagements, she had entered in 1978 into a deep-therapeutic training program at the Rattner Institute with which she is still connected with to this day.

In 1977 Dörthe became acquainted with and entered into a relationship with Günter Klingebeil, a judge. in 1984 the two purchased a house in a Berlin suburb, which they transformed into a beautiful home with an elaborate garden. Dörthe and Günter married in 1993. Until 1999 Dörthe conducted a small practice in their home, treating children and adults. Administrative regulations and the resulting problems caused her to terminate her operation. In 2003 Günter took early retirement, whereafter the couple enjoyed their home, the garden with its many flowers and fruit trees, and, last but not least, the many sculptures dotting the greenery, Dörthe had created and still is.

I do not recall precisely, when, seen through the fog of times past, I first met Ute, who was born on November 10, 1936, just six weeks younger than I. She schooled with my favorite cousin, Gerda, and, at times, visited at my uncle, Fritz Michels' home in Amöneburg, which occasionally became a meeting place for the extended family age-mates, Fritz, son of Fritz Michels, his daughters Liesel and Gerda, and, eventually, the girls' boyfriends, and myself. There were sing-alongs – in which I did not care to participate – and dancing. I loved to dance the tango with Ute.

Right from seeing her the first time, I was enchanted by the fair and lithe girl, but as inhibited as I was in my teenage years, I kept my distance. After her graduation studying as a dietitian in Bad Hersfeld, Ute prepared a ristafel at my uncle's to which my family was invited. I savored the many different tastes and was smitten – now also by her cooking. At some time in my later teens I gathered my courage and called Ute's home to invite her to the movie 'An American in Paris.' The phone was answered by a gruff voice, her father's, who told me in no uncertain terms that "Ute has a cold." And that was the end of it – at least for years to come!

Ute left home in 1955 for her dietitian studies in Bad Königstein, then continued the same in Bad Hersfeld until 1958.

When, first Ute's father in 1955, then her mother with Dörthe, left in December of 1957, the Rutkowsky household was dissolved with the adult, or near-adult children 'thrown adrift.' Ute had 'drifted' closer and closer to my cousin Fritz, and the couple married some time in the summer of 1960 – much to my regret. To maintain contact and to bring some life into their lives – so I thought – my friend Milton Guha from Calcutta and I kept visiting the pair for outings. Later that year the couple, plus cousin Renate Otto and I, traveled in my car to Spain. Whatever happened there drove home to Ute that her marriage was on shaky ground, as her brother had earlier so astutely observed. In the months to come, the couple split, and Ute and I became closer. After her divorce in early 1961, we married on July 8, 1961.

We quickly had two, then three children, and despite having a very good job and a nice apartment north of the Taunus Mountains, I became itchy, and felt confined, having traveled much before. When I asked Ute whether she would come with me to wherever in the world I could find new employment, my intrepid wife, without hesitation, said "yes." Several overseas job applications resulted in my employment with a German company in Canada in 1964. Now, Ute had to deal with three small children, aged two and one year, and a five month old, with no family support in a foreign country! Some help came in the form of an American neighbor couple we became friends with.

Six years later, in 1970, I transferred with my employer to Chicago. Two years later, the company fell on hard times with everyone being laid off, except myself, to continue a downscaled operation. To stand 'on two legs,' Ute went to college to acquire an associate degree in nursing, and, eventually, a bachelor's degree. We both did well. The children grew up and left the house. Then, in 1992 we found a new home in Prescott, Arizona, where Ute joined the Art Docents, and I was able to remain employed part-time by my old company. I then became a consultant to the company's new owners and eventually began an importing business. Ute was happy to leave work behind and eventually became involved in black-and-white photography, then digital photography.

After living now for more than 18 years in Prescott, we will celebrate our 50th wedding anniversary this year, 2011.

Lake Toba

Günter, Dörthe, and Herbert. Ute taking picture on Mt. Sibayak

5. Epilog

A Third Generation's Visit to Sumatra

In 1989 I asked my wife Ute if she wanted to visit her country of birth, Sumatra. We discussed the idea with her sister, Dorothea and her partner, Günter. Dörthe was thrilled. Dörthe brushed up on her knowledge of the Indonesian language and was to be our translator.

It did not take long for us to meet in Singapore, they coming from Berlin, we from Chicago. A joint flight took us from Singapore to Medan on Sumatra. Just prior to landing in Medan, Dörthe, overcome by her memories of the past, began to cry, caused by the thought: "Finally, I'm home again."

In retrospect, Dörthe's memories of this trip were ambivalent and, for her, difficult to describe. As often happens, when we return after some time to a place of which we retained fond memories, the 'new' reality does not match the past. Dörthe remembered the three formative years she had spent in Sumatra, her paradise of 31 years ago, and thought to recapture that which, unfortunately, was no more. She had hoped to connect once more with an important period of her past – impossible to accomplish. Her subsequent experiences alternated between feelings of loss and rediscovery of the familiar.

The sterile, monotonous oil palm plantations that had replaced the dense woods and some rubber plantations along the route of our two hour taxi ride to the Siantar Hotel in Pematang Siantar came as a disappointment to Dörthe. Then there was the garbage strewn about. In earlier times everything had been wrapped in banana leaves, which then ended up on the road or in the adjacent drainage channels, where, while producing a pungent odor for awhile, they eventually rotted away. Now, everything was packed in plastic bags, tossed away as before but without rotting, causing an impression of indescribable filth.

My wife Ute described her 44-year old recollections, somewhat more distant than Dörthe's, and, because of the internment, not as paradisiacal: "Some memories of my childhood came tumbling forth along the drive: The smells, some familiar, some not yet identified."

The ride introduced us to a strange, foreign world, a chaos of all kinds of vehicles, driving on the left side, too fast and too close, and honking for numerous reasons. Vendor stalls lined the road, from which various kinds of 'fast' food, durian, rambutan, and other fruits were sold. And people, especially children, were everywhere. But, oh, the stink of all the two-stroke engines propelling the various types of vehicles!

We arrived at the hotel and Dörthe recalled that, "this was where our parents dined once a week with the Hotel's owners, the Ottos, a Swiss couple, friends of my folks."

Mrs. Otto had been born on Sumatra, and her family had obviously been well off. Her parents had established the Siantar Hotel as well as the pabrik es, the ice plant, where block ice and soft drinks were made. The Ottos had a beautiful garden. Dörthe recalled that, "their son Hansli had a tree house on one of the big trees, something I had always dreamt of. Hansli and I, joined by the cook's son, Temiran, played up there, while the adults entertained themselves otherwise." The garden surrounding the building was absolutely luxuriant with blooming orchids and old Balinese stone sculptures placed everywhere. Around a pond quacked and chattered white and black turkeys, Manila ducks and Guinea fowl. Just prior to Dörthe's arrival in 1957, Mrs. Otto had given Alfred two black-iridescent turkeys which later proliferated aplenty, just as she provided the Rutkowskys with plenty of plant cuttings.

Mrs. Otto was highly creative, inviting the children to making handicrafts for Christmas, and providing them with wonderful birthday presents. Dörthe especially remembered an about two foot (60 cm) long Noah's Ark, made of solid wood, for which she had carved the animal figures herself. She arranged trips in which only Dörthe and her mother joined, since Alfred was busy at the university. However, he was able to join in two weekend excursions to islands in the Strait of Malacca.

The Ottos lived in a world separate from church and the Mission. They enjoyed a very different cultural life-style, whose quality was nevertheless valued by the Rutkowskys. Being close friends, this couple's lifestyle and interests became, according to Dörthe, in some ways a model for Alfred and Gertrud.

Since it had been important for Dörthe to stay at the Siantar Hotel, I had made telephone reservations from Chicago. To Dörthe the hotel had barely changed, but the people, previously so much a part of it, were missing. She said: "Nevertheless, now sitting at the tables, where in earlier times the parents had been sitting with the Ottos, joined by other European doctors and plantation owners, dinner smelled just as delightful as before and tasted as good."

After dinner, we found comfortable seating on the rattan armchairs on the covered verandah. Darkness lay warm over the city with crickets chirping in the surrounding bushes. Titjaks, geckos, hung from and skittered over the ceiling and walls, making their soft smacking sounds. Temporarily, everything seemed to be as unchanged and home-like to Dörthe as it had been in earlier times.

The following morning we enjoyed a typical Indonesian breakfast of strong coffee, nasi goreng (fried rice), and bami goreng (fried noodles), passion fruit juice and papaya. Then we left for a bank to exchange our currencies for wads of Indonesian rupees. The armed but friendly guards outside the bank asked for their picture to be taken, just as many of the children and adults did on our later sojourn.

Thereafter, we visited Adalbert Sitompul, the Dean of Nommensen University's theological faculty, a former student of Alfred Rutkowsky's, who had taught at the university from 1954 to 1966. Dr. Sitompul spoke highly of Alfred and expressed his gratitude for Alfred's donation of numerous books to the university from his extensive library.

The next morning we were invited to a traditional Indonesian breakfast at the Sitompuls' house. Meeting his wife, we enjoyed a delightful hour with this highly educated couple, both speaking several languages. The conversation jumped back and forth between English and German, with many memories going back to father Rutkowsky's activities and the Mission's work, now the H.K.B.P. This being a Lutheran organization, grace was spoken in Batak, a touching experience for Ute and Dörthe, despite their distance from their forbears' religious background. Dr. Sitompul spoke with great respect of Alfred Rutkowsky's contributions to the university, but emphasized that the invitation to us was meant as homage to Dörthe's and Ute's father. Dörthe's covert reaction at the time, while she took a little swallow, was: "It sounded as if he meant to say, 'not that you think I invited you for your own merit!' Well, and why should he have invited us? Just because we were who we were? But his 'laudatio' for our father felt good, anyway."

While he expressed his gratitude, he was able to skillfully connect it with the question of what we could still do for the university. This sounded familiar to Dörthe as being typical of Batak nature, where one always entertained the consideration of how to benefit from one's vis-à-vis. Of course, this question, at least in the past, often originated from some need. In the past, Alfred Rutkowsky had often helped in making something available to someone, at one time a bicycle ricksha so that its owner could make a living. In gratitude the man painted 'Rutkowsky' in large letters on his contraption.

Dr. Sitompul also pointed out the university gardens, where many palm trees had been planted under Alfred's supervision, and, forming a boulevard, had now attained a respectable height. Dörthe recalled the large pits dug for planting the young trees, which were first filled with 'compost' from the pasar, the market, to give the trees a good start.

We walked the grounds to look at the former Rutkowsky house, now a shadow of its former beauty which made recognition for Dörthe difficult. The tulip tree, however, that her father had planted 30 years ago, had become a giant, on top displaying its fire-red blossoms. Dörthe was full of stories, the layout of the rooms, the furniture, their dachshund, memories of this part of her life, so precious to her. When her parents left for good in 1966, parting from their garden was most difficult for both of them.

In the afternoon, Ute and Dörthe went to town. They walked through a park with a monument to Indonesia's independence. Sitting on a bench, they were quickly surrounded by a group of girls, giggling and moving in close, with their typical Batak lack of concern for personal space. No way these two German women were concerned with maintaining their customary western distance; no, they felt 'at home', having truly arrived again in the land of their parents. Their parents had lost their hearts to these people, and late in his age, Alfred wrote to a Batak in Hamburg: "My heart has remained in Indonesia."

Then the girls' questions came: "Who are you? Where are you from? What are you doing here, and where will you go?"

Dörthe had to answer to these same questions many more times on our subsequent travels. And before leaving, the girls, of course, wanted their picture taken.

Dörthe and Ute returned with a durian: green, spiny, somewhat larger than a head, and 'smelly,' although Dörthe called it 'having a scent.' It had been their mother's favorite fruit. My three companions ate it with relish, even Günter. I, considering the foul odor, said to myself, "Try everything once." But that was enough, and never again. In the future, every time I had to pass by one of the huge piles of durian, stacked by street vendors, I took a deep breath, then quickly left the terrible odor behind – many of the merchants giving me a knowing grin, for there are only lovers and haters of durian!

We called on Elisabeth Steinhardt, an old playmate of Ute's from internment times, these days working as a Missionary Sister in Siantar. She was an 'open,' direct and 'take charge' person. While sitting in the comfortable rattan furniture in her house, drinking tea, we talked about her work for the Mission and the Indonesian political situation. Mother Rutkowsky had given Dörthe some presents to hand to Gertrud's valued and beloved cook of times past, Lasinah. Elisabeth had inquired about her, but sadly, Lasinah had died a year earlier. However, her son-in-law, Pairin, whom Alfred had helped to get his driver's license, and who had then been his chauffeur for many years, was found and was brought to Elisabeth's house. The old man had only one tooth left. Not being able to hand the gifts to Lasinah, Dörthe gave him the presents, which he did not open, though. Later, Elisabeth explained that it was Batak custom not to open presents immediately, so as not to hurt a donor's feelings, should a gift not be pleasing. Dörthe missed very much not seeing Lasinah again, a woman she had also treasured. She had come too late.

Many years earlier, in 1962, I myself had an 'encounter' with Lasinah, when the Rutkowskys came visiting Germany. They brought along a jar of sambal, a very hot, spicy pork 'goulash,' Lasinah had made. (While Muslim Bataks do not, Christian Bataks eat and love pork) It was very hot, and I relished it, eating the entire jar in one setting by myself. We have a saying in German that, "a Hungarian goulash must burn twice." Well, this was no Hungarian goulash – it burned four times!

Someone at the university recommended a Muslim Batak, the owner of a well-kept van, to drive us for a number of days to the various places we intended to visit in the vicinity of Lake Toba. With him, we took off from Siantar to Parapat and the Lake, where the Weissenbruchs' first Mission Station was located at Si Piak, when Batakland was still 'wild.'

The landscape became hillier and wilder, and we now passed more of the old gabled Batak houses. Then, suddenly, Lake Toba in all its glory lay before us. We stopped and viewed its huge, shimmering expanse from an overlook. Mountains rose straight from its shores. This was the place of Weissenbruch and Rutkowsky family legends, so often told stories Ute and Dörthe had grown up with – this was 'home'! Ute said: "How often had this lake with its people been mentioned in family lore, how its name had permeated our family history. We had always retained a nostalgia, a longing for this paradise."

We found Parapat dirty with plenty of garbage strewn about. Stalls, offering fast food Indonesian style, lined the streets. It was hard to believe, but Parapat's main street was lined with the remnants of mango trees grandfather Weissenbruch had planted eight decades ago, which now still bore witness of his former presence. These trees bore small, extremely sweet fruit. Now Dörthe could tell the people that she and Ute were the ones, whose grandfather had planted these trees, and once more, she was asked: "Where do you come from? What are you doing here? Do you have children and how many?" Or: "Why don't you have any children? Don't you have a man? Why aren't you married?" Again and again, Dörthe had to tell the story of grandfather, who built the no longer standing church in Si Piak, now integrated with Parapat, and the big church he built in Balige. She had to repeat the story of her mother, who had been born in Si Piak/Parapat, and of her parents living in Sipirok and Siantar.

Grandfather Hermann and father Alfred had been panditas, pastors, as Dörthe told her listeners. This led to comments and questions by some inquisitive folks about the differences that had by now arisen between different local religious directions. "Then you, too, must be of the H.K.B.P. persuasion," concluded some, putting their minds to rest.

We walked the market in Parapat with its profusion of goods, its many kinds of fruit and vegetables, spices, live chickens, eggs, dry goods, etc., along its meter-long rows of tables, from where dried fish, sorted by size in baskets, were sold. Dörthe recalled her grandmother's dislike of dried-fish smell. When, later, in Wiesbaden ristafel was served and ikan teri, tiny dried fish, were fried in preparation for this dinner, she left the house, only to return once the rooms had been sufficiently aired. Dörthe could not help thinking that, "considering all these smells, how much grandmother Martha, with all her love for Sumatra, had nevertheless remained the European. I just couldn't imagine her being a durian aficionado."

And while standing by this fried fish monger another one of the already well-known conversations ensued. While Dörthe recounted her story, ever more women joined the group, some peering over the wooden back wall to partake of the entertainment these orang bolanda, these white people, brought them. Maybe they only enjoyed hearing of the old times, but Bataks are certainly very much aware, interested in all kinds of things, but also very conscious of their traditions. There is barely a Batak who cannot quickly name several generations of his forebears, including their relatives related by marriage.

We had found overnight accommodation at Tor na uli, the university's guest house, where the Rutkowskys had stayed years ago when vacationing at Lake Toba. The place, with its beautiful garden, provided a nice, broad vista of the lake.

Next day's half hour ferry ride from Parapat was to take us to Samosir Island. We carried our luggage on board, but when the captain told us a way-too-high price, we readied to leave the boat again. After some haggling, we paid an acceptable fare. Dörthe claimed that one must haggle with these folks as a matter of course and that they enjoyed doing it; without haggling life to them would be so much duller. Mother Rutkowsky often bargained for a bunch of bananas, refusing to be taken just because she was European.

Once we got under way, I was "assaulted" by two, about 12-year old Chinese boys who wanted to practice English. During the crossing, Dörthe became engaged in conversation with a young, open-minded Batak woman by the name of Theresa. Theresa told Dörthe about her life and in the course of the conversation, bemoaned that adat, Batak custom, was still strong and alive. When Dörthe pursued this direction, she was told that her family still required that the oldest daughter had to marry first, with the younger ones following. She, herself, was the third daughter. She was less than happy about this situation and asked Dörthe whether she wouldn't know a European man, who would marry her, then all would be all right. Maybe there would be a suitable friend in Germany? Dörthe was rather nonplussed and tried diplomatically to disengage from the situation. What Dörthe took away from this encounter was that Bataks, too, like most societies, face conflicts between tradition and modernity.

Dörthe found Lake Toba no longer as blue as she recalled it, attributing it to the fertilizer run-off from the surrounding rice fields. But then, did her memory perhaps deceive her just a little? Nevertheless, at least to us newcomers, Günter and myself, and Ute's memories going much further back, the lake looked crystal-clear and one could still see every pebble on the shore's bottom.

Our island hotel somewhat resembled Batak houses. With its simple but comfortable ambiance, the view from our balcony across the broad expanse of the lake was incredibly beautiful. For breakfast we received, among other things, pisang goreng, fried bananas, which we devoured with ardor. We watched women washing laundry on some rocks and fishermen in their solus. The air was balmy and we swam to our heart's content.

After our morning's breakfast, we walked to a couple of Batak villages, where women still wore traditional garb. We looked into an old Batak house, then visited some Batak grave sites. These images evoked the past, stories of the last heathen chiefs, when some of these people were still practicing cannibalism. In the evening, we participated in a huge dinner. It was followed by singing and instrumental music, performed by the hotel employees. Bataks love to sing, and these people were very good. Dörthe joyfully recalled such songs as, 'a sing sing so' and 'o tao toba.' She also remembered her mother, when she was very old, still singing along and waving her head, following the rhythm of the Batak songs played from a tape her children had given her. Thinking of this, Dörthe sensed how much her mother had been at 'home' in Batakland.

Walks took us through rice fields and past water buffalos. This brought back the story of her mother, when, as a youngster, she was picked up by the horns of one of these sometimes mighty creatures. In one of the customary conversations, a woman, working in the field, suddenly pronounced: "You are siblings!" referring, of course to Dörthe and Ute. "How do you know?" came the retort. "You have the same teeth." Dörthe was amazed by the woman's observation. In the West, we judge by the nose, the eyes, and such. But by the teeth? Well, why not, especially when teeth commonly go missing at a much earlier age in developing countries.

Our next stop was the town of Balige, another place with strong familial memories, and where brother Michael was born. We wanted to visit the beautiful church Opu Weissenbruch had built. Its entrance hall featured two commemorative stones, the one on the left honoring the Mission's founder, Ingwer Nommensen, the one on the right, Hermann Weissenbruch. Ute said that, "entering this place, I felt a sense of history and the connection with my roots. I tried to imagine what it must have been like to live and work here as a missionary in the beginning nineteen hundreds. I could almost hear my grandfather speaking from the pulpit. Both Dörthe and I were very much touched."

We had lunch in a Chinese restaurant, where Dörthe found the smells she had forever missed in Europe, the smells so familiar to her from back in Siantar. That's where the Rutkowskys ate once a week, whenever their cook, Lasinah, had her day off. It must have been a particular oil or spice that had left its indelible impression on a little girl's mind.

We visited with Dr. Fritz in town, a friend of the family. Dörthe remembered him when he had worked at the hospital in Tarutung. This German family had had the only two children of Dörthe's age she could comfortably play with, when her family happened to visit Siantar. Dr. Fritz must also have lost his heart to Sumatra to have returned. He now worked at the Balige hospital. One of his daughters had also returned for her doctoral training in tropical medicine at the local hospital. Dörthe could not help but envy her her renewed connection with Sumatra. We spent a pleasant afternoon with tea and cookies on the emper of their house.

Dr. Fritz recommended staying in a Batak guesthouse, which introduced us to the customary Indonesian bathroom facilities. Everything was sparkling clean; a hole in the tiled floor represented the toilet and a two-by-two-foot wide and four-foot high tiled basin held cold water with a ladle to douse and clean

265

oneself. However, our nightly stay turned out rather restless with too much activity going on through most of the night.

After our driver picked us up the following morning, we soon left the touristy area behind, seeing more of the old-type Batak kampongs with their steeple-roofed buildings, in which people lived 'upstairs,' their fenced-in animals, 'downstairs.' These settlements of maybe six to eight houses were surrounded by an earthen mound with trees and bamboo growing along its ridge for protection against wild animals. Only two gates at each end offered access to a kampong.

Narrow side roads took us into the hills to Sitorang, the last mission station of grandparents Weissenbruch, where they had spent six years. It was a beautiful area of valleys with rice fields, surrounded by mountains. Bent down, women were working in the fields. The area looked rather isolated. Grandmother Martha had been warned by the Sitorang Station's predecessor of its remoteness, prior to their move from Balige. Definitely few tourists found their way here.

When we walked towards the village, people, but especially children, surrounded us quickly to ask the already all-too-well-known questions. We foreigners became the 'excitement' of the day. We looked at the church, where we found a picture of Opu Nommensen, but none of Opu Weissenbruch. Then, a man, roughly our age, clad in a sarong, a loin cloth, approached us and introduced himself as belonging to the Panjaitan clan. When Dörthe explained the reason for our visit, telling him that her grandfather had once lived here, the man, to our surprise, said, "My grandfather gave your grandfather the land to build his house on." He led us to the place where the house had once stood, followed by the gaggle of children. But except for a number of fruit trees Hermann Weissenbruch had planted, no remnants of a structure were visible any longer. Our guide told us, "It was once a Garden of Eden." Our contact asked whether he could get photos of people of the old times, which Dörthe promised him. Once back home, she was able to find a few and mail them to him. Sitorang was known for its Batak wood carvings. When grandfather Weissenbruch left the village to return to Germany, he was given a specially-made, beautifully carved Batak chest with the dates of his stay incised in the Batak language. Today, it stands in Dörthe's house in Berlin.

From Sitorang, we were driven through the surroundings of Lake Toba, stopping at old villages where we were invited into some houses. There were children everywhere. One old woman said she had 13! Usually, people we met were very friendly. The building of an old Karo Batak King, now a museum, had housed 13 generations of Rajas, 'Kings,' each with up to 22 wives and up to 117 children. The sturdily-built structure stood raised on approximately 10 foot (3 m) tall, solid poles for protection from tigers and other wild beasts. The 'king' slept up front, from where a door led to the women's quarters, each having their own fire place and bamboo pipe water supply, all guarded by a eunuch. Refuse was apparently dropped through the gaps between the horizontal poles.

Our continuing ride took us to Brastagi, located northeast of Lake Toba in the direction of Medan. Gertrud Rutkowsky lived here with the children for a short time in 1942, then again from 1944 to 1946, during the Japanese occupation. When the Rutkowskys returned in the late 1950s, they enjoyed a vacation here with their friends, the Ottos, of Siantar Hotel fame. Aside from strawberries that grew here, Ute remembered two volcanos nearby, the Sibayak and Sinagung, both dormant. Entering Brastagi was confusing for Ute, for much had changed in the intervening years. Driving around Mount Gundaling, a prominent landmark, she spotted the house they had once lived in. Walking into town the following day, we asked for directions to Djalan Udara #1, the street address of the house. Approaching the location, a number of houses triggered the memory of 'having lived there.' Then, a long driveway leading up to a house on a hill, made Ute certain: "This is it. I can almost see myself as a young girl walking from here through the adjacent canyon to school. I can see the bamboo growth I walked through. I can see myself playing on the hill with other children. I recall making kites and flying them over the canyon. Feelings surfaced from down deep! Again, they meant I was back to my roots!"

Our accommodation in town was the Bukit Kubu Hotel, an old colonial structure in a beautifully manicured garden. Dörthe recalled staying here with her parents as guests of the Ottos. To Dörthe, the place brought back memories of her first horseback ride, with Hansli Otto on his horse, and she farther back on her 'Blacky.' It was her first try, and her steed decided to join his companion farther in front, and took off straight across the meadow, with Dörthe clinging to her saddle. And while she prayed to the heavens, her mother was sitting higher up by a window, wondering why Dörthe was galloping across the golf course.

The next morning our hired driver did not show up. No matter, we found ready transportation. In the meantime we visited a market with much-too-muddy pathways, but a multitude of fruit and dried fish, the latter sorted by size, from 2 inches to 15 inches, in big baskets. In the late afternoon, a taxi driver suggested taking us to a village of Karo Bataks for a native dance, celebrating the change of police chiefs. It sounded interesting, so we took off with him – to a place far removed from Western customs and yet retaining some of its trappings. We, being the sole Westerners, were greeted by the two police chiefs, their wives, and the village elders; later, we were invited to partake in their common dinner. This being a Muslim community, the women ate separately from the men, while our two wives were allowed to sit cross-legged with us and the men. Before dinner, small water bowls were passed around to wash fingers. Dinner, which was served on waxed brown paper, consisted of rice with one piece of meat and a couple of vegetable pieces on top, tasty and spicy, all eaten by hand. Ute, being left-handed, automatically used this hand which, in southeast Asian countries, is considered 'unclean.' I had to covertly urge her to switch sides.

After the meal we were invited to sit in the front row on benches, together with the 'big shots,' to watch the forthcoming performance on the raised stage. It had turned night. More and more people from outlying villages had drifted in, and with the Indonesians' smaller personal space requirement, we were soon tightly surrounded by humanity. Electric lights illuminated the stage, then some typical Batak musical instruments were played. Various groups of old and young danced, speeches were held, and a lone singer performed. Eventually, six professional male and female dancers with incredible grace and agility entered the stage. Some of the postures of their dance must have conveyed specific meanings unknown to us, for the audience broke into laughter a number of times. Then we were invited on stage to dance with the 'professionals.' After some hesitation we agreed, but in no way were we able to match the grace of these men and women. Did we hear some subdued snickers from the huge, but polite crowd? Eventually, after I had made a covert 'donation' to the new police chief, we slipped away and our taxi took us back to the hotel, which we now found completely occupied by noisy Chinese.

The Chinese New Year is not celebrated on only one day, but over a number of days. There is a large Chinese population living in Indonesia, and these visitors had driven from low-elevation, humid Medan to the higher-elevation, cooler Brastagi to celebrate New Year. The celebration went through the entire night! People talking, radios blaring, children screaming – were they never going to stop? Our plans were to rise early in the morning and climb the Sibayak volcano, but sleep was impossible.

Rather bedraggled, we left early for our volcanic ascent. The trail eventually led through what looked like jungle, but wherein people lived. Then we passed by a giant, staked-down water buffalo. I tried to demonstrate that one could safely approach such a beast, but when I came close, there sounded this unpleasant growl, and I thought it better to retreat. Just when we were to go on, a loin-cloth-clad boy of about five years appeared from the bushes, pulled out the stake, and led the beast away. Did I feel silly! The trail eventually turned into a very steep concrete stairway dating back to Dutch colonial times.

There is the story of my mother-in-law ascending these very steps in the early 1960s. The husbands were already way ahead, mother Rutkowsky following, with Julie Denkhaus somewhere below. Suddenly, she heard loud screams behind her, and when she turned, saw Julie lying on the stairs with a Batak youth threatening her with a knife. Both were struggling, one to get, the other to keep, Julie's purse. Gertrud ran down the stairs, and being fluent in Batak and knowledgeable of the customs, assaulted the youth with a flood of Batak admonitions about what his ancestors would think of such behavior. Despite being Christians or Muslims, Bataks are beholden by ancestor worship. And, lo and behold, shamed, the boy apologized, then quickly disappeared into the surrounding woods. It occurred to Dörthe that it was rather lonely up here, and she regretted not having her mother along, able to scold fluently in Batak.

Climbing on, we reached the tree line, where the steps ended, and eventually entered the nearly 650 ft (200 m) wide caldera. Sulfuric vapors escaped, hissing, from multiple vents, from which the natives caught the sulfur by affixing burlap bags over the major outlets. Then we walked down an apparently new, but extremely muddy path. Ute promptly slipped and fell, to end up rather messy. I cut four walking sticks for us after which, now three-legged, we were able to descent safely, but only by carrying plenty of Sumatran clay with us, sticking to the soles of our shoes.

Prior to our departure, we explored Medan a bit, today a city of over one million people, its streets pervaded by two-stroke vehicles, which left a bluish tint to the air and a terrible stink. Ute and Dörthe ventured alone to the Tip-Top Restaurant of old, once 'the' place to dine for their parents when visiting Medan. Dörthe recalled having eaten there the hottest, spiciest saté skewers of her life. They brought back some utterly delicious sticky-rice pastry to us men (and women), and we retired to a hotel lobby for some tea. The pastry was so good that Günter willingly braved the smelly streets to fetch some more.

Our journey to today's Sumatra and some of its past, the past of grandparents and parents, had come to an end. Our venture had been a wonderful recapture of past memories for Ute and Dörthe, but they also faced dealing with the reality of today's Sumatra, comparing it with the memories and their nostalgia of past experiences.

There were plenty of new impressions for Günter, most of which were the exotic strangeness of the country. He did not find all experiences positive and the climate, at times, stressful. He enjoyed observing Dörthe's and Ute's delight in recapturing some of the images of their past and their getting in touch with people known and unknown. Since Dörthe had been in Sumatra for only about three years, he was surprised at the strength of impressions left behind from this short period. But as I have found, it is not the length but the intensity of experiences that make a place feel like home. Sadly, we can never fully recapture these images of the past.

Yet, writing this biography twenty years later – this bridge to the past – vividly recalled my own experiences in Sumatra.

From the time I made her acquaintance at age fifteen and learned of Ute's "exotic" background, she and her origin had fascinated me. Back then, when the time came, with other trips completed, I was and am glad to have suggested this journey to my wife. It was first of all to be for her benefit, only secondarily to bring some of the places of her stories from this exotic land alive for me. Thus, when we found 'Ute's old house,' where she had lived with her mother and siblings in Brastagi, and I saw her break into tears, it became a grateful experience also for me.

May I therefore say in closing: "While our destiny is known, we do not know our destination." In my collecting of aphorisms and mottos, I have come across an African proverb: "When you don't know where you're going, it's important to remember where you came from."

Glossary

H.K.B.P. = Huria Kristen Batak Protestan, translating to: Batak Christian Protestant Church

Pandita = native pastor

Adat = traditional law

Radja = King, ruler, chief, or village leader; generally a wealthy and powerful man

The prefix 'Si', similar to the English 'the' is used for place names and people's names, when not talking to the latter. 'Si' can stand separately from the place name, or it can join the name, as in Siantar or Simalungen, instead of Si Antar or Si Malungen.

Also written as Prapat or Perapat

Tuan = mister or master

Nyonya = Wife

At the time, Penang was part of the colony of British Malaya, which is nowadays independent Malaysia. Penang is not to be confused with Padang on Sumatra's west coast.

Ceylon = now called Sri Lanka

Solu = a boat

Rijsttafel = a sumptuous Dutch-Indonesian meal

Pisang goreng = pisang = banana, goreng = fried banana

Quinine was the only malaria medication available at the time, and at that, not very effective

Durian = a somewhat larger than an American football, green, bumpy tree fruit. Its inside holds several golfball-size pits, immersed in a white fruit flesh. The fruit, but especially its interior smells like a rotting corpse. There are only lovers and haters for this delicacy.

Ephorus = Vicar or Bishop, from Greek historian Ephorus

Singamangaraja was finally killed by Dutch government troops in 1911

In German Muslims are or were called Mohammedans, derived from the name of the Muslim prophet Mohammed, in an analogy to the name Christians, being derived from Christ. Muslim means being an adherent of Islam, in turn meaning Submission to God.

Tole, in Batak = "Forward"

Sprue = a disease preventing effective absorption of food

At the time, Germany held the colonial port city of Tsing Tao in China. Japan, in W.W.I on the side of the Western Powers, attacked the city, together with British forces, taking 50 days to conquer it.

What was then called Malay, is today called Bahasa Indonesia, the Indonesian national language based on Malay

Allow me, the author, to confirm this. My wife, Ute Windolf, née Rutkowsky, and I, together with Dorothea Rutkowsky and her husband

272

to-be, Günter Klingebeil, stood in 1991 before this church. When we entered it, its entry hall featured two memorial stones, the one on the left inscribed with the mission's founder, Nommensen, the one on the right with that of its builder, Weissenbruch. It was a touching moment! "So silent looks the Moon at me, so quietly flows the Rhine."

Batavia, seat of the colonial Dutch government, nowadays called Jakarta, Indonesia's capital.

Cassava aka tapioca

During the Japanese occupation, Germany operated more than 40 U-boats in the Indian Ocean and the Pacific, as well as a umber of Raiders. Resupply-bases had been established in several southeast Asian countries

Klapper = Coconut

Babu = housemaid and/or cook

Katjang = Peanuts

For the time, Alfred's observation was very astute and prescient!

The logistics would have been formidable, and it was probably more wishful thinking

A reminder: Heinrich de Kleine is a Dutch national, married to a German woman, Friedchen

Bombay = today called Mumbai

Lesser celandine = Ranunculus ficaria, early spring growing

Tropics Recuperation Institute

Dorothea = "Gift of God"

Bahasa Indonesia = The Indonesian language

Passar = market

Sintua = village elder

Gondang = drum music, accompanied by gongs, an oboe-like instrument.

A Final Note

Dear Reader

Ten years have passed since I wrote this biography. In the intervening years much has happened, personally and on the world stage. Christa and Michael have gone the way of all flesh, and, for two years now, the world is ravaged by the contagious virus of the Covid-19 pandemic. By the time this book is printed, hopefully before the end of 2021, I will be 85 years of age. Some luck!

If you have perused this biography, you will know that I, the author, have known all members of the Rutkowsky family, parents and siblings, some more, some less, through many years. I actually married the second-born, Ute. By now married for sixty years, I am, however, sad to say that our togetherness lasted only fifty-five years.

I collected the information for this biography and wrote it in English in the course of a year, completing it in 2011. A limited number of illustrated copies were published for the extended family. This biographical text includes only a limited number of pictures.
I then translated the text into German and forwarded my translation to Dorothea Rutkowsky, suggesting that she transcribe my translation into perfect German. I further proposed that she publish this work under her name with me as second author. Except for the Introduction, I believe that my original English text has largely been maintained in the German edition. The Otto family story was expanded by Dorothea's further data collection.

Having been intrigued by James Michener's novella introductions in which he first enters into the historical background of the story, I followed his example in my introduction, whereas Dorothea immediately came to the heart of the subject, the family history. It took three years to complete a proper German edition, after which she had it published in hardcover under the title *Brücken über Zeiten und Kontinente, Die Geschichte dreier Generationen einer deutschen Missionarsfamilie auf Sumatra,* by Verlag für Tiefenpsychologie und Anthropologie, in 2015. The appendix of the German edition is somewhat more substantial than my English original.

I, of course, never met Hermann and Martha Weissenbruch, the older generation, but became acquainted with their adult daughters Else (Otto) and Gertrud (Rutkowsky). It has always been my impression that Gertrud, Ute's mother, had she been able to distance herself from her Lutheran background, might have become quite a different person with her musical talent.

Gertrud bore four children prior to the outbreak of WWII, one of whom died as a baby. Dorothea was born in 1947 after the couple reunited in Germany. Despite its hardship and pain, the seven year separation of the couple during WWII may have been a blessing in disguise. Had the War not happened and living circumstances had remained peaceful, the family might very well have grown to eight, even ten children.

Alfred, her husband, a strict Lutheran, was, according to what little filtered through to me, afraid to meet his Maker. Was it, that he was concerned not to have fulfilled his missionary duty? A highly intelligent and educated man, but also practical, he was always out to explore the world around him. He would quiz his vis-à-vis on all kinds of subjects. However, I often found that the answers he received, went in one ear, and out the other. To what extent did he integrate the information he received?

What struck me in my research, going through the plentiful material, was the focus of the missionary members on the here and now and, foremost, on the promulgation and maintenance of their faith. What lay beyond, the manifestations touching their lives were, maybe noted, but not pursued. Thus tigers and snakes are repeatedly mentioned, also their concern of cholera. New foods and agricultural methods were introduced by them to the native population. Monkeys are mentioned but any details are missing. They must have heard gibbons, the "singing" lesser apes, in the jungle canopy. Even orangutans may have been in their larger environment. None are mentioned by name. The appearance of a comet in 1910 is noted. It was a return of Halley's comet. Nothing beyond the sighting itself is mentioned. Grandmother Martha's seeing the ocean surface shimmer in an eery glow (bioluminescence) on her voyage from Genoa to Sumatra, is all there is noted. That the northern celestial constellation are all turned upside down once one gets close to the equator is never mentioned, maybe was never noticed.

I cannot help thinking that our forebears, whose faith took up a considerable part of their education, knew very well how to deal with the contingencies of their world. But they could not know what was then unknown. We have progressed in scientific knowledge. I, the author, am a man of no religious faith but of the broader contemporary knowledge base (just think of gibbons "singing" and being lesser apes).

But then, the people of this story lived their lives, I only wrote their biography.

Herbert Windolf   Prescott, AZ, August 2021

Other **Publications and Activities by Herbert Windolf,**

As Translator of Karl May

Published by Washington State University Press:
The Oil Prince

Published through BookSurge:
Black Mustang
with Marlies Bugman

Published by Nemsi Books:
The Treasure of Silver Lake
The Ghost of Llano Estacado
The Son of the Bear Hunter
Imaginary Journeys I
Imaginary Journeys II
Imaginary Journeys III
Thoughts of Heaven
Winnetou IV
Pacific Shores
The Inca's Legacy
The Scout
Deadly Dust
The Mahdi I

Published through CreateSpace:
The Mahdi II
The Mahdi III
One More Day . . .
As Translator of Autobiography of Isabell Steiner

As Author of Poetic Prose:
Through Booksurge:
Observations and Reflections
Pondering What Is
Otherwise
Musings
Contemplations

Through Kindle Direct Publishing:
Thoughts
Searching
Shadows and Light
Insights

Private Printing:
Biography – Bridges Across Times and Continents

Published by Verlag für Tiefenpsychologie und Anthropologie:
Brücken über Zeiten und Kontinente,
Biography – with Dorothea Rutkowsky

Planetary Studies Foundation Quarterly
Travelogues:
A Hike in Provence
A Safari Through Namibia
Alaska, the Last Terrestrial Frontier of the US
Galápagos
Excursions in Saxony's Switzerland
Monumental Sights, in Grand Staircase/Escalante, Utah, and
Northernmost Arizona
Journey to Sumatra
Zambezi
Moroccan Impressions
The Lure of Africa
Tanzania Redux, unpublished

Planetary Studies Foundation Quarterly
Ten Explorations, six published:
The likely Futility of S.E.T.I. Programs
Snowball Earth
Wondrous Water
The Probability for Intelligent Life in the Universe
A Personal View of Existentialism
Tsunami
Pragmatism
Forty billion Potentially Habitable Planets
Exceptionalism
December 26, 1776

Annemarie Schnitt - Willkommen Website
Translations of Poems and Stories

Unpublished – for Private Use
Autobiography
Translations:
The Texas War of Independence in 1836
by Herman Ehrenberg
Letters to David Walter
Heinrich Himmler, by Franz Wegener
Ukraine Letters, by Hans Windolf
Germany's Final Months of WWII, Diary of Hans Windolf
The Forgotten Generation, by Sabine Bode
War's Grandchildren, by Sabine Bode
Genesis, by Dorothea Rutkowsky

Courses facilitated:
From the Spice Trade to Globalization
Cataclysms and Extinctions
The Likely Futility of SETI Programs
The Cambrian Explosion
Human Evolution and Migration
The American National Mind vis-à-vis the Rest of the World

Addendum
in *Thoughts*
A Collection of Haiku Verses
in *Searching*
Three African Stories
in *Shadows and Light*
Ten Explorations
in *Insights*
Comments &Autobiography
in *Favorite Poems*
Fourteen Travelogues
in *Stayin' Alive*
Five Years Behind Barbed Wire

Made in the USA
Middletown, DE
08 April 2022